Goodnight Campers!

GOODNIGHT CAMPERS!

◇

The History of the British Holiday Camp

Colin Ward and Dennis Hardy

AN ALEXANDRINE PRESS BOOK

Mansell Publishing Limited
London and New York

This book is part of the series
Studies in History, Planning and the Environment
edited by Gordon E. Cherry and Anthony Sutcliffe

First published 1986 by
Mansell Publishing Limited
(A subsidiary of The H. W. Wilson Company)
6 All Saints Street, London N1 9RL, England
950 University Avenue, Bronx, New York 10452, U.S.A.

British Library Cataloguing in Publication Data

Ward, Colin
    Goodnight campers!: the history of the British holiday camp
    — (Studies in history, planning and the environment)
    — (Alexandrine Press book)
    1. Tourist camps, hostels, etc.—Great Britain—History
    I. Title   II. Hardy, Dennis—III. Series
    647'.9441   G155.G7

    ISBN 0–7201–1835–2
    ISBN 0–7201–1836–0 Pbk

Designed and typeset by Katerprint Typesetting Services, Oxford
Printed and bound by Alden Press Ltd., Oxford

CONTENTS

PREFACE

> Roll out of bed in the morning
> With a great big smile and a good good morning –
> Get up with a grin
> There's a good day tumbling in!
> Wake with the sun and the rooster,
> Cock-a-doodle-do like the rooster use'ter,
> How can you go wrong
> If you roll out of bed with a song?
> (Traditional start to the day's broadcasting at Butlin's)

It is enough just to mention the subject of holiday camps to bring on a knowing grin. Like the seaside landlady, the saucy postcard and the garish kiosks along the front, holiday camps are part of a rich and colourful folklore of the seaside holiday. An amused reaction is brought about, not so much because of what the camps are in themselves as for what they trigger off in one's imagination. Their meaning lies less in what is often a rather unexceptional collection of buildings and activities, but rather more in their associations. Holiday camps are popularly linked with the idea of fun, with getting away from the everyday routine, with a sense of togetherness, with being looked after, and with a promise of romance, glitter and fantasy.

But is there anything more to holiday camps than this? Is it mere pretension to venture a serious study of a topic that is, by its very nature, lighthearted? Certainly, we have been drawn to the subject in part at least by this very quality, and by the fact that it has been enjoyable to research. Fun is infectious, and writing about holiday camps has been all the easier for this. At the same time, we have also been drawn to the subject because we believe there is a wider story to tell. The era of the holiday camp, dating from the end of the last century, is also an era of radical social change. Looking back on this era we may find that holiday camps tell us something of these broader changes.

Four themes in particular have interested us. The first is that, in terms of their enduring popularity in the twentieth century, holiday camps merit attention as an institution in their own right. Since the turn of the century, literally millions have poured through the camp gates for a week or two of communal living. Many have returned year after year. This annual process is in itself a story worth telling, and one thing we do is simply to record the rise and changes in holiday camps as a chapter in modern social history.

A second theme is to probe the motives for providing holiday camps in the first place. These motives, too, are interesting in themselves but also reveal some of the wider conflicts of interest that characterize the present century. Inevitably, commercial motives loom large, and modern camps catering for thousands of visitors at any one time are linked exclusively with the profit-making side of the leisure industry. Commercialism, however, offers only a partial explanation of camps in general. Educational ideals, trade unions and welfare considerations, the cult of the outdoor life, and political utopianism have all played their part. We try to unravel the various motives, to see how they have changed over time, and to look at the different types of camp that have resulted.

Another source of interest lies in the planning and design of holiday camps. What we find is that this process is itself entangled within the wider concerns of an environmental lobby and of an emergent planning system. Camps were seen to pose both a threat and an opportunity. They were a threat in the sense that here was yet another source of development in a coastal or countryside setting that was already under immense pressure. And yet, there was also a sense of opportunity, for no matter what went on within the camp compounds, the fact was that it could all be contained. Perhaps, too, the new buildings could even be well-designed. As such, the evolution of holiday camps is part of a broader history of planning and architectural control.

Finally, holiday camps are without doubt a source of contention. Are they one of the great products of the twentieth century, making their own contribution to an era of consumption? Should they be recorded in the same category as the cinema, Woolworth's and the universal hamburger? Are they part of the same package as sliced bread? Do we recall holiday camps as a source of social opportunity, offering to millions the kind of release from daily toil that had previously been known to a privileged few? Or are they to be regarded as an opportunity missed, consigned to the cultural dustbin along with the daily tabloids, soap operas and junk foods? A study of the holiday camp offers no easy answers, but it will at least draw one into this wider and crucial debate about mass society and related issues of individual freedom and popular culture.

Colin Ward
Dennis Hardy
August 1986

ACKNOWLEDGEMENTS

The research for this book was based at Middlesex Polytechnic, and we are indebted for an internal research award to support the work, as well as the friendly and helpful support of our colleagues. Edmund Penning-Rowsell encouraged us 'to do something interesting' (which we hope we have), and Annabel Coker and Audrey Hardwick came up with some interesting source material. We are also indebted to the British Academy for an award to enable us to visit various parts of the country.

Sources had to be dug out from the most unlikely places, and we are grateful to Bronwen Hardy for applying her skills as a librarian to such good effect. Once located, doors were willingly opened, and our thanks are due to many people, including Clive Bush of the CPSA, Michael Dempsey of NALGO, Robert Hamlin of the Bognor library of the West Sussex Institute of Higher Education, Roy Garratt of the Co-operative Union Library, Manchester, Malcolm Hornsby of the Co-operative College, Loughborough, and Michael Bean, of the local history collection, Great Yarmouth Library, and to the public library staff at Scarborough, Hull, Lincoln, and Lowestoft. Our thanks are also due to the many planning officers who replied to our enquiries about camps within their areas.

Everyone we meet seems to have a holiday camp story to tell, whether as campers, as temporary staff or as managers. To thank just a few, we acknowledge the help of Richard Page, Margaret Jones, Don Waterman, Della Chapman, Lynn and Brian Edwards, Ron Griffiths, Shirley Ward, Arthur Foster, Victor Dodd, Bob Greenfield of Warners, David Thacker of Butlins, Sir Fred Pontin, Margaret Partridge, Ray Gosling, Harold Worthington, Minnie Edwards, Sylvia Sutcliffe, Roger Milne, Tom Starbuck of Ladbrokes, and Steve Humphries of LWT.

In recapturing the spirit and image of holiday camps, illustrations play an important part in this book. Our prime debt in this respect is to Dot Davies, who has combined her considerable technical skills as a photographer with a subtle understanding and enthusiasm for the topic. We have also gained from the technical assistance of Alison Shepherd (who drew the maps) and Steve Nutt. For the use of photographs we are much obliged to Jill Drower (whose own book on the first holiday camp was a considerable source of inspiration), John Tovey, Victor Dodd, Harold Worthington, Fred Gray, Alan McDonald, Sue Munt, Richard Govett, Marjorie Ward, Tim and Shirley Ward, Richard Govett, Brian Pearce and Kenneth Sampson.

Finally, work on this book has been assisted from the outset by the encouragement and valued advice of Ann Drybrough-Smith of Alexandrine Press and, in turn, of Terry Renshaw of Katerprint, and John Duncan, June Eaton, Catherine Johnston and Joe Smith at Mansell.

With all this help, we hope that we have done justice to a topic that, we have discovered, has touched on so many people's lives.

Illustration Credits

The list below details the credits for individual illustrations according to the pages on which they appear.

Chapter 1

page 4 top picture: John Tovey; bottom right-hand picture: Patrick Creek; pages 9 and 10: Tim and Shirley Ward; pages 15 and 16: Brian Pearce; page 19: John Tovey; page 20, top picture: Jill Drower; bottom left-hand picture: Jill Drower; bottom right-hand picture: John Tovey.

Chapter 2

page 26: Brian Pearce; page 27 top picture: John Tovey; page 28: Richard Govett; page 29 bottom picture: Victor Dodd; page 33: Malcolm Hornsby; page 37: John Tovey; page 38: Harold Worthington; page 40: Lowestoft Public Library; page 44: John Tovey; page 46: Marjorie Ward.

Chapter 3

page 55: John Tovey; page 58: Sue Munt; page 61: Tim and Shirley Ward; page 62: BBC Hulton Picture Library; page 65 left-hand picture: Sue Munt; pages 66/67: Sue Munt; page 71: Victor Dodd; pages 74 and 75: Kenneth Sampson.

Chapter 4

page 80: John Tovey; page 82: Sue Munt; page 85, top picture: Victor Dodd; page 86, bottom picture: BBC Hulton Picture Library; page 89: Ladbrokes; page 91: Tim and Shirley Ward; page 93: Victor Dodd; page 94: Ron Renshaw; page 95: Dot Davies; page 107: Portsmouth and Sunderland Newspapers.

Chapter 5

pages 116, 117 and 118: the Royal Institute of British Architects; pages 120 and 121: John Tovey; page 125 and bottom of page 128: West Sussex Institute of Higher Education; page 130: Fred Gray; page 137: Sue Munt.

Chapter 6

page 144: Fred Gray.

CHAPTER
1 Togetherness in Tents

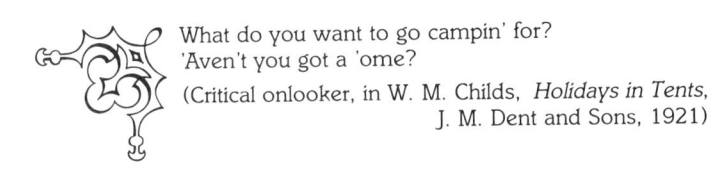

What do you want to go campin' for?
'Aven't you got a 'ome?
(Critical onlooker, in W. M. Childs, *Holidays in Tents*,
J. M. Dent and Sons, 1921)

From bell-tents to ballrooms and beyond, holiday camps have evolved in order to survive. Over the years, social idealists and commercial entrepreneurs have each been forced to adapt to changing demands. The holiday camp (now typically a leisure complex, renamed a holiday centre) is a world away from the hopes of its pioneers, the non-conformist philanthropists, evangelizing socialists, trade unionists and co-operative societies who simply aspired to comradeship in the fresh air and togetherness in tents.

Under Canvas

In the pre-railway days of 1853, I crossed the Prairees of America. My first experience of Camping was above the wooded slope on the plateau behind Kairkock on the Mississippi, when a lad of nine. There, 300 of us camped in tents and wagons, which camp lasted for about five weeks. It remains the longest 'fixed camp' that I have attended, but it was only the beginning of a prolongation, for it was a case of Camping entirely across the prairees over a distance of 1,200 miles, and it lasted from the Spring until August. The plains were then uninhabited save for a few wandering tribes of Indians, probably a million antelopes, and possibly half-a-million of wary buffaloes. In the following Spring a wild and dangerous wagon trip and camp-back from Salt Lake City, up and through the Rockies, back to the States, closed that experience.

A good many years passed. I was engaged to lecture in Sunderland on the subject of 'Muscular Christianity' in the Spring of 1877. It led to the purchase of a canoe, the canoe led to Camping and to a canoe cruise in the Highlands of Scotland...From 1877 to 1907 is 30 years, during which, on every conceivable opportunity, and in 95 per cent of all the counties of Great Britain and Ireland, camping has continued without a break.

(T. H. Holding, 'A Camper's Story', in *The Camper's Handbook*, 1908)

For many centuries the word *camp* had a purely military connotation: the temporary accommodation of armies in the field, using tents and portable huts. Its meaning slowly extended to cover the improvised settlements of migratory farm workers, nomads, gypsies, tinkers, explorers and populations fleeing from persecution, war and pestilence. Camping was an inevitable accompaniment to human activities in locations where permanent buildings were not available. It was a necessary evil, not an activity undertaken for its own sake. It was a penance not a pleasure.

The nineteenth century changed the popular perception of camps and camping. It was, first, the age of romanticism. The romantic movement glorified the outlaw, the bandit, the lone outsider at war with organized society. Works like Schiller's *The Robbers*, Merimée's *Carmen* and Borrow's gypsy stories, with their innumerable imitators in popular fiction and theatre, idealized the brigand or gypsy camp whose carefree occupants lived a simple, heroic life under the

A JOURNEY INTO THE CANADIAN WILDS

stars, contemptuous of settled town dwellers in their smug, dull comfort.

Secondly it was the age of empire. Expeditionary forces of the European powers were conquering new territories in Africa and Asia, colonizing, 'pacifying' the hinterland, establishing their networks of permanent and temporary camps, setting up their 'lines' of bell tents and barrack huts. The Bible followed the sword. Missionaries and explorers penetrated where no white man had been before.

Thirdly it was the age of emigration. Every family had sons, brothers, uncles or cousins 'roughing it' as they sought a new life in Canada, America, South Africa and Australasia. There were fur trappers, lumberjacks, sheep and cattle ranchers, hundreds of thousands of men lured by gold rushes, as well as big game hunters and collectors of botanical and zoological specimens and railway builders. A whole specialist industry grew up manufacturing camping equipment, camp chairs, camp beds, camp stoves and camp kettles for the camp fire. Camp Coffee and Camp Matches remain from that era. Letters home were cherished. Every Sunday school showed its children lantern slides of missionaries like Livingstone and the self-publicizing explorer Stanley. The popular press thrilled its readers with exciting stories from camps in far-away places.

The link between camping as a necessity in the outposts of empire and camping in Britain for sheer pleasure was T. H. Holding, 'the greatest known authority on Camping', whose early experiences in the United States and Canada led him to pioneer first camping with canoes, and then cycle-camping. He was, he claimed, the originator of the Cyclists' Touring Club, then of the Association of Cycle-Campers, (for having concluded that the old 'ordinary' bicycle or penny-farthing was 'practically an impossible machine with which to camp', he welcomed the invention of the modern 'safety' bicycle), and finally in April 1906, of the National Camping Club.

These were immediately successful organizations, and Holding wrote in his *Cycle and Camp*, that 'It is now clear that the poor clerk or workman who wishes to see fresh countries at home and abroad, may gratify his whim and have a fine holiday on the weekly expenditure of his pocket money and be independent of weather, distance, or, to him, the prohibitive tariff of hotels.'[1] And in his subsequent *Campers' Handbook*, he stressed the joys of the family camp, though hardly that of a poor family:

> I have just visited an ideal family camp. It is on an island in a river. There was the eating tent, the sleeping tent, the servant's tent, the cooking tent for wet weather, and the over-boat tent. Here the family and their servants were spending a 'savage' holiday. The scenery was pleasant and they were adjacent to a town. I asked if they liked it, for they have a fine home on a beautiful lake...They were having a delightful time. The brown limbs of the children, the bronzed faces of the parents and grown-up branches of the family, the enjoyment of the servants and the 'handy-man', all was complete. At the end of a month they were not tired, but were counting with regret the remaining days in camp.[2]

Already, he pointed out, 'we take the poor errand boys — orphan or otherwise — and give them a camp at the seaside' and camping was bound to spread to all classes of society. Campers, he claimed, 'are a growing force, and destined to grow more.'

3

Errand Boys at the Seaside

> We with our fair conditions of life at home and school do not realize even one little bit what the poor lads of our busy manufacturing towns have to live amongst and endure. The Boys' Brigade, its drill and festivities, and more than all, its annual camp, is indeed a boon and a blessing – a bright star in their lives pointing to so much that is higher and nobler than anything else around them.
>
> (A. Hume Smith, 'A Company Camp', in *The Boys' Brigade Gazette*, March, 1903)

Hayling Island, south of Havant in Hampshire, was first connected to the mainland by a bridge in 1823. Soon afterwards a developer judged that with its sandy southern shore, it could rival Brighton as a holiday resort, and laid out a crescent of houses facing the sea. 'But the enterprise was clearly a failure, for only half the crescent was ever built, and this genteel, urban group of tall houses, with basements and areas, looking as if a section of Bayswater had been transported to the seaside, remains as an uncomfortable memorial of an over-optimistic scheme.'[3]

But all through the twentieth century, a humbler kind of holiday-maker has found Hayling an accessible and inexpensive venue. Weekend chalets, holiday camps, caravan and camping sites occupy the greater part of the island, and old residents recall the long queues of vehicles at summer weekends, waiting to cross the old narrow bridge which was finally replaced after the Second World War. The pioneers of organized camping there were the members of the St Andrew's Home and Club for Working-boys, founded in Soho in 1866, and moved to Great Peter Street, Westminster in 1885. In 1867 the club 'acquired for £11 a ship's cutter and christened it The Merry Andrew. Its eight oars were manned by lads in blue jerseys and navy-style caps, who rowed it merrily up river on Saturdays and on camping weekends at Sunbury-on-Thames at Whitsun.'[4] By 1889 the club was camping annually under canvas at Hayling Island over the August Bank Holiday weekend.

The foundation of organized youth movements like the Boys' Brigade, the Church Lads' Brigade, and subsequently the Scouts and Guides brought the experience of camping to hundreds of thousands of boys all through this century. At first the proportion of girls was far smaller, but today a much larger number of girls join the Brownies than do boys the Cub Scouts, and virtually all urban schools take their pupils camping at some stage in their school life. However, in the early years of the century, when family holidays were far from universal and when paid holidays were the exception rather than the rule, it was the prospect of camping which drew boys into clubs and youth organizations, just as it was the Sunday School Outing that ensured the attendance of younger children at Sunday schools. John Springhall in his study of *Youth Empire and Society*, while wary of the lyrical reminiscences of elderly scoutmasters, finds that 'there is no denying the profound impact of a summer camp by the seaside on the boys' consciousness', and that 'to most boys who joined an organised youth movement, camping was by far the greatest attraction it could offer.'

The boys who flocked to the Boys' Brigade in its early years were usually working boys, and the first camps were held over Bank Holiday weekends. When the camp was held for a week, the campers had to find five shillings as their contribution and to forego a week's wages. Camping had to be justified to their employers, and an editorial in the journal of the Church Lads' Brigade (an Anglican breakaway from the predominantly nonconformist Boys' Brigade) declared in 1898:

> We hope that employers of our lads will read the accounts given in this number, and we believe, to hear of the happy time they have had and of the good behaviour, will be of some reward to them for the inconvenience they have been put to in giving their lads a holiday. We are confident that the sacrifices they have made will be made up to them by the better service which the lads will render during the year, from the habits of order and discipline, and the new stock of health they will have acquired.[5]

John Springhall provides a composite account of a typical day in camp, which before 1914 would start with reveillé at 6 a.m.

> After breakfast at 7.30 came morning prayers, the hearty singing of the boys often being led by a quartette of the band. Camp inspection came next, after the 'fatigue squad' had done their work, and this was usually followed by a route march with the band at its head. The 1st Glasgow Company at camp in the Kyles of Bute would then go out in four-oared boats to pull across to the bathing place. After dinner the boys were usually free to roam over the hills surrounding the camp alongside the Loch, to play cricket, or to visit the nearby small resorts of Portvadie and Tighnabruaich in Argyll. It was near here at Auchenlochan that the first ever Boys' Brigade camp was held in 1886 during Glasgow Fairs Week. After tea there might be a fishing parade in the camp boats, the long eventful day usually closing with a supper of cocoa and biscuits, evening prayers and 'Lights Out' at 10.30....At the first Jewish Lads' Brigade Camp at Deal, Kent, in 1897, the routine was slightly different: for at 6.30 morning prayers, 'all but one lad came down duly provided with his *Tephillin* and everyone without exception displays his *Arbang Confes.*' Some of the boys who went for an early morning bathe had never even seen the sea before, while the majority had only spent a day at Clacton. Physical drill was followed by breakfast; then the boys 'brailled-up' their sleeping tents and generally tidied up the camp: this was followed by an hour of rifle drill. Basically, the morning was for work and the rest of the day for play, including cricket and chess. All the meals were strictly kosher. Games continued until a little before supper at 9.00, and 'Lights Out' was at 10.15.[6]

By contrast, the Scout movement's camps were smaller, more flexible and spontaneous, 'more relaxed and less well organised, lacking in military precision and a sense of order'. When Baden-Powell's *Scouting for Boys* was published in serial form groups of boys all over the country set up their own groups before any central organization had been formed. Leslie Paul recalls how 'With an astonishing perception they leapt at Scouting as at something for which they had been waiting, divining that this was a movement which took the side of the natural inquisitive, adventuring boy against the repressive schoolmaster, the moralising parson and the coddling parent. Before the leaders knew what was happening groups were springing up spontaneously and everywhere bands of boys, with bare knees, and armed with broomsticks, began foraging through the countryside.'[7]

A Woodcraft Folk emblem of the 1920s.

Camping was popularized in dozens of schoolgirl stories. Elsie J. Oxenham wrote four books a year. This picture comes from her 1918 book *The School of Ups and Downs: The Story of a Summer Camp*.

Baden-Powell had met while on a fishing holiday in Ireland a Mr Charles Van Raalte, who owned Brownsea Island in Poole Harbour, Dorset, and there, from 29 July to 9 August 1907, twenty boys camped under canvas on the south shore in the first experimental Scout camp. By the 1930s more than a million boys and girls in Britain were members of the movement at any one time, and virtually all of them had experienced camp life.

Of the various alternative youth organizations which eschewed the patriotic religious or militarist indoctrination which they discerned in the existing single-sex movements, the most successful was and is the Woodcraft Folk. Its inspiration came ultimately from the United States, where Ernest Thompson Seton's Woodcraft League had been founded in 1902. The organized camping of the Woodcraft Folk, its founders stressed in the 1930s, 'differs from holiday camping in that it is – or should be – organized upon an educational basis.' To the child, Leslie Paul wrote, 'the camps are the principal events of the movement. The red-letter days in the calendar are those spent at camp, for camp life combines the general romance of the movement with the material delight of sleeping in tents, of making fires, bathing in sun and water, tramping over the hills, and singing round the fire. The leisure-time group becomes, for a little while, the full-time tribe with its own laws, practices and traditions.'[8]

The purposes of Woodcraft Folk camping were summarized as

1. To give pioneers a well-organized communal life.
2. To provide them with opportunities for healthy outdoor activity.
3. To train them in self-reliance and communal responsibility.
4. To counterbalance the monotony of factory and school life and the complexity of an industrial civilization with a life that is simpler, freer and more spontaneous.

The nineteenth-century discovery of 'Nature', coinciding with the extraordinary pace of the growth of the cities of both Britain and the United States, led to a variety of attempts to give some kind of rural experience to the urban child. The *New York Times* programme of one-day excursions for slum children began in 1872, the *New York Tribune*'s Fresh Air Fund in 1877. By 1897 seventeen American cities had organized Fresh Air Relief, and in London the Children's Country Holiday Fund sought to fulfil the same function and was followed by similar projects in other cities.

An American innovation which became an institution for middle-class children but which has had few equivalents in Britain was the Summer Camp. Hardly known at the beginning of the century, it had become 'the customary thing' in America by 1915, and involved a million children and seven thousand camps by 1929.[9] They range from the deliberately primitive tented camp to highly sophisticated and luxurious permanent sites.

But in Britain the event which guaranteed that the majority of the male population at least, had experienced camp life, was the First World War. It was the nation's first conscript war, and with the usual paradox of the glow of nostalgia, its veterans remembered the comradeship, the sing-songs and the shared adventures, and obliterated from their recollections not just the horrors of war, but the ordinary discomforts, the mud and the rain, the improvised cooking and squalid latrines. Camping, just like scouting, acquired in retrospect, a rosy glow of communal experience and excitement.

The war also left behind vast stocks of bell tents which could be bought in the 1920s for less than ten pounds each and of army huts similarly available at knock-down prices, as well as innumerable 'temporary gentlemen' who as officers had learned all about the organization of camps and needed a way of making a living in the land fit for heroes.

The East-Ender's Holiday

> See! from the great metropolis they rush,
> The industrious vulgar! They, like prudent bees
> In Kent's wide garden road, expert to crop
> The flow'ry hop, and provident to work
> Ere winter numbe their sunburnt hands and winds
> Engaol them, murmuring their gloomy cells....
>
> (Christopher Smart, 'The Hop Garden', 1752)

Everyone over fifty who lived as a child in the inner boroughs of East and South-East London knows some variant of a song with dozens of verses that begins

> When we went down hopping,
> Hopping down in Kent,
> Saw old mother Murphy
> Living in a tent,
> With an EIO, EIO, EIEIO.

It is part of the folklore of the annual migration to the hop gardens of Kent in September which was the nearest thing in Britain to the grape-picking festivals of the vineyards of Europe. The hop bine, *humulus lupulus*, whose clusters of flowers are used for flavouring beer, was brought to England in 1524 by Flemish refugees and is still grown in the places where they settled. The hop belt in Kent roughly coincided with the fruit-farming districts. It used to begin in neighbourhoods like Bromley and Bexley which have since been absorbed by London's southern suburbs, stretching down to Sevenoaks, with another large area between Maidstone and Tonbridge, Edenbridge and Tenterden, and further east around Canterbury and along the North Kent coast.

Picking the flowers is concentrated into a short period, usually the first few weeks of September, and before mechanization took over in the 1950s and 1960s, the growers had relied for at least two hundred years, not only on casual labour from the surrounding towns and countryside, but on a mass-migration of Londoners: poor people welcoming the chance to pick up a little money in the autumn sun. In the nineteenth century the beer consumption of a rapidly increasing population led to a huge increase in the acreage devoted to hops. This and the expansion of the railway network turned hop-picking into a vast Cockney family holiday with its own rituals and traditions.

In both atmosphere and appearance the hop gardens are like vineyards. The plant is grown in rows on tall poles linked together by overhead wires along which the bines are trained. At the picking time bines are pulled down into the alleys between the rows and the flowers stripped off, today by machinery, but for generations by hands which were blackened and made sore by the prickly surface of the plant. In alternate rows were the bins, which were long loose bags of sacking supported on poles which extended at the ends to enable the bin to be carried. Each family group picked from both sides and, working from seven-thirty in the morning to four in the afternoon, might pick forty bushels a day in a year when the weather had been kind to the hops. In a good year, enough was earned to buy new clothes for the winter in the Kent market towns. Eighty years ago Sir Walter Besant was astonished by the piles of worn-out boots discarded by returning hoppers who had bought new ones on the way home.

There were always arguments when the measurer came round with a bushel basket or a 'poke' of brightly coloured sacking, to empty the bins and call out the number to the 'bookie' to write in the tally book. Old hoppers knew exactly the quantity of leaves which the measurer would tolerate among the hops, but since the flowers are spongy, he could squash a very large quantity in his bushel measure while the hoppers looked on furiously. The scene was accurately described in George Orwell's early novel *A Clergyman's Daughter*. In the diary he kept of his experiences picking hops in 1931 (a very bad year for the industry) he remarked that 'It was humiliating to see that most of the people there looked on it as a holiday — in fact, it is because hopping is regarded as a holiday that the pickers will take such starvation wages.'[10]

The historian of the Londoners' hop-picking exodus, Alan Bignell, sees the same paradox of working and holiday-making slightly differently. The whole history, he says, 'is corrugated with little outbursts of passion — strikes, fights, demonstrations, occasionally riots — always on a fairly small, localized scale, but at the same time a constant symptom of discontent and simmering revolt. Yet that history is also decked out with reminders that these same people could change very quickly from sullen malcontents or impassioned would-be revolutionaries, into apparently carefree, happy holidaymakers, at least superficially as well satisfied with the good things that hopping had to offer as ever they were angered by its less attractive features. Time and time again, reformers found themselves thwarted in their attempts to champion the hoppers by completely misunderstanding the priorities of the hoppers themselves.'[11]

Bignell's researches in railway archives reveal how ready the railway companies were to take advantage of the traffic generated by this huge movement of whole families, and what organizational problems they faced since it was confined to a few weekends. Hoppers' Specials with reduced fares were run from the mid-1850s until 1960. In the first of these, cattle trucks were used, and all through the period more trains were required on the journey back, since those hoppers who could not afford the outward fare walked, but felt they could spare enough from their earnings for the luxury of a train ride home. Additional special trains were run for Hop-Pickers' Friends, bringing weekend visitors, relations, husbands and fathers, for a trip to the hoppers' camps. 'In one year, 1925, the Southern Railway ran 71 hoppers' specials into Kent and 75 for the return journey. They carried 34,448 hoppers by special and ordinary trains. During five weekends that season, the trains carried 33,980 Hoppers' Friends in to Kent on the Saturdays, 13,854 on the Sundays, and 43,410 back again on the Sunday evenings.' As late as 1945 the special trains still brought 30,000

The Easter-Enders' hop-picking holiday.

hoppers in sixty trains. Their belongings were piled into old perambulators or little carts made from mounting boxes on pram wheels. Farm waggons brought them from the usually quiet rural stations to the hoppers' camps.

These could range from incredible squalor and overcrowding in farm sheds, barns and stables to tents, long subdivided ex-army huts and 'chalets' of the holiday camp pattern. 'Until well into the 19th century farmers made up little hoppers' lodges from hurdles laced with straw and fastened together with hazel bands. Later on, tents became common as temporary homes for the 'foreigners', but they were often not much better than the straw huts. Many of them were acquired by farmers from the Army which had condemned them as no longer suitable for soldiers.'[12]

As early as 1866, land-owners and tenant farmers formed a Society for the Employment and Improved Lodgings of Hop-pickers which recommended standards of accommodation which were hardly ever put into practice until long afterwards. Nevertheless it was possible for the author of *Chamber's Book of Days* in 1869 to see the hoppers' camps as one of the prettiest English pictures of the Autumn scene:

> Merry people, too, are the hop-pickers, whether at their work, or when going to or returning from the hop-plantations. The little huts they run up to sleep in, their places of cooking, washing, and other domestic contrivances, tell that they belong to the race who have heralded the way into many a wilderness, lived there and founded colonies, that are now springing up as great nations...We see them travelling to the hop-grounds with baby on back, and leading children by the hand, carrying nearly everything their humble home contained.[13]

They had to bring bedding and utensils from home since few farmers would provide more than a hop-poke for sleeping on, straw to fill it and a tin basin for washing. But of course for most of them their homes were almost equally humble in Poplar, Bermondsey and Southwark, and some would use the

Homeward-bound.

hopping holiday to save rent and take all their belongings while 'flitting' from one landlord's room to another. An observer of 1883 makes the same point as did the advocates of children's camps, on the healthy escape provided by a holiday in the sun. 'Imagine for a moment the change from a stifling court and room where the sun never shines, where pure air is never breathed, where cleanliness is unknown, to sudden transportation to one of these hop-gardens.'[14]

Local residents looked with disgust at the Cockney invasion, the pubs locked up their glasses and served their beer in cut down bottles, putting up segregated sheds marked 'Hop Pickers and Friends', but the pickers were not worried. Some East London shop-keepers made the migration too, and opened temporary shops, while itinerant vendors wandered the gardens with sweets and ices which mothers would offer as rewards for children once they had picked their quota for the family bin and were freed to play.

The same families went year after year, even generation after generation, to the same farmer, and regular pickers would often paint their habitual hut and would go down on August Bank Holiday before the season began, to paste wallpaper over the black tarred walls of corrugated iron huts and even bring linoleum and curtains. 'It's like your own 'ome 'ere,' said Nell, an old lady who had actually been born in a hoppers' camp, to Cyril Ray in 1959, 'and if you like to be as clean as you are at 'ome you can be.'

At Paddock Wood, he talked to sixty-three year old Florence from Rother-hithe, who had first come to the same garden when ten weeks old and was then leading a family of nine. 'That's me eldest daughter; she's forty-two now, but I used to bring 'er 'ere in long clothes and thought nothink of it. Me Muvver's muvver fetched 'er kid 'ere, and that's what started us off. Not that me old man'll come — 'e's a docker and 'e likes 'is drink, but don't like 'opping, never did: meself, I'd rarver 'ave this than a mumf's 'oliday at the seaside. And I've *been* to the seaside, too.'[15]

The end of the picking was always celebrated by a feast with a big bonfire of accumulated rubbish. There was music, dancing, community singing and improvised entertainments. In the larger gardens a marquee was hired for the occasion. All through the 1950s and 1960s the supply of pickers declined and the pace of mechanization increased. Whitbreads, with their big farms at Beltring used to say that as long as there were people willing to pick they would continue to employ hand-pickers. By 1968 the cost of hand-picking was twice as much as that of using machines. At Beltring, 'Last-night celebrations were continued as enthusiastically as ever, but observers who remembered the "good old days" recognised subtle differences. There was a band, and dancing, a children's fancy dress competition and a yard-of-ale drinking contest, with a silver tankard prize presented by the farm. There were talent contests too, and no shortage of entertainers of all ages. It was all very much in the old traditions – and yet...'[16]

And yet it was the last of the great celebrations of the hopping holiday. Improved social conditions, the declining population of the inner London boroughs, the fact that the education authority was no longer willing to extend the school holiday to include the hopping season, the fact that properly equipped modern homes made hopping huts less attractive even if they were renamed chalets, the fact that all employed people now had holiday pay and that the revolution of rising expectations had made us all consumers of holidays rather than improvisers of a change of work, had all removed the incentive to go hop-picking. Tending the modern machines is usually done by students on vacation.

There are still families who make the annual pilgrimage to Kent because of long-standing connections with individual hop-farmers who need a particular kind of seasonal labour. In the secret world of preparing hops for the dozen wholesalers in the hop trade, they have an expertise which cannot be replaced. But is is not unknown for elderly visitors to holiday camps in Britain or to holiday villages in southern Spain to sigh nostalgically at the end of an evening and say 'It makes you think of the old days, hopping down in Kent.'

Brown Bread and Dewy Mornings

> It was a very sociable politics. He used to play the harmonium at socialist meetings and he collected socialist songs together in a book called *Chants of Labour*. This was characteristic of organisation in this period. The socialist movement created a whole network of cultural forms. There were cafes, meals for schoolchildren, rambles in the countryside. From the 1890s the Clarion cycling club and the Clarion choir continued this tradition...
>
> They saw socialism as an inner transformation which meant change in the here and now. They sought this new life in the everyday, in their stress on the warmth of fellowship and comradeship, in their clothes and furnishings, in a network of associations from those cycling clubs to Socialist Sunday Schools...
>
> (Sheila Rowbotham, 'In Search of Carpenter', *History Workshop*, Spring, 1977)

The mentors of the socialist movement in Britain in the last decades of the last century were not simply in revolt against the injustices of capitalism, they were appalled, like Morris, by 'the sheer damned ugliness' of urban life, and like Edward Carpenter, at the dreadful respectability of Victorian family life and its dependence on a submerged class of domestic servants. Life must be simplified and brought closer to nature. 'Plain food, the open air, the hardiness of sun and wind, are things practically unobtainable in a complex *ménage*', and 'No individual or class can travel far from the native life of the race without becoming shrivelled, corrupt, diseased...'[17]

Carpenter's view was echoed by the philosopher of Arts and Crafts architecture, W. R. Lethaby, who was converted to socialism because 'to live on the labour of others is a form of cannibalism'. He noted that there was a brown bread and dewy morning ideal of civilization and a champagne and late night supper ideal.[18] We had to choose the former, he felt, if only for the sake of our health. And Carpenter's feeling that 'the race' was becoming 'shrivelled, corrupt and diseased', was upheld by the Report of the Inter-departmental Committee on Physical Deterioration, where the Inspector-General of Recruiting spoke of 'the gradual deterioration of the physique of the working classes' as revealed by army recruits for the South African War.[19]

In 1891 Robert Blatchford started the *Clarion*, 'the first working-class paper since the *Northern Star* to have gained a mass circulation and pay for itself.' He serialized in it between 1892 and 1893 his *Merrie England*, which, published as a book, sold nearly a million copies in the next few years. A Clarion Fellowship grew up as a loose federation of innumerable clubs and associations which had arisen around the paper, and the most significant of these were the Clarion Cycling Clubs, seizing upon the newly invented 'safety' bicycle and the opportunities it brought for fresh air, exercise and fun.

Not the least interesting aspect of Blatchford's book, almost a hundred years since it was written, is that the first of his objections to the factory system is based on what today would be called environmental grounds, contrasting not only the environments of factory owners and factory workers but the locations and qualities of their holidays. In a passage worth quoting at length, he argues with his readers thus:

> You know the factory districts of Lancashire. I ask you is it not true that they are ugly, and dirty, and smoky, and disagreeable? Compare the busy towns of Lancashire, of Staffordshire, of Durham, and of South Wales, with the country towns of Surrey, Suffolk, and Hants.
>
> In the latter counties you will get pure air, bright skies, clear rivers, clean streets, and beautiful fields, woods and gardens; you will get cattle and streams, and birds and flowers, and you know that all those things are well worth having, and that none of them can exist side by side with the factory system.
>
> I know that the Manchester School will tell you that this is a 'mere sentiment'. But compare their actions with their words.
>
> Do you find the champions of the factory system despising nature, and beauty and art, and health — except in their speeches and lectures to you? No. You will find these people living as far from the factories as they can get; and you will find them spending their long holidays in the most beautiful parts of England, Scotland, Ireland, or the Continent...To make wealth for themselves they destroy the beauty and the health of your dwelling places;

and then they sit in their suburban villas, or on the hills and terraces of the lovely southern countries, and sneer at the 'sentimentality' of the men who ask you to cherish beauty and to prize health.

Or they point out to you the value of the 'wages' which the factory system brings you, reminding you that you have carpets on your floors, and pianos in your parlours, and a week's holiday at Blackpool once a year.

But how much health or pleasure can you get out of a cheap and vulgar carpet? And what is the use of a piano if you have neither leisure nor means to learn to play it? And why should you prize that one week in the crowded, noisy watering-place, if health and fresh air and the great salt sea are mere sentimental follies?...And does a week at a spoiled and vulgar watering place repay you for fifty-one weeks' toil and smother in a hideous and stinking town?[20]

Shrewdly, Blatchford touched upon an aspect of life much closer to the experience of his audience than the carpets or the pianos, the annual holiday at Blackpool, paid for by weekly contributions. The mill shut down for a week, and the employees moved as a body to the sea. Blackpool and similar resorts on the west coast, Scarborough and its satellites on the east coast, were their destinations. When they got there, by special trains, as the railway companies ran their holiday services to coincide with the Wakes Week of any particular town, they found holiday accommodation as carefully stratified as their experience of the work they were employed in back home.

The employers were booked at the Grand Hotel, though naturally they were actually going to Weymouth or Lake Como, and so, in a generous mood, were able to depute their places to their faithful assistants in top management. The rest of the workforce found its own level in holiday accommodation. Middle-class families would rent a whole house, except the basement and attics, where the staff attending to their needs migrated, and others rented 'lodgings' or 'diggings' where the guests did the daily shopping, which was cooked by their landlady and served in their rooms. 'Lancashire millworkers slept three or four to a bed in "company houses" in Blackpool.'[21]

The dreary seaside boarding house and its formidable landlady have passed into English mythology, and the popularity of holiday camps in this century can be seen as a revolt against both. The house with its durable and dingy brown paint, lincrusta or anaglypta wall coverings, its lumpy mattresses, its morning queue for the bathroom and its smell of cabbages, was the epitome of down-at-heel shabby gentility. The landlady was a figure of fun, but also of resentment, with her charge for the use of the cruet or the bath, her fixed mealtimes and her insistence that the family should be off the premises between meals, rain or shine. The children, for whose sake the holiday had been planned, were a source of embarrassment because of their table manners or their habit of emptying the sand from their plimsolls on the carpet, or of scraping the hallstand with their buckets and spades.

By comparison, the prospect of cycling and camping brought the promise of freedom, health, independence and comradeship, a new style of informal clothing, a new kind of relationship between the sexes, fresh air and exercise, in a period when tuberculosis was the scourge of the overcrowded cities. The atmosphere of the Clarion Fellowship can be tasted in the recollections of Walter Southgate, trade unionist and founder member of the Labour Party. 'We were familiar with the countryside, because I can say truthfully that one of the best periods of my life was the days I spent cycling through the Essex countryside before motor cars and lorries came to spoil it all.' He explains that,

> In 1910 I had founded the North East London Clarion Cycling Club and when members were too numerous for safety on the road I founded various offshoots. Membership was open to both sexes and we explored the rustic villages and pubs for drinks and teas; there was plenty of bread and butter, cake, shrimps and lettuce. We rode two abreast with the captain in front and vice-captain at the rear, giving signals to one another by coded whistles. A puncture meant that two of us would drop out for the repair, the rest slowing down speed. Our journeys were accompanied by singing and the ringing of our bells – it was a real fraternal outing in the fresh air, far from the stinks and grime of East End life. In those groups many found their marriage partners over the years. In the years after the clubs had ended, we celebrated with an annual dinner, remembering, too, those who had fallen in the war. These events carried on until the 1930s.[22]

One such Clarion cyclist, according to some accounts, was John Fletcher Dodd, who, it is said, camped with his two sons at a lonely seaside site a mile from the village of Caister on the Norfolk coast three miles from Yarmouth. They fell in love with the place and determined to set up a camping ground for socialists. Others suggest that he owned the land there and, as a keen member of the Independent Labour Party, opened the camp to provide holidays for East Londoners: 'In 1906 J. Fletcher Dodd took ten friends from the East End and they camped in tents by the shore at Caister. The venture was a tremendous success. In the years that followed the fame and repute of the camp grew until nearly 1,000 people a week were staying there in the summer...The campers

Early days at Caister
Holiday Camp.

shared in the work of running the camp. The women would be responsible for all the cooking. The men would share the camp's chores and had the task of picking the day's supply of vegetables from the gardens which adjoined the camping area.'[23]

The campers slept under canvas and sang around the camp-fire within sound of the waves. 'The camp committee, many of them trade union leaders, organized socials, dances, lectures and debates. Every Sunday there was a lecture in the afternoon, and for many of the campers this was one of the most exciting moments in the week.'[24]

The 'Caister Socialist Holiday Camp' of 1906 soon became simply the Caister Holiday Camp and attracted a different clientele, as tents were replaced by huts and chalets. Mr George Stokes, who first camped there as a boy in 1911, recalls that 'In the years before and just after the First World War, these came mainly from the professional and business classes seeking freedom from the restrictions of the hotels and boarding houses of the time. In my teens, for example, I met Duncan Grant and Sir Alexander Gibson there, neither of them "Knees up, Mother Brown" types.'[25]

By 1949 the Caister Camp, still run by the long-lived John Fletcher Dodd and his family, accommodated 800, catered for every kind of sport, and had in the season a resident dance band and weekly cinema shows. In its 90 acres, the owners claimed, 'Everything is provided for, from the energetic round of sport to that quiet cosy armchair with a favourite book. You can do as you please and go as you please. There is no regimentation at Caister.'[26] After the Dodd family finally sold the camp, it changed hands several times and is now completely rebuilt as Ladbroke's Caister Supercentre. Wartime apart, the site has been in continuous use as a holiday camp for eighty years.

The Clarion Cycling Clubs faded away during the First World War, never to be revived, but the Cyclists' Touring Club and the National Cyclists' Union prospered, and by the 1930s they had nearly 60,000 members in 3,500 clubs. And the Camping Club of Great Britain, whose membership was 820 in 1910, had over 7,000 by 1935, with a network of sites around the country where they could pitch their tents for eightpence a night. In the 1920s and 1930s rambling and hiking grew in popularity, and the Youth Hostels Association, founded at the initiative of the National Council of Social Service, first opened the doors of its chain of hostels in 1931. By the last pre–war summer it had reached a membership of 83,418.[27] One of the earliest members told us, 'I was intoxicated with the poetry of people like Whitman and with books like Carpenter's *Towards Democracy*. I wanted the simplification of life. 1932 was the first summer when I didn't have to go on a stuffy, fussy seaside holiday with my parents. I was trusted to go hostelling at a shilling a night. The more primitive it was the more I liked it. Best of all was the hostel at Chepstow, which was simply a row of bell tents.' At the Geographical Association's Manchester conference in 1931, a speaker welcomed the YHA, remarking that 'the advantage of such hostels...over holiday camps is that they give the user the priceless asset of mobility.'[28]

The Labour movement, and its offshoots as Fabians, trade unionists or co-operators, played an important part in the growth of holiday camps of every kind. In 1910 Beatrice Webb found herself the chairman of the Fabian summer school, managed year after year by Mary Hankinson, gymnastic instructor and captain of the Fabian cricket team. This was not held under canvas, but in a country house in Wales, with 'overflows' rented next door. Mrs Webb found her fellow holiday-makers 'a miscellaneous crowd, all kindly and well-bred and interesting, but not exciting in themselves, and some of them ugly and crude in mind and manners. Still, my dominant impression is the "well-bredness" of this extraordinarily mixed assembly: ILP organizers, medical officers of health, teachers, minor officials of all sorts, social workers, literary men, journalists and even such out-of-the-way recruits as auctioneers and unregistered dentists, all living in extremely close quarters, and yet not getting on each others' nerves through too great a disparity of speech and behaviour. It is a wonderful instance of the civilising effect of a common purpose and a common faith.'[29]

Beatrice Webb was describing the dilemmas of anyone who sought, like J. Fletcher Dodd, to run a holiday camp on socialist principles. With a wonderful unconsciousness of the difficulty of organizing anything for anyone, Beatrice Webb wrote in her diary that the trouble with Miss Hankinson as general manager was that she wanted 'a co-operative country holiday made up, in the main, of organised games, excursions and evening entertainments, with a few lectures and discussions thrown in to give subjects for conversation,' whereas 'Our conception is that of an organised school — teaching, learning and discussing, with some off-days and off-hours for recreation and social intercourse...For the first fortnight *our* conception was carried out; for the second fortnight there was a rather unsatisfactory compromise. But this third fortnight has been practically given over to Miss Hankinson's "pleasuring", and the lectures and discussions have suffered in consequence...'

She concluded that 'another time we must, somehow or other, select our staff and even our guests, and take a great deal more trouble to plan out an intellectually varied bill of fare, and a far more *technical* and *specialized* kind of discussion which will attract a better type...'[30]

For this reason she was 'rather against having professional gymnastics instructors', but it was they who won the day against the ideologists, whether in the summer camps of the Progressive League in the 1930s or the Liverpool Young Socialists providing a cheap holiday in Wales for their unemployed comrades in the 1980s.

Our informants, recollecting the blend of socialism, physical culture and the simple life in holiday camps of the 1920s and 1930s remember not the message but the incidental discomforts or delights. One tells us of the sheer painfulness and embarrassment of a naturist holiday among the pine-cones of Ash Vale in Surrey, another of a Communist drama camp in Hampshire where the proletarian struggle was reenacted among the chalky uplands. Alan Albon recalled the camp at Walderslade in Kent, made from army huts of the First World War, run by conscientious objectors who survived it, where the great delight of children like him was to get covered in mud in their allocated task of digging out a duckpond.

The First Holiday Camp

ARE WE
DOWNHEARTED?
NO !

ARE WE
COMING BACK
AGAIN ?
YES !

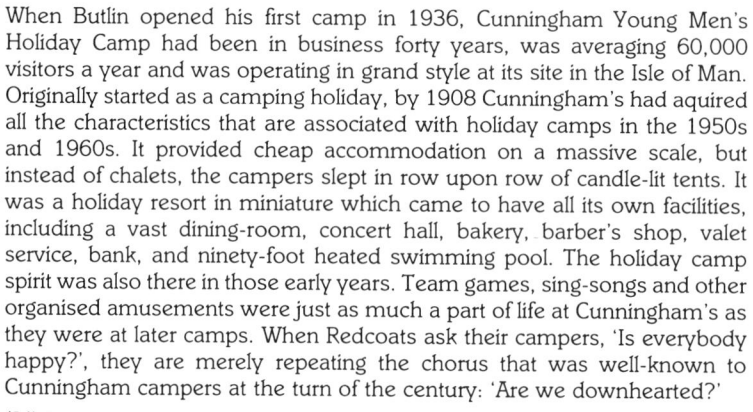

When Butlin opened his first camp in 1936, Cunningham Young Men's Holiday Camp had been in business forty years, was averaging 60,000 visitors a year and was operating in grand style at its site in the Isle of Man. Originally started as a camping holiday, by 1908 Cunningham's had aquired all the characteristics that are associated with holiday camps in the 1950s and 1960s. It provided cheap accommodation on a massive scale, but instead of chalets, the campers slept in row upon row of candle-lit tents. It was a holiday resort in miniature which came to have all its own facilities, including a vast dining-room, concert hall, bakery, barber's shop, valet service, bank, and ninety-foot heated swimming pool. The holiday camp spirit was also there in those early years. Team games, sing-songs and other organised amusements were just as much a part of life at Cunningham's as they were at later camps. When Redcoats ask their campers, 'Is everybody happy?', they are merely repeating the chorus that was well-known to Cunningham campers at the turn of the century: 'Are we downhearted?'

(Jill Drower, *Good Clean Fun: The Story of Britain's First Holiday Camp*, 1982)

The first holiday camp entrepreneur was not Billy Butlin, nor a demobilized army captain at Hayling Island, but a Presbyterian teetotaler from the nineteenth-century world of Working Lads' Institutes in Liverpool. Joseph Cunningham's great-granddaughter Jill Drower, has told his story in a delightful book which stresses how many features of the modern commercial holiday camp were present in his venture before Billy Butlin was born. Cunningham was a flour merchant and Sunday School superintendent from Toxteth, Liverpool, and his 'Cunningham Juvenile Songsters' were well known in the city's religious life. Starting in 1887, he and his wife used to run an annual summer camp for the boys of the Gordon and Florence Institutes. After sampling various locations,

THE CUNNINGHAM CAMP, DOUGLAS

they moved their annual week of camping to Great Orme's Head near Llandudno in 1891 and in the next two years to Laxey in the Isle of Man. The hire of bell tents was paid for by holding concerts and each boy had to save ten shillings for the week in the Florence Institute's savings bank.

But they were undercharging and the Institute's committee decided to dispense with the Cunninghams' services. They resolved in 1894 to set up in business on their own at a new site near Groudle Glen overlooking the sea, two miles from Douglas. Their campers could now be collected not only from the Florence Institute boys but from all round Liverpool among the members of Sunday schools, harriers' clubs and temperance leagues. They were now losing their own money, and Elizabeth Cunningham insisted on taking control of the catering. By the turn of the century the weekly charge was seventeen shillings and sixpence and the camp was open from May to October. One thing made it different from all earlier camping holidays, and this was the fact that it was run like a hotel.

> The timetable no longer revolved around tent inspections and the care of guy ropes. The emphasis was now on leisure and fun. The management had to please its customers and tempt them back next year. They were told that their duties were limited to eating, sleeping and enjoying themselves. As a result the Camp soon began to attract members of the regular holiday-going public. Textile workers, office clerks and shop assistants who were used to saving for an annual holiday could now enjoy a well organised camp that did not have charitable overtones. Parents could rest assured that their sons would be closely supervised while the campers themselves could enjoy the feeling of freedom and adventure that could not be found under the watchful eye of a boarding house landlady.[31]

The first holiday camp: the Cunningham Camp, Isle of Man. On the back of the card sent to Miss Treloar, Barnsley, in 1910 is the message: 'Had some excitement this afternoon. The tent to the left of ours caught fire with the sun (you can imagine how hot it is) and burnt everything to ashes . . .'.

Smart young men at Cunningham's.

The formula was wildly successful in spite of its all-male, non-drinking, non-gambling regulations and in spite of the fact that campers were fined if they came in after lights-out (11.45 on week-days, 10.30 on Sundays). In 1904 the Camp moved to the site it occupied until 1939, immediately above the seafront at Douglas, close to the resort's own amenities. A hundred foot long dining hall was built and every conceivable facility was provided. The camp had electric lighting before the town had a supply. The steam from the generators heated the swimming pool and waste food from the kitchen went to the camp pigsty. 'Of all the Camp buildings, the most original was the miniature castle housing washrooms and latrines. This was to become the essence of holiday camp architecture: the functional disguised as the fantastic.'

The humble tents which remained as the sleeping accommodation provided the capital for the expensive and expansive public parts of the camp which were far more luxurious than those of the usual run of boarding houses and hotels. The camp had, Jill Drower explains, 'class': 'For the first time in British seaside history, the middle classes were choosing to spend their holidays alongside their social inferiors. The camping holiday that had been started for the good of working lads in Liverpool was, by the end of the Edwardian period, attracting young men from most walks of life.' It was not, she notes, until after the Second World War that holiday camps became distinctly 'non-U'. At Cunningham Camp conviviality arose quite spontaneously, and the campers themselves 'performed a function which in later years Redcoats would be paid to do: to make sure that everyone was having a good time.'

But like Butlin years later, Joseph Cunningham aroused the antagonism of the local holiday industry. However, after legal wrangling, the Manx Parliament passed a Bill giving legal status to holiday camps, with certain restrictions. 'It was felt that camps for women were undesirable. It was decided that while ladies could not be prevented from camping "at their own sweet will", they should not be allowed to pay for their board and lodging.'

In the First World War, the camp was used to accommodate 3,300 interned enemy aliens. Six were shot dead by their guards in a 'riot' while the popular press fulminated about the luxury in which they were assumed to be living. Even in March 1919 three hundred were still there, and 'their despairing letters home' crossed in the post with the avalanche of letters to Cunningham requesting the *Camp Herald*, the annual publicity magazine describing the attractions of the new season. The surviving campers from the 1913 and 1914 summers came back in droves, but 'it was a different breed of camper who visited Cunningham's during the 1920s.' The difference, Jill Drower explains, was that,

> Before the War, middle-aged campers could behave like overgrown schoolboys and nobody had minded. Now, even the youngest of schoolboys comported themselves like gentlemen. Gone was all the boisterous over-eagerness, the banging of plates on the tables and the stampede for the dining-hall at mealtimes. This was not to say that the high spirits had disappeared. Quite the contrary — the feeling of camaraderie was never stronger than in those first heady days of peace. No, it was just that young people had become more sophisticated. The campers looked different too. Cumbersome three piece suits and those stiff meddlesome collars were replaced by more casual sporting wear...The 1920s was to be a decade of

crazes, and in particular, crazes identified with youth, vigour and the outdoor life. All of this fitted in perfectly with the mixture of fresh air and entertainment offered at a holiday camp and the Cunningham management, aware of changing expectations, adapted to most, if not all of the new conventions.[32]

After Joseph Cunningham's death, even women were allowed into the camp for the morning and evening dances. Some of the campers brought their sisters, who stayed in the boarding houses of Douglas, to meet their tent mates.

Part of the Cunningham family folklore is about the way they foiled Billy Butlin when he was entering the holiday business and wanted to see the kitchens and grasp the new techniques of mass catering developed there. There were no convenience foods. 'Virtually every stage of culinary preparation was carried out at the camp itself – in the case of vegetables, this included farm production.' The facilities were continually improved:

> By 1933 three quarters of the campers slept in bungalows or dormitory accommodation. New 'chalet tents', which gave extra headroom and had their own front doors were introduced in 1936 and entirely replaced the old 'bell' design the following year. Tents were never entirely phased out, and some holidaymakers preferred to 'camp out' in the old Cunningham style.[33]

In 1939 the camp was requisitioned by the Admiralty to serve as HMS St. George, and when it was returned in 1945, the Cunningham family sold it to a Blackpool business man for £500,000 and the site was redeveloped as holiday homes, shops and offices. It had seen the whole evolution of the British camping holiday from the working boy's week in the sun to the second home by the sea.

2 Pioneer Camps

The time to be happy is now. The place to be happy is here. The way to be happy is by making others happy.

Those are the rules when you are at camp. Why put them into cold storage for the remainder of the year?

(Editorial, *Holiday Camp Review*, Vol. 1, No. 1, April, 1938).

Well before the large commercial camps arrived on the scene in the 1930s there was already a generation of holiday camps with a headstart. These were, in the words of their devotees, the *genuine* holiday camps or as they were also known, the *pioneer camps*.

In the latter half of the 1930s commercial camps and pioneer camps lived side by side, each drawing on their own sectors of an expanding holiday market, yet beyond sharing common classification as holiday camps the two types of venture were worlds apart. The new commercial camps were on an altogether different scale, catering for thousands rather than hundreds. Investment and organization reflected a corporate pursuit of profits, capitalizing on the fact that each year more people were taking holidays away from home. Huge white-painted concrete buildings with bright neon lights and tropical blue-lined swimming pools offered excitement and glamour for thousands who had been seduced by Hollywood on the screen and who had seen pictures of high living on the luxury trans-Atlantic liners, but for whom Skegness and Clacton marked the practical limits of their journeys into fantasy. For these the new camps hit just the right note. And over time it was the commercial camps (or *mass camps* as they were sometimes known) which wrested the initiative from their forerunners to set the pace and image for post-1945 developments.

HOLIDAY CAMP REVIEW

Editorial and Advertising Offices :
173, Fleet Street, London, E.C.4.
Telephone : Central 5610.

Vol. I No. I	APRIL, 1938	Threepence

Yet the original holiday camps were not to give ground easily. Theirs was a world that sought to turn away from the trappings of mass commercialism in search of the simpler qualities of fresh air, wholesome cooking and good, clean fun. It was an ideal that was closer to the more general pursuit of camping under canvas than to that of new developments in holiday camps.

For a couple of years (immediately before the outbreak of the Second World War ended the pursuit of innocent pleasures) the pioneers had their own magazine, *Holiday Camp Review*.[1] It was a cheerful, optimistic magazine, rooted in the belief that 'the Holiday Camp movement has come to stay...[and] is destined to spread its influence far wider and even more rapidly than it has done during the past few years.'[2] In its columns it expressed the spirit of what had by the end of the 1930s become something of a cult in itself – an offshoot of earlier, more broadly-based movements in pursuit of the simple life, a return to the land and co-operation rather than competition. The whole emphasis was on community rather than commerce.

These were broad principles, subscribed to by varied sources. Pioneer camps were sometimes simply family ventures, modest in scale and offering plenty of fun at reasonable charges. In other instances, camps were sponsored by organizations for their members. They, too, were offering relaxing holidays in convivial surroundings, though sometimes with a dose of education and self-improvement to enrichen the experience. Local authorities, co-operative societies, trade unions and special interest groups shared a common interest in the holiday camp as a new and challenging dimension to their activities.

All the signs are that the pioneer camps were popular places. Each year more people spent their holiday in a camp. Fresh investments were made throughout the 1930s, and campers themselves were keen to tell the world of the wonders of a holiday in camp.

But, in a growing market for holidays, the early camps – generally small-scale and often run as family businesses – came under increasing competition from the much larger, 'mass' camps. The pioneers responded, not by trying to emulate the newcomers, but by championing their own special qualities. Above all, the 'true camp spirit' was something they claimed was theirs alone. The larger enterprises had appropriated the name 'holiday camp' but there the similarity ended. They were, in reality, nothing less than 'holiday towns masquerading as holiday camps'.[3]

At times the criticism of the new camps became quite vitriolic. 'Concentration

Camps' was the heading of one diatribe, which then went on to describe them as 'the negation of everything that holiday camps have hitherto stood for. More, they are a definite menace to the future of genuine camps...High-powered publicity allied to a Woolworth technique may temporarily add enormously to the population of mass camps. In the long run it must pervert the principles of holiday camps and destroy the camp spirit.'[4]

Visitors to the new camps were measured in thousands — 5,000 weekly at Skegness for instance — but the pioneer campers were less than impressed. Some looked back nostalgically (albeit over no more than a decade) to the real pioneering days of tents and oil-lamps. Those who liked the pioneer camps invariably spurned the regimentation that went with the larger numbers. Typical was the comment of one camper who spent 'fifty-one weeks working in a factory. During the remaining week I like to escape from a factory, even though it is by the seashore.'[5]

In *Holiday Camp Review* the case for the pioneer camps was put by a group of journalists who 'have tasted the joys of camp holidays and...want others to do the same.' Write to us, they asked, 'not as impersonal scribes in distant Fleet Street, but as, say, Jimmy, Harry or Bill, Peggy, Dorothy or Grace of Hut 16, 60 or 90.' Their aims were to keep holiday campers in touch with one another and also to widen the circle and generally to spread the benefits of 'the true camp spirit'.[6] They were also at pains to respond to critics of the movement — some (like seaside landladies) who saw their own holiday businesses under threat from the growing popularity of the camps, and others who tarred the movement with accusations of widespread immorality and sub-standard conditions that were a threat to public health.

As well as the campers' own magazine there was also a formal organization, the National Federation of Permanent Holiday Camps, to further the cause.[7] The Federation had its roots in an association of holiday camps in Norfolk and Suffolk that was formed in 1933. Two years later, in 1935, the National Federation (with representatives of the great majority of existing holiday camps) was established with the aim of guaranteeing basic standards of food, comfort, accommodation, conduct and amenities in its camps. In an attempt to shake off an image of primitive camps (with likenesses drawn even to the rough conditions of military encampments experienced on overseas campaigns), eligibility to join the Federation depended on meeting certain requirements. Most of the accommodation had to be permanent (as opposed to tents), with an acceptable water supply and sanitary system, dining and dance halls had to be large enough for the size of the camp, kitchens were required to be open to inspection, and unseemly conduct by visitors was not to be tolerated. The day of simplicity for its own sake was already over. Pioneer camps were coming of age.

The Real Pioneers

> What shall it profit a camper if he gain the service of a Grand Hotel and lose the easy camaraderie which made a holiday camp so refreshingly different from anywhere else?
>
> (View of correspondent to *Holiday Camp Review*, Vol. 2, No. 1, May 1939).

Pride of place for the first holiday camp goes to the Cunningham Camp on the Isle of Man from as early as 1894 – starting life in tented accommodation and remaining throughout an all-male camp.[8] Mixed and family camps emerged some ten years later, amongst the first of these being Harsent's Camp at Pensarn in North Wales and the camp at Otley Chevin on the Yorkshire Moors.[9] These were the real pioneering days, when a rough wooden hut served as the common room for the campers who lived in tents and did most of the camp work themselves:

> We prepared vegetables, laid tables, served meals, did the washing up, and looked after our tents and their contents. Chores were meticulously shared out. First business on arrival was to appoint the daily committees. Each camper, young or old, served one day on the 'committee' and helped in practically all the essential work on the camp apart from cooking...For the evening concert or camp sing-song a swinging oil lamp provided dim illumination in the common room. We stepped up one when the tents were given boarded floors; the advance from camp beds to regular bedsteads made us marvel at our good fortune; and when the first huts were introduced we could scarcely believe that such 'magnificence' was possible for the money we paid.[10]

Also in the early years of this century J. Fletcher Dodd opened a holiday camp at Caister-on-Sea, on the East Coast a few miles north of Great Yarmouth. In its later advertisements the Caister camp was to claim that it was the oldest established camp and also that it was the only camp with its own railway station. It was followed, especially after the First World War, with a succession of new camps, starting in 1920 with Potter's camp at Hemsby in Norfolk.

These were invariably small-scale family ventures and 'Pa' Potter's camp was typical. Inspired by visits to Caister, Potter set about raising capital through

Pioneer campers at Caister Holiday Camp.

The Square, Hemsby Camp.

'Maddy' Maddieson's Hemsby Holiday Camp.

Another East Coast holiday camp was Pakefield Hall in Suffolk.

competitions in newspapers. With £950 from that source he joined with his brother on demobilization to start his first camp at Hemsby. From there he moved down the coast to a new site at Hopton-on-Sea in 1925 and then, eight years later, in 1933 opened nearby his famous 'Potter's Hopton Beach Camp' complete with all 'mod. cons.'. 'Gone are the days of candlelit huts. They have given place to brick verandah chalets with electric light and modern toilet conveniences.' In spite of the obvious improvements in the material well-being of the camp, Potter retained happy memories of the real camp spirit which abounded in the pioneer days. He was looking back nostalgically to the days when 'white American cloth was considered a luxury table cover and the few camps then in existence did a roaring trade on Saturday evenings with their penny candles which lit the sleeping quarters. Loud cheers used to proclaim my arrival with the pressure oil lamp which cast a dim religious light over the bare tables of the common room after supper had been served.'[11]

Typically, the pioneer proprietors liked to be seen as 'characters'. As well as Fletcher Dodd and 'Pa' Potter, there was 'Maddy' Maddieson of Hemsby and Littlestone, and the jovial 'G.A.' (G. A. Price) of Bramble Chines. Invariably they took an active part in the life of their camp – organizing games and competitions, getting to know their visitors, and generally keeping a watchful eye on what went on. It was a paternalistic role with utilitarian aims, 'pulling together in a spirit of co-operation and goodwill, to the one common end so that the greatest number of campers can get the maximum amount of happiness.'[12]

Still in operation today, and typical of the cheap and simple holiday camps of the inter-war years, is Golden Sands, at Voryd, Rhyl. It was started in 1933 by Arthur Jones, formerly of the merchant navy, who had a timber yard in the town. It had both one-room chalets and tents as well as a vast pavilion, built entirely of wood, for dining and entertainments. The 20-acre site, bought from a local farmer, was by the sea, 'Right on the Beach' as its slogans proclaimed. So

Coach trip from Golden Sands Holiday Camp in the 1930s.

that the name could be seen from the road, it was carried on letters 6 feet high held by 60-foot poles, and Mr. Jones, the founder 'was able to climb to the top of these poles without aids of any kind – a skill he had learned as a cadet in sailing ships.'

The camp was immediately successful, and in 1937 the Golden Sands Chorus, written by two campers from Birmingham and Sheffield was broadcast by the BBC and relayed 'to the Empire'. The words (to the tune of *Back to Those Happy Days*) were,

> Back to the Golden Sands
> Campers have congregated.
> Back to the Golden Sands
> Well worth the year we've waited,
> There's lots of Girls and Boys,
> The skies are always sunny;
> We are right on the beach,
> Rhyl is within our reach,
> Back to the *Golden* Golden Sands.

By 1939, when Mr. Jones's business was 'on its feet' the war brought an end to the annual holiday. The pavilion was used as a factory for making anti-gas capes, but the camp itself was not requisitioned for military use as the drains were not considered capable of coping, so it continued to be used to provide short breaks for people from Liverpool. A communal cook-house was equipped with rows of gas rings.

After the war, the founder was joined by his son-in-law, Victor Dodd, who has seen generations of the same families returning year after year. The Golden Sands publicity is disarmingly honest: 'Our chalets continue to be very well booked year after year. We ourselves feel they are somewhat dated, but they are well maintained and easy on the pocket.'

Another aspect of Golden Sands links the holiday camp with the caravan sites that proliferate on the North Wales coast. In the 1930s, plots on the site were rented to people who wanted a seaside caravan but who also wanted to use the facilities of the holiday camp. At the same time, a camp was developed on the other side of Rhyl, on a seaside site of 34 acres on the road to Prestatyn. The owner was a Mr. Hargreaves from Nottingham who began by renting bell-tents, and then employing out-of-work men from Liverpool to build three-room chalets, as well as renting caravan plots. The Robin Hood Camp (with its Maid Marion Store and its former Friar Tuck Café) now belongs to Golden Sands. All its chalets and caravans are privately owned, and all bookings arranged between the owners and campers, as with the caravans at Golden Sands itself.

The Rhyl Urban District Council obtained a private Act of Parliament to control camps, which are licenced from Easter to October. Standards of accommodation and the rules for lettings are closely supervised by the camp proprietors: 'Any owner who does not look after your interests doesn't last long at Robin Hood!', they claim in their advice to campers.[13]

Just as it was difficult in the 1930s to make a hard-and-fast distinction between holiday camps and caravan sites, so it was not easy to distinguish between organized holiday camps and colonies of individually-owned holiday chalets, like the 'bungalow town' of Shoreham Beach in Sussex, or like Jaywick

Sands on the Essex coast, which we have described elsewhere, with its 'permanent carnival atmosphere'.[14] Colley's Camp at Withernsea on Humberside is typical of many such seaside plotlands. Mr. Colley senior started the camp in 1932, using unemployed joiners from Hull to build thirty-five chalets of timber, clad with match-boarding, asbestos-cement sheeting on timber framing. The price of a chalet was £75. An adjoining site with twenty-five plots, called Kenwood's Camp was bought by the present Mr. Colley in 1966. The Public Health Act of 1936 was used to prevent permanent occupation by limiting the period of use to the period between 1st March and 31st October each year. Most of the owners come from the Sheffield and Doncaster areas. A recent visitor concluded that 'even on a rainy day the place has a delightful atmosphere and the feeling of a backwater is emphasised by its concealed entrance. The bright colours, neat gardens and painted fences make a gentle and poetic image in stark contrast to the alien atmosphere of the nearby modern chalet and caravan camps with rows of identical and impersonal units.'[15]

Most of the early camps were on the coast, offering a popular blend of sea air and camp jollities. A few, however, took advantage of an inland site, like the Robinson Crusoe Club and Holiday Camp in Berkshire which used its woodland setting to create an image as 'the camp that is different'. Chalets were built in the trees and, as well as the usual range of camp activities 'in the happy company of campers', Robinson Crusoe offered the unusual quality of solitude and an opportunity 'to retire to bed to the song of the nightingale.'[16]

As well as the private entrepreneurs the Holiday Fellowship also made its mark in developing the early camps. A non-profit-making organization formed in 1913 'to provide healthy holidays, and to encourage love of the open air', the Fellowship promoted holiday centres as well as camps.[17] Of the latter, holiday camps were initially seen as a way of offering cheap holidays for parties of children, though later there were camps for families as well.

A Fellowship brochure in 1932 advertised three seaside holiday camps for parties of boys and girls – at Staithes on the Yorkshire coast, at Conway in North Wales and on the Isle of Sheppey in the Thames Estuary. Together they could accommodate up to 500 children in a week, all in 'well-built army huts'. It was all very basic, but cheerful and well-organized. Campers who wrote to the Fellowship were more than pleased with the experience: 'The holiday was the best we have had...can think of nothing that would improve present conditions...the whole camp arrangements are A1.'

Family camps later in the 1930s could boast superior accommodation for those who could afford it. At Kessingland in 1938 a family could be housed in wooden blocks of bedrooms for 43/6d each. There was also an option of cheaper garden huts and sheds, for which 'great delight has been expressed by families'. In the true spirit of camping, guests were expected to keep their bedrooms and tents tidy and to take their turn at waiting at table.

The prospect of cheap, healthy holidays encouraged other organizations to launch their own schemes. Towards the end of the 1930s the National Fitness Campaign was active in spreading the word about holiday camps and also had plans of its own.[18] In 1938 a scheme was announced in which the Campaign was to sponsor a camp on the Lincolnshire coast, with the work to be carried out by Mablethorpe Council. The intention was to subdivide the 60-acre site into eight sections, each of which would receive 'poorer people' from eight counties in the Midlands and East Anglia. It was one of a number of plans that was foiled by the start of the Second World War, after which the holiday camp movement was to take a decidedly different direction.

Children in Camp

> Summer camp is a hallowed North American tradition. For close to 125 years large numbers of young Americans between the ages of six and 18 have set off each summer for their annual rest from tiresome parents. Parents over the years have had their own reasons for forking out the camp fees; this year, between June and August, some four million young Americans are expected to sign in at more than 10,000 summer camps across the country.
>
> (*The Economist*, June 30, 1984)

Since the very first British holiday camp grew out of the effort to provide a summer camp for poor Liverpool boys, and since bodies like the Scouts and the Boys' Brigade were pioneers of organized camping, it is very surprising that children's camps on the American pattern have not developed here on anything like the trans-Atlantic scale. There, summer camps are part of the folklore of growing up in America. They have inspired several minor literary classics, (and it is interesting to learn that the Camp Keyumah of Herman Wouk's *The City Boy* is the very same institution as the Camp Katonah of Paul Goodman's *The Break-up of our Camp*.[19] They have inspired dozens of collections of 'camp-fire songs' which must be engraved on the American heart, though they probably don't include satires like *Hello mudder, hello fader*, or even an unofficial camp song that runs

> No more days of vacation!
> Off to the railroad station!
> Back to civilisation!

In France the *colonies de vacances* were flourishing by 1920, but it was not until much later that organizations like the Forest School Camps and Colony Holidays were started in England. PGL, the largest British company providing children's adventure holidays (55,000 boys and girls at fifty centres by 1984) was founded as recently as 1957, when its founder, Peter Gordon Lawrence, first took canoe-camping expeditions down the River Wye in Herefordshire. Like its even more recent imitators running computer camps, it depends heavily on using preparatory and public schools during the summer holidays.

All these initiatives have catered for middle-class children at middle-class prices, but there have always been those who, true to the origins of the holiday camp movement, have pressed for an extension of their use for poor urban children. Apart from the work of the Holiday Fellowship and the pioneer work of the uniformed youth organizations, the propagandists for children's holiday camps earlier in the century frequently turned to the progressive example of the Scandinavian countries.

In an article in 1927, 'For England's Sake and the Children's', the author

The children's camp run by Birmingham Co-operative Society at Dunton Woods, Lea Marston from 1930 to 1939.

pointed to the growth of holiday camps in Denmark for children from the towns. Initiated in 1903 – with the support of municipal corporations, trade unions, newspaper appeals for funds, and the State Railway which carried the children free to the camps – the system had grown to the extent of accommodating some 6,000 children in the year of the article. The camp system itself grew out of a longer tradition of sending children into the country, not simply to fill their lungs with fresh air but also to absorb some of the solid qualities and uncomplicated values of peasant life. Health and patriotism were intertwined and that, claimed the author, was why a comparable system of holiday camps was essential. 'England has no use for "little old men and women"...while of sturdy, hardy boys and girls she can never have too many. And the great majority of our little East Enders might be turned into staunch patriots, in time, if only they were caught early enough, and enough trouble was taken.'[20]

By the end of the 1930s, some progress had been made in providing camps for children but the system was by no means as widespread nor as well-organized as it had already become in North America and Northern Europe. In addition to Denmark, the examples of Sweden, Germany and Poland were often cited. Reminiscing in the House of Commons, Philip Noel-Baker recalled how one of his most vivid memories remained that of going to the Stockholm Olympics in 1912 and being taken to a school camp in a forest outside the capital. It was something in which he regarded that Britain had been far outstripped.[21]

Apart from limited examples of therapeutic camps, the main thrust in Britain had come from welfare organizations and education authorities which had established school camps for their children. Where this had been done the record was encouraging, and initiatives date back in most cases to the beginning of the 1930s, and in some cases even before.

The Education Department of Glasgow Corporation, for instance, set up a Necessitous Children's Holiday Camp Fund and made fifteen films for fund-raising purposes to be shown in Scottish cinemas, illustrating the benefits that camp life gave to poor city children. In 1928 it provided holidays for 6,000 Glasgow children in ten locations by the sea and in the country.

Of the welfare organizations, the National Council of Social Service made an important contribution. Through grants from the Commissioner for the Special Areas, the Council had been involved with setting up and maintaining sixteen school camps in the North of England and South Wales. Between 1935 and 1939 over 141,000 children spent a fortnight's holiday in one of these camps.[22]

Reviewing the role of education authorities in 1939, the Chief Education Officer for Birmingham, for instance, used the evidence of 25,000 elementary school children to exhort councillors to extend the practice. He pointed to a discernible gain in health and physique amongst children from the city who consumed the regular meals, fresh air and sleep with voracious appetites. For many of the children a stay in a camp was their first visit to the country, and although at first 'the children were inclined to be undisciplined, and sometimes even frightened by the loneliness of the countryside after the busy hustle of town life...they quickly settled down and were really happy.'[23] Wolverhampton was another example of an education authority that had pioneered its own school camp, a start having been made as early as 1923.[24]

By 1939 there were some twenty school camps in England and Wales provided by education authorities. About half the camps catered for under-nourished and weakly children at no charge to their parents. The other camps were intended for use by children with no particular problems, who were simply offered the chance of doing their normal school work for a week or two in healthy surroundings. Parents contributed to costs according to their means, the average payment being between 2s.6d and 7s. weekly.[25]

The success of school camps encouraged the view that the children of every education authority should enjoy this type of facility. At an exhibition at the Housing Centre in 1939 the planning and provision of school camps was one of the topics on display. Amidst talk of mass evacuations and impending war, the idea of school camps was couched in terms of the very health of the nation. Indeed, it was argued, not only would it contribute to a healthier population but children would grow up with a better attitude to life in general and with a more responsible approach to the countryside in particular.[26]

Camps for the Workers

The development of large-scale holiday services by private enterprise has been rapid and successful during recent years, and more particularly during the last two years. Our members and their families have made this development possible: it is their savings that are pouring into the pockets of the owners of the modern luxury camps and similar services.

The members of the co-operative movement and their families represent one-half of the population, and, if one may assume a similar proportion of holiday makers and holiday makers to be, one can see at once the tremendous possibilities of co-operative holiday catering. There is no reason to believe that, properly undertaken, the movement within a very short time could not capture 30 per cent of the present holiday camp business...

(John Corina (Director, Royal Arsenal Co-operative Society), 26 May 1938)

A key element in the development of pioneer holiday camps is the contribution of workers' organizations – set up specifically for the purpose of promoting holiday camps or, more generally, as part of the co-operative and trade union movement. The attraction of holiday camps to this type of movement is twofold – serving both welfare objectives (in the sense of enhancing the quality of life for working people) and, at the same time, encouraging communal activity and a spirit of camaraderie.

The first co-operative holiday camp was started by the United Co-operative Baking Society at Roseland, on Canada Hill, overlooking Rothesay Bay, and lasted from 1911 to 1974. The Society had begun a holiday club in 1899 and in 1908 had sent twenty-five young people to the YMCA camp at Ardgoil. John

---

Dewar, president of the Renfrewshire Co-operative Conference Association was keen on camping because of his annual experience with the Volunteers (a precursor of the territorial army) and his propaganda for a co-op camp was supported by another Renfrew co-operator, John Paton, who had been converted through a visit to the Cunningham Camp at Douglas.

A site was found on the Ayrshire coast but the tenant farmer's landlord stepped in to veto the proposal. Then the little farm of Rosedale came on the market. The committee thought that to purchase it was 'too bold a step' and decided to lease the site for six months only. The staff were accommodated in the farmhouse, the campers in bell-tents with their meals served in a large marquee. They were 'unanimous in their praise of the beautiful situation, privacy and perfect catering' and the farm was bought for £600. The following summer showed that the water supply was inadequate in dry weather but also that in wet weather 'something more impervious to rain than a marquee was desirable for the gatherings of campers'. To put both defects right, the Committee sought a loan of £1,000 on the security of the property and before opening in 1913 had erected both a water tank and a dining hall to cater for several hundred campers. At the same time they urged the Baking Society to take it over as a going concern. 'They explained to the directors of the Baking Society that they were not taking this step because they disbelieved in its success, but solely on the ground that they considered dual control was not good for discipline and did not make for good management.'[27]

After the First World War (when the camp was requisitioned for military purposes) improvements were made, and chalets built. It held 400 people and was very popular among Scottish co-op members for decades. The Baking Society was finally merged with the Scottish Co-operative Wholesale Society and, in turn, in 1973 with the Co-operative Wholesale Society. It was this latter body which decided to close the camp at the end of the 1974 season, to the regret of those veterans who remembered the days when the seven-acre hillside site, next to Rothesay golf course, was 'covered in the summer and autumn months with picturesque pyramids of white canvas.'[28]

It has always been one of the principles of the co-operative movement that a certain proportion of trading surpluses should be set aside for education, and it was the education committees of co-operative societies that sought to promote holidays for members. In 1893 a Congregational minister in Colne, Lancashire started the Co-operative Holidays Association, of which the Holiday Fellowship was an eventual offshoot. Around the period of the First World War the Co-operative Wholesale Society ran an inland holiday camp on one of its farms outside Manchester, and various retail societies, in their long history, sought to follow the example of the Scots in venturing into the field of holiday camps.

The Plymouth Society had, before the end of that war, adapted some houses for use by members as holiday homes 'though this experiment was to prove costly and shortlived. There still remains from this venture the holiday camp at Stoke House.' By 1953 'a number of members who were actively interested in using the facilities at Stoke Beach attended a special meeting to give their advice and opinion, the result of which was that the committee did not go forward with its plan to cease operating Stoke House.' But they did so soon afterwards.[29]

As another example of co-operative society involvement, the Birmingham

A quiet game of cards at the C.W.S. Holiday Camp on its Crumpsall farm site outside Manchester.

Society ran 'the only children's camp in the movement', from 1930 until the Second World War, on its farm at Dunton Woods, Lea Marston, nine miles from the city. 'The days are spent in a joyous round of adventures – swimming, hiking, tours, cricket matches, hay-making, deck quoits, and games of all kinds, interspersed with a little "fatigue duty". It appeals to the children as part of the novel experience of camp life, and it is realised – only dimly, perhaps – that communal life means sharing the duties, as well as the pleasures.'[30]

Apart from the Roseland Camp, the most durable co-operative camp was the one established by the Coventry Co-operative Society at Voryd, Kinmel Bay, near Rhyl. It had its origins in 1929, when a small party of co-operators spent their Whitsun under canvas in the Peak District. One of the campers, Tom Snowdon, urged the society's education secretary to find a permanent site for annual camps, and part of a field near the seashore was rented. The equipment for the first camp in 1930 consisted of six sleeping huts, an old railway coach and an ex-army hut, two dozen square tents and some old bell tents. In July it was announced that 'no accommodation is available for the last week in July and the first two weeks in August. The bookings for these periods have passed our expectations, and only go to prove that the education committee was fully justified in its experiment.'[31]

In Coventry, as in most of the country, the last week in July was 'holiday week', so that the August Bank Holiday (then the first Monday) could be tacked on. People queued in February outside the Coventry Co-op offices to win a place in the ballot for that week. The immense popularity of the camp enabled the education committee to persuade the management committee to buy the whole of the field and to build about sixty chalets as well as providing space for campers to pitch their tents. Campers made their own meals with primus stoves, pans and crockery provided. The Rhyl Co-operative Society operated a shop with the dividend credited to the sports and entertainment fund.[32] The camp was run on a non-profit basis from the education committee's share of

Happy campers at the Coventry Co-operative Society Camp at Voryd.

The Ladies' Race at the Coventry Co-operative Society Camp at Voryd, 1948.

trading surpluses in Coventry and its education grant from the Co-operative Wholesale Society.

Harold Worthington, who took over as manager in 1948 when the last of the evacuees had finally left, recalls how the weekly charge of two pounds ten shillings a week for a chalet for four left nothing for maintenance and improvement. 'I remember, after a lengthy discussion, getting permission to line with hardboard about a dozen chalets, which internally were simply the rough unfinished side of the external lap-boarding, with the $3'' \times 2''$ framework showing inside. I did this, then realised that because of the uneven floorboards (no lino or carpets) a skirting board was necessary. Not forthcoming, so I finished off the job by using the crates in which the hardboard had been delivered.'

Even the primus stoves remained until the 1950s. 'This entailed me selling paraffin by the pint in ex-lemonade bottles, and methylated spirit to get the wretched things going. I was hauled over the coals by (I think) a local inspector of the Board of Trade for selling meths, obtained in 'six-penn'orths' from the local chemist, without a licence, so we stopped. Instead we sold small sticks of formaldehyde at a penny a time.'[33] Services were later improved, and as late as 1966 when a quarter of a million people had stayed there, 'queues form outside the Education Department Offices in King Street at least 24 hours before the first day of booking.' But the stage was reached when only a wholesale rebuilding, beyond the budget of the education department, could bring it up to modern public expectations. The chalets were bulldozed in the late-1970s and the site remains empty as the right buyer has not been found.

But its beginnings in the 1930s had been full of promise: that of cheap holidays for the workers without the taint of charity or patronage. It seemed to many to be the way forward. At every co-operative conference in the late-1930s there were voices urging that the movement was 'missing the bus' in meeting the challenges both of the forthcoming legislation for holidays with pay and of the new commercial holiday camps. Finally, a new joint organization, Travco Ltd, sponsored equally by the Co-operative Wholesale Society and the Workers' Travel Association was formed. The Workers' Travel Association had been founded in 1922 and by the Second World War had become the second largest holiday organization in Britain. The new non-profit company was intended to make 'a practical contribution towards the holiday problem of the family as well as individual workers of limited means', and it sought to ensure that its camps would be as modern as possible in ideas, while at the same time in keeping with the best camp traditions.

Rogerson Hall at Corton, just north of Lowestoft in Suffolk (now a Holimarine Holiday Centre) was the first of these new-style camps intended to provide a 'luxury' holiday for lower-paid workers, drawn from the co-operative movement, the trade unions and workers' organizations generally. Rates to stay there were competitive, though a scheme was introduced in which deserving cases were nominated each week for a free place. Opened in August 1938 the camp took 200 campers a week in its first season, with early plans for 360 weekly and an ultimate ceiling of 500. It offered a full range of accommodation, communal facilities and gardens, though certain features attracted their critics. Single and double accommodation, for instance, was not segregated in separate blocks (which was common practice), and huts were linked in continuous terraces. 'Arrangement of the huts in long continuous rows is surely a mistake,' wrote the editor of *Holiday Camp Review* 'but the architect may have been more influenced by town planning than camp planning.'[34]

The *Architectural Review*, needless to say, saw this as a virtue: 'The fact that the architect has organized its chalets into unified blocks alone represents a

Rogerson Hall: the W.T.A.
Camp opened in 1938.

great advance on the rows of individual shacks found in most speculative holiday camps.'[35] It was planned to follow Rogerson Hall with five more camps – on coastal sites in the South, the South West, South Wales, the North West and the North East. Although this particular strategy was not to materialize, other schemes in the 1930s certainly did.

A variety of welfare organizations showed an interest in the holiday camp idea. Along the Yorkshire coast, for instance, there was a Co-operative Holiday Association camp at Whitby, and at Hornsea a private firm (Needlers the chocolate-makers of Hull) had established their own camp for employees. In the 1930s the unemployed were not forgotten, but (in the workhouse tradition) strictly one sex at a time. It was women and children only at the Yorkshire Unemployment Advisory Council's camps at Cloughton and Filey. Unemployed men could stay at the Redcar School Camp in August but only in the weeks when no women were booked in.[36]

In contrast to holidays on sufferance, a more progressive scheme was that of the Derbyshire miners. After a lengthy campaign for holidays with pay ('could anything be more absurd...?' was the view of one colliery owner in the 1920s) an agreement was reached shortly before the advent of national legislation. This, combined with a Holiday Savings scheme organized by the Derbyshire Mining Association, provided the basis for the miners' own holiday camp by the sea (at Skegness, only a short distance from the first Butlin camp).[37]

Opened in 1939 (and still in business) the Derbyshire Miners Holiday Centre

The Derbyshire Miners Holiday Centre at Skegness, opened in 1939, continues in business.

catered at the outset for nearly a thousand visitors a week. A capital sum of £40,000 had been raised by the Miners' Welfare Fund and by contributions from colliery owners. Miners and their families arrived with £4 per week (£3 for single men) from the savings scheme, and the weekly charges were very low. A miner and his wife could enjoy a week's holiday for 33s., with an extra 8s. 6d. for each child, and they also benefited from a special rate negotiated with the railway companies to take them on Sundays to and from Derbyshire and Skegness.

Families lived in chalets ('in a general colour scheme which will be expressive of the holiday spirit') and single visitors were accommodated in what were termed 'cubicles'. Apart from the expansive beach on the doorstep, camp life revolved around the dining-hall (with seating for 500) with its well-regarded cuisine and, when meals were not being served, the nightly concerts and dances. A week at the camp meant good food and fresh air for workers who knew only dust and darkness for most of the year, and a real holiday for their wives who could leave behind their usual tasks and whose 'day of rest and enjoyment [at the centre] begins when she rises.' In its first year, some 15,000 visitors took advantage of what must have been one of the most successful schemes of its kind, and Sir Frederick Sykes (Chairman of the Miners' Welfare Central Committee) was probably right when he claimed that there was nothing comparable and that it was a pioneer venture that was being watched with close interest.

The popularity of these various initiatives in the 1930s, and the continuing demand for cheap holidays encouraged the Trade Union Congress to take a more global look at the potential for more camps. A proposal was considered

41

by the General Council for funds to be invested in a company to be formed jointly by the T.U.C. and the Workers' Travel Association to promote the building of a network of holiday camps and guest houses throughout the country.[38]

Although the Second World War was to intervene before plans could be implemented, the prospect of the T.U.C. (whose members and their families comprise a quarter of the population, and whose assets numbered millions of pounds) investing in the holiday industry encouraged fierce protests from traditional holiday interests. The plight of the seaside landlady was invoked in a cry of 'unfair competition'. But by 1939 the holiday camp had its own lobby and the legendary landladies, for years the butt of music-hall jokes, were given short shrift:

> Seaside landladies are doomed. The decent ones among them should realise that in time. Some of them might find worthwhile jobs in the camps. As for the rest, their passing will be a national benefit. Too long their indifferent catering, their musty rooms, their decrepit furniture fit only for the junk heap, and their methods of drawing up the bill have been sorry jests...It is a waste of time for them now to indulge in protests.[39]

By 1939 it was estimated that a million and a half people spent their holidays under canvas and in camps of all kinds. But compare this with the figures claimed by the traditional resorts. Blackpool estimated that it had 7 millions a year (including day trippers), Southend 5.5 million, Hastings nearly 3 million, Bournemouth and Southport, 2 million each.[40] All the same, the holiday industry felt that change was coming. Putting publicity claims aside, the resorts were uncomfortably aware that the number of summer visitors was declining year by year. At a meeting in January 1939 of the Chamber of Commerce in Lowestoft, one hotelier declared, 'It is time we faced up to the simple truth. We have got to recognise the competition of holiday camps, continental tours, cruises and motor tours at home. We have arrived at a period of great change and we have got to consider the new methods of taking holidays.'[41]

Pen-Pushers at Play

> When the Gods look down and see the bronzed body of the young labourer they smile.
> When they see the pale-faced clerk crouched over his desk, they drop tears of sorrow.
>
> (*The Clerk*, quoted by David Lockwood in *The Blackcoated Worker*, 1958)

The envy of the clerkly classes for the physical well-being of the manual labourer was founded on a fallacy. Statistical surveys in the interwar years showed without any doubt that unskilled workers had a lower life-expectation and a higher mortality rate than office workers. But, following the principle that a change is as good as a rest, it was the lower middle-class holidaymakers who most exploited the new opportunities for an active holiday in the sun, housed in tent, hut, cabin, chalet or sun-trap bungalow.

When the Industrial Welfare Society held a conference on Workers' Holidays in 1938, the Society reported that 'Holiday camps, private camping and visiting relations appeared to account for very few. The commercial holiday camp seemed to be hardly used at all by the average worker...Very few go abroad or to the country; fewer still take holidays through organizations such as the Holiday Fellowship, Co-operative Holidays Association, and the Workers' Travel Association.' The proprietors of commercial holiday camps similarly found that 'their visitors were not drawn from the factory floor but consisted mainly of the smaller salaried people, the black-coated worker and his family.' Even the new Rogerson Hall Holiday Camp, started specifically to extend holiday opportunities to working-class families, was booked up long in advance by school-teachers, minor Civil Servants, etc, and the people for whom it was designed were crowded out.[42]

And when Elizabeth Brunner compiled her remarkably informative survey of trends in holidaymaking at the end of the war, the secretary of the Workers' Travel Association told her sadly that 'It does seem to me that one of the disadvantages of present arrangements is that we cannot provide the working man and his wife with a holiday cheap enough to attract them, under decent conditions, and we fill our guest houses with middle-class people. If the WTA had to give a summary of genuine manual workers who went to their holiday centres, I do not think it would amount to 10 per cent.'[43] Two of the large unions of white-collar public employees were the pioneers of trade union holiday camps.

It was W. J. Brown, for many decades the ebullient general secretary of the Civil Service Clerical Association, the largest of the clerical unions, who claimed to have 'quite by chance set going what is now a very big and flourishing industry in Britain – the modern Holiday Camp industry.' He had found, as a parent, that to be at a seaside boarding house in wet weather with young children was 'purgatory', and at the same time he had recollections of the Caister Holiday Camp. He had spent a holiday there as a young man, in a bell tent, which was 'full of discomfort. One had to walk a hundred yards to get water for washing. The only light at night was candlelight: and the food was very poor, and the countryside bleak.'[44]

The idea that occurred to him in the early 1920s was, 'Suppose that instead of a bleak field we could have wooden chalets, with running water and electric light. Suppose we could have a recreation hall for dancing, concerts and the rest. Suppose we could have a place where, wet or fine, the children could make all the noise they liked, in circumstances where they wouldn't upset the adults who wanted quiet? Surely this would be a vast improvement on the seaside boarding house.'

He obtained the approval of his Executive Committee and found a site of wooded gardens by the sea at Corton, which had been laid out with loving care by the mustard magnate Jeremiah Colman. Brown wanted the camp to be a co-operative enterprise, run by his Association on non-profit lines. But then both his Executive and the Branches of the union got cold feet and found the enterprise too risky. 'Very well, I'd do it myself one way or another. I got together a few of my friends, and each of us contributed what we could, a few hundred pounds in all. Then I invited the members to take up shares at £1 a piece at 5 per cent. This raised the derisory figure of about £240. So, my friends having failed me, I went to the "enemy".' By this he meant the chiefs of various

Civil servants at their own holiday camp at Corton.

government departments, who lent £50 apiece. 'By one means and another we raised enough to justify us in placing an order for the erection of the camp, borrowing the balance from the bank as building got under way, and we had some security to offer. Altogether we spent many thousands of pounds, and we awaited the upshot of the venture with great anxiety.'[45]

The company Brown formed, 'Civil Service Holiday Camps Limited' opened Corton Camp on 7 June 1924, though in the May issue of *Red Tape* he was still urging members to take up shares, which they were not doing 'anything like as rapidly as we hoped they would do.'[46] On the other hand the accommodation was very quickly booked for the summer. The terms were £2.2s a week, with children under 12 at half price. Members were delighted, one of them writing, 'when I heard Brown say during a speech on the camp at Conference, "Corton is as near an earthly paradise as I ever hope to see," I thought he was being carried away by his enthusiasm. After a week at Corton my chief impression is that Brown understated this case. Corton is not "nearly an earthly paradise" – it *is* earthly paradise.'[47]

In the following year, would-be campers were having to be turned away, and it was announced that 'the time has arrived to consider the formation of a further camp on the South or West coasts.'[48] A second site was bought, the Orchard Lease Estate at Hayling Island, and opened in 1930. It was announced that between 170 and 200 people would be 'very adequately accommodated' and that 'profiting by the results of experiments at Corton, the huts will be built on the detached principle, each from its fellows, and their distribution will be artistically arranged to overcome that feeling of sameness which tends to result from rows of huts.'[49]

The columnist of the Association's journal *Red Tape* glowed over the luxuriousness of the new camp, which he felt had secured 'the absolute maximum of comfort for everyone consistent with not destroying the essential feeling that one is a camper and not a mere resident in a hotel or boarding house.'[50] By now annual reunions of campers were being held in London, and civil servants who booked for Corton in the 1930s found that the original camp could hardly be recognized, so much improved was it. In 1936 it was enlarged to take 200 campers.[51] Prices scarcely rose from their 1920s level all through the decade.

Brown was triumphant, and when the Association's annual conferences were held at Corton, would silence criticism on other issues, by reminding delegates of their lack of faith in the holiday camp venture when he first mooted it.[52] Was he tempted to give up the hectic life of a union boss and become a full-time camp entrepreneur? 'I suppose I should,' he mused, 'have set to work to do, what could easily have been done and has, in fact, been done by others – the building of a chain of such camps. But I confess that a life devoted to the making of money strikes me as the dullest kind of life of all.' He felt that Butlin had imitated his success, but commented that 'in my opinion, (pace my friend Bill Butlin) no camp should accommodate more than 500 people. Up to this number a very rich and full corporate life can be achieved. Beyond this number it cannot, and one of the best features of camp life disappears.'[53]

The other union which to this day still operates the first of its holiday centres is NALGO, now the National and Local Government Officers Association. Like W. J. Brown in the CSCA (now CPSA) the officers of the association 'were men of exceptional business flair to which the restricted field of local government gave little scope,'[54] but who were anxious to put it at the service of the union. They were aware that it was the multitude of ancillary services that the union gave to its members that drew potential members to the union and which held them there. Consequently, when at the 1930 conference of NALGO there was a call from the Manchester branch for the union to build a holiday camp for its members, this was both endorsed and eagerly accepted by the National Executive and the honorary treasurer, 'Billy' Lloyd, the borough treasurer of Hampstead. They appointed a committee to look for sites on the south and west coasts. They did not have to look far for the committee chairman W. G. Auger, a sanitary inspector from St. Pancras, had found the 'ideal spot' at Croyde Bay, North Devon, a newly built commercial holiday camp where he had spent his own holiday that year.

> It was perfectly sited on the edge of a deserted, surf-washed beach. Sheltered from the north by the whale-backed mass of Baggy Point, from the east by the foothills of Exmoor, from the sea by low sand-dunes, it lay trapped in sunshine and rural peace. It had ninety-five asbestos huts, a recreation room and dining hall, a tennis court and putting green, a garage, and its own electricity plant and artesian well. Auger asked the owners if they were prepared to sell. They were, asking £13,000. NALGO offered £12,000 and the owners accepted the offer, plus £428 for stock. The former manager and assistant manager were taken over, and the camp was opened to members on 2 April 1931.
>
> Fired by this success the NEC itself went to the 1932 Conference seeking authority to acquire a second holiday camp in the north. This was readily given. Within two months, after inspecting ten sites, the Council's 'special activities' committee had agreed to buy one of 94 acres at the top of a wooded cliff at Cayton Bay, south of Scarborough. Before the year ended, plans had been prepared and building begun – for this camp was to be NALGO's own, to its own design. It comprised 124 wooden bungalows,

Views from the NALGO camp at Croyde Bay, Devon, in 1935.

housing 252 guests, plus dining hall, recreation room, billiards room, card room, bowling green, children's playground, and a separate bungalow on the beach below. The camp cost £25,000 and was opened in July 1933.[55]

Croyde Bay was instantly popular, even though for half its pre-war years it had a financial deficit. Almost every post-war year has shown a surplus. Cayton Bay was always less popular and in most years resulted in a deficit. Some members began to criticize the association for concentrating on the 'frills' and not on the bread-and-butter issues of trade unionism. Our informants who as children saw the earliest days of Croyde Bay remember the 'spartan' accommodation but the beautiful surroundings, but in 1937 the wood-and-asbestos huts were replaced by brick bungalows with heating and hot water, and the recreation room by a concert hall with stage and dance-floor. The association's executive committee declared it to be 'several years ahead of any other holiday centre in the country,' for NALGO was one of the first camp operators to change from the title 'camp' to that of 'centre'. In the post-war decades Croyde Bay continued to be popular and profitable, but at Cayton Bay it remained 'difficult to attract a sufficient number of members for profitable operation' and the problem was made worse by a landslip in 1969 which necessitated the removal of eighteen chalets to new positions. The association's Council reported in 1970 that 'Between 1959 and 1979 the substantial profits produced by the Croyde Bay centre have been applied largely to offset losses at Cayton Bay. This has been frustrating to the management of the centre who have clearly demonstrated the ability to operate the centre successfully and profitably but have been unable to utilise the profits for the benefit of the centre.'[56] Already in 1959 the Council had recommended to the annual conference that Cayton Bay should be sold, but a strong lobby of local supporters led the conference to decide that it should be retained and improved.

The issue brought arguments year after year. 'Some members thought it was not a union's role to run holiday centres and wanted to dispose of them. Most members favoured the facilities provided the centres were self-supporting financially. A small core of seasoned campers wanted the centres maintained and enlarged regardless of the cost to the union funds. Such was their enthusiasm for the camps that they fought tenaciously whenever necessary to preserve them.'[57]

A Save Cayton Group was formed, and NALGO members throughout the country were urged to lend their support. An independent site survey and financial appraisal were commissioned, and details were circulated to show that the image of Cayton slipping into the sea, along with the association's money, was quite false. With modest changes in management and refurbishment, an attractive and viable recreational and educational centre could be created.[58] But the campaign failed, and at the end of 1976 the centre was sold for about £100,000.

In spite of its chequered history, the centre is still remembered with affection by former visitors. Alan McDonald was taken as a child to Cayton Bay every year in the 1950s. The children were organized into teams by 'Skipper', and known as Yorkshire Lads or Lancashire Lasses. Each wore a badge with a nickname. As he belonged to the Yorkshire Cricketers, his was Freddie Trueman. He remembers the long walk down to the sea on the winding path through the woods, and he remembers the weekly camp-fire sing-songs which ended, inevitably, with the lugubrious *Goodnight Campers*, a parody of Jack Buchanan's song from the 1930s, *Goodnight Sweetheart*.[59] Croyde Bay remains, completely modernized and rebuilt, as a monument to trade union involvement in the holiday camp adventure.

Camps on the Rates

> In the past camps have mainly been provided by voluntary bodies, and public authorities have only been concerned under recent legislation to exercise some measure of supervision. But the camps provided by voluntary agencies by no means meet the great needs of the urban population today, particularly the London population...
>
> (Secretary of the Area Committee for National Fitness, 24 May, 1938).

Some of the more progressive local authorities also began to look to the holiday camp as a way of bringing relief to people living in unhealthy surroundings.

Lambeth Borough Council, for instance, was a pioneering authority in this respect. In 1938 plans were announced for a municipal camp that could offer a week's holiday at a maintenance cost of not more than 45 shillings for adults and less for children.[60] Councillors were told that after the initial costs the camp could be expected to pay for itself and would not be a burden on the ratepayers. As well as being of general social benefit it would also have an important welfare function, with health visitors alerted to identify families in need of a good holiday by the sea.

There was some discussion as to whether a local authority could lawfully involve itself in this form of activity. Reference was made, however, to the Physical Recreation and Training Act, 1937, as a source of intervention and it was also established that the Board of Education could contribute to capital costs. Thus empowered, negotiations were opened for a 50-acre site at Hillborough, Herne Bay and the architects Max Lock and Judith Ledeboer were commissioned to prepare plans. It was envisaged that the site could accommodate up to 500 campers, 400 in chalets and 100 in tents. The huts were to be constructed in timber, using prefabricated sections. As the social focus for the camp, there was to be a community block with facilities for games, recreation and children's play as well as rest rooms.

It was a progressive plan and there was optimism in the air. Lambeth's Alderman Wilmot expressed a common view amongst his fellow councillors when he said he was sure that the municipal camp idea was the beginning of a great development. The London Area Committee of the National Fitness Council promptly called a conference to discuss possible cooperation between all those councils intending to follow the Lambeth example. It was argued that camps so far provided by voluntary agencies fell short of the growing demands of the urban population, particularly in London. Areas of cooperation included ways of preventing competition in acquiring sites, reducing construction costs through placing bulk orders, and achieving a rational distribution of sites.

More than forty local authorities subsequently attended a conference on the theme of Camps for the Nation.[61] Some authorities, like Chesterfield Borough Council, were already making similar plans to those of Lambeth.[62] The focus of concern at the conference was for the 70 per cent of the population who were earning £3 a week or less and who were unable to afford traditional forms of holiday. It was argued that there was little point in legislating for 'holidays with pay' if most people could still not afford to go away for a week. To redress this had become nothing short of a 'national responsibility'.[63]

For local authorities in areas of high unemployment the attraction of holiday camps was especially strong. In this context the Commissioner for the Special Areas in 1938 recommended the building of camps for the mutual assistance of the workers, their children and the unemployed in the distressed areas. Apart from the end product in the form of healthy holidays, the very process of construction could bring relief to the unemployed.[64]

There was certainly, by the end of the 1930s, no shortage of ideas and enthusiasm for camps in one form or another. Undoubtedly, various local authorities would soon have established their own outposts by the sea. In the event, however, the outbreak of war dashed so many of these plans, including that of Lambeth.

Camps for the Nation

> It is all very well for the Hon. Member, in kind and soothing terms to say that if we had these State camps they would do good by advertising holidays. In another sphere he reminded me very much of Hitler. When he walked into Czecho-Slovakia and took over the country and put its people into concentration camps, he said it was all for their good. When the Government walk in and set up state competition to the holiday industry the Hon. Member says that it is very good for us.
>
> (Mr. Robinson, in debate on Camps Bill, House of Commons, 29 March, 1939).

Preparations for war and thoughts of mass evacuation from the cities brought a new and more serious meaning to the idea of the planned camp. In debates on civil defence in 1938 and 1939 the question was addressed as to how and where to relocate children especially from urban areas in the event of a threat of enemy bombing. It was always expected that the great majority of children would be billeted in private homes away from congested areas. At the same time, purpose-built camps were considered as a partial solution, offering the dual benefit of being useful in peacetime as well as in the eventuality of war. To fulfil their implementation the Camps Act was passed in 1939 and the National Camps Corporation Ltd. was established by Parliament.[65]

The very idea of government-sponsored camps was of obvious interest to existing holiday camp operators. Their interest was twofold. As the acknowledged experts in the business of building and managing camps they had a part to play in the government programme. There was also the question of what would happen to the new camps in peacetime, and whether or not the existing operators would find themselves in competition with the State. In Parliamentary debates on the issue there were certainly those on the Opposition benches who welcomed the possibility of a degree of national planning to enable the entire population (including the unemployed and lower-paid) to enjoy a holiday away from home. Others welcomed the possibility of the emergency camps being used for holidays in peacetime, but did not envisage the continuing involvement of the State. It was probably a fair reflection of opinion at that time to claim that 'in this country there is strong and healthy opposition to bureaucratic incursions into the spare time activities of the individual.'[66]

In itself, the idea of planning a network of camps on a national basis attracted support on both sides of the House. Arrangements for evacuation had been found wanting and camps seemed a sensible answer. Criticism was more about the inadequacy of finance to provide a sufficient number of camps to a suitable standard, and about details of design, rather than about whether to have them at all. The pioneer camp lobby welcomed the spread of camps but was opposed in principle to any that were too large. 'Mass camps are not a desirable development in times of peace. In the event of war they would provide targets for enemy action far more vulnerable than any town.'[67] A few politicians, representing seaside towns, also raised a note of dissent. What they feared was the use of government money to create what might become unfair competition with the landladies and small hoteliers in their towns.

This possible growth in State investment was, of course, precisely what

National Camps Corporation sites, 1939.

others were to welcome. Labour politicians regarded the camps as an overdue measure in social progress although it could at best, as it stood, be regarded only as a small experiment. More camps were needed and in peacetime they should be open to adults as well as for use by schools. The belief was that the need and demand for well-planned holiday camps was well in excess of what the government had indicated.[68]

A month before the outbreak of the Second World War the Minister of Health reported on progress to date.[69] At that time there were plans for between thirty and forty camps in England and Wales, each to be built at a cost of £20,000. One hundred and fifty-five sites had been investigated and thirty had been found suitable. For strategic reasons they were all in the countryside rather than along the coast. There had been some discussion about the ideal size of camps (with early plans for as many as 10,000 in a single camp) but a maximum of about 350 in each case was the general target.

Design and construction was standardized through the National Camps Corporation. Swedish-style timber hutments were favoured, using Canadian cedar with cedar shingle roofs. The units were standardized and contracts were shared between four firms.

In spite of a call to see the camps used for family holidays in peacetime, the National Camps Corporation was required to give first preference to education authorities who could use them as school camps. Politicians spoke euphorically of the prospect of giving every child a holiday in the country. It was regarded as a social experiment, and there were '...substantial hopes that these camps would be the means of building up a fit race; fit not only in body, but fit as citizens.'[70]

By the end of the 1930s, then, the potential moral and social contribution of camps to the life of the nation (which had always been a part of the debate surrounding their origins) had acquired a new meaning. The imminence of war created its own priorities, and camp planning could no longer be left to the mere whim of individuals and voluntary organizations. Inevitably, the State was itself drawn into the business of what had previously seemed a marginal issue. In 1939 there seemed little likelihood that in peacetime the State would wish to retain a major interest. Yet the fact was already noted that camps, of all forms of holiday provision, lend themselves to an overall system of planning. And, in the ensuing years, when State planning became more widely understood and accepted, the possibility of a continuing role in this field became distinctly less remote. Though anathema to some, the idea of State holiday camps appealed to others as a practical means to bring the rhetoric of holidays for all into the realms of reality.

Happy Campers

Old campers, I am sure all agree that the real camp spirit, which counts for more than anything else, cannot be found in the 'Town' Camps. The smaller camps will continue to maintain and strengthen their hold on the real camper, who, once a camper, is always a camper.

(Camp pioneer, H. E. Potter, in *Holiday Camp Review*, May, 1939).

The pioneer camps, then, had come a long way in the 1930s. In 1938 the Labour politician George Lansbury could rightly claim that 'holiday camps are now part of our national life.' As a socialist, though, he added a note of reservation, observing that it was not like other parts of Europe where 'Governments organize this and other social efforts.'[71]

Before the 1930s examples had been few, and with their rudimentary conditions some were more akin to army camps than holiday centres. By the end of the decade there were more camps, the range was more diverse and the standards had improved enormously. Each year more people visited a holiday camp (the figure was some 30,000 for all types of commercial camp in 1939)[72] and although it was still a minority form of holidaymaking the trend was clear.

Various factors had contributed to their growth in this period. Throughout the 1930s (with the help of the 1938 Holidays with Pay Act) more people were taking a holiday away from home. Although manual workers suffered long periods of unemployment, for artisans and white-collar workers it was a time of rising incomes – enough, at least, to pay for a week if not a fortnight at a camp. Getting away to the sea with its 'bracing air' and open skies was also a fashionable and enviable thing to do. 'Wishing you were here' had real meaning for those left behind in the dreary, smoke-laden environment of the industrial cities. The omnibus also played its part in carrying families with their luggage from the railway station to the holiday camp that would invariably be away from established centres. And, finally, the pioneer camps also benefited from the growing involvement and investments by the labour movement and local authorities in welfare issues.

More, though, than simply profiting from external circumstances the pioneer camps were nourished on a reputation of their own. Happy campers returned from one year to the next, and word spread that this was the way to spend a holiday. 'It is something good in life and needs to be exercised to the full...The Holiday Camp ministers to every rational need of entertainment and healthful recreation at a cost which is well within the means of millions of people.'[73]

In fact, the cost claim was true in one sense but it was also true that many with lower incomes were still excluded. Particularly as facilities were improved weekly rates were raised to a level that was beyond the reach of many working people. At a time when the average wage was about £3 weekly, holiday camp charges of about 50 shillings each made it very difficult to take a family.[74] In the 1930s holiday campers were more likely to be clerks and skilled workers than dock labourers and factory hands. Another problem in terms of securing the best use of the camps was that of the people who could afford to pay more taking some of the cheaper accommodation. While the problem was not easily soluble there was agreement that a means test would be objectionable while, in any case, the segregation of poorer holidaymakers was undesirable.[75]

For the lucky ones, though, it seemed like fun all the way. The story of 'T.S.' a 23-year old clerk, printed under the heading 'First Time at a camp but Going Back for More' is typical:

> I am a clerk, 23 years of age, of good health and hearty appetite. Last year I went to a holiday camp for the first time...
>
> I arrived on a Saturday evening after a sticky and crowded train journey (I found afterwards that I could have gone by coach but it never occurred to me).
>
> I won't say that the management brought out the red carpet and brass band because they didn't, but I was met immediately by a very pleasant manager chap who saw that I got a good meal right away. Then I was shown to my hut, a roomy enough place with running water.
>
> I found that I was in time for the regular evening dance and after a quick change I beetled in to survey my fellow campers.
>
> There were two or three hundred dancing. You know how it is when you walk right in among a crowd of strangers? Fortunately no one tried to introduce me to anyone – because I hate that sort of gushiness. Makes you feel a fool.
>
> It wasn't long before I was dancing and the company looked pretty good.
>
> At breakfast next morning I got to know a decent crowd of chaps who were sitting at my table. We quickly arranged a foursome at tennis and by the time I had met a lot of others swimming and sun-bathing on the beach I felt thoroughly at home.
>
> I've rambled on like this just to show that there's nothing like a holiday camp for good companionship. It's easy to get to know people, everybody's friendly and there's plenty of social life.
>
> The campers elected a committee to organize all sorts of events and the

management helped in every possible way. We had physical jerks before breakfast for the energetic early-risers, sports, tennis and ping-pong tournaments, beach games, rambles, cricket matches, sing-songs, whist drives and concerts. In fact there was something doing every minute of the day and the beauty of it was that if you wanted to be alone there was plenty of room to do it in – if you know what I mean.

We got up to all sorts of stunts – we found moonlight rambles and moonlight bathing highly popular and with the help of a B.B.C. artist and a group of amateur actors we put on a revue that would have made Cochran himself sit up.

I stayed for two weeks and was pretty fed up at having to go back to work. The whole holiday cost me not a penny more than ten pounds. There was £2 10s. a week for the camp, about 30/- railway fares and the rest on personal expenses. There were absolutely no extras at the camp – all games and sports were free, although we sometimes subscribed sixpence each for our tournaments.

And £10 for a fortnight's holiday, living right on the edge of the sea and feeding like fighting-cocks is, I submit, pretty good value for money.

That's why I shall be going again this year. I'll be seeing you![76]

Different advocates cited more specific advantages of holiday camps. 'C.J.' was a doctor in Manchester who each year not only prescribed the restorative qualities of a week at a camp but like many other doctors he knew, took his own medicine to spend his own holidays in this way.[77] In medical terms, camps were the perfect antidote to urban life – offering the means for rest, fresh air and a wholesome diet. For many of his patients – 'the victims of bad housing, poor food, and indifferent factory conditions' – a stay in a camp would have been of more value than any medicine he could prescribe. But 'as it is, the majority are too poor to pay even the modest charges of a camp. I have, however, been instrumental in inducing scores of better-placed patients to visit camps. They all came back to thank me...'

In contrast, for Peter Howarth of Derby, the great attraction of holiday camps was that as you entered the gates the class distinctions that plagued the rest of society somehow disappeared.[78] 'Take your old school tie off and put your old camp shirt on...when I enter through the gateway of a camp I get that Liberty Hall feeling.' If camps do this for something as basic as class divisions, then what might they contribute to international relations? Supposing, imagined Howarth, that Hitler, Mussolini, Stalin and Chamberlain were to get together in a camp, what then? It was, at least, a colourful thought.

Another interesting claim for holiday camps was that they offered a fair deal for women.[79] Pamela Frith of Putney was a typist, 'not a rabid feminist' but someone who found it 'annoying to have so many men admiring the hat that I have on my head instead of appreciating the thoughts inside my head.' In camps (like Peter Howarth said about classes) everyone was treated equally. 'At a camp alone a woman gains that pleasing sense of equality. The girl of 8, the maiden of 18, the grandma of 80 rank with the boy, youth and grandpa without any sort of distinction. They are campers first, last and all the time. Age and sex do not matter.

CHAPTER

3 Chalets and Chandeliers

 Once or twice a week during the summer of 1934, a maroon, fabric-topped Austin Seven, driven by a stocky man in his mid-thirties, roundish-faced and smooth-haired, trundled along the narrow winding road between Skegness and Mablethorpe on the flat Lincolnshire coast. The man at the wheel was me, and though I did not know it then, I was travelling a road that was not only to change my life dramatically, but was to start a social revolution in Britain.

(Sir Billy Butlin, *The Billy Butlin Story*, Robson Books, 1982)

It is not the pioneer camps which are best remembered. Mention holiday camps now to anyone in Britain and they think of three names: Billy Butlin, Harry Warner and Fred Pontin. The familiar personal images are out of date of course: Butlin's now belongs to the Rank Organisation, Warner's is part of the Mecca empire, and Pontin's is a member of the Bass-Charrington conglomerate, but in each case holidaymakers associate their experiences with the familiar household names of the firms that bear these names.

Harry Warner, who died at 75 in 1964, retired from the Royal Artillery in 1925 and started a small seaside catering business. Six years later he began his first holiday camp at Hayling Island, profiting from his association with W. J. Brown, who had set up the second Civil Service holiday camp there in 1930. By the outbreak of the war Captain Warner, as he was always known, was operating four camps, with plans for more, and by the time of his death he had fourteen, in a huge holiday enterprise worth £2$\frac{1}{2}$ million. He was one of the founders, and was the first chairman, of the National Federation of Permanent Holiday

Harry Warner's first holiday camp, Hayling Island, 1931.

Camps, and he deplored the idea that there was any difference of interest between the 'pioneer' and the 'commercial' camps. As a military man he knew the value of spheres of influence and he made a deal with Butlin that the latter should confine himself to the coasts north of the Thames and Severn, while he should attend to the South Coast market. (It was in repudiation of this gentlemen's agreement that Butlin eventually opened his camp at Bognor.)

Fred Pontin came, as we shall see, into the holiday scene after the war, and built up his own huge slice of the industry, but the name that comes to everyone's mind, as personally epitomizing the holiday camp, is that of Billy Butlin. He was the kind of public figure that the British take to their hearts, since as the Duke of Edinburgh put it, 'Billy Butlin started poor and became rich by his own intelligence and enterprise, but he then proceeded to give away his wealth with typically realistic and perceptive compassion.' It was Butlin who set the pattern for the huge donations to charity associated with the show business organization, the Variety Club of Great Britain: 'He was the instigator of what I call the Big Givers. It was he who inspired the Michael Sobells of this world, who inspired the Charlie Clores of this world and all the other generous benefactors who somehow made it the right thing to support Variety Club charity projects.'[1]

But like many such big givers, he had another reputation among his associates and employees: that of a ruthless entrepreneur with an absolute unwillingness to delegate responsiblity. 'You either loved him or loathed him, I suppose,' a former Butlin's manager reflected, and like many other people who spent many years working for Butlin, he had tales of The Boss's continual preoccupation with the idea that his staff were defrauding him, as well as of his alternating harshness with magnanimity.

His son Bobby Butlin says 'I genuinely believe that the immense amount of charity work he did for under-privileged children, and children without a happy home environment, in his retirement was part of a guilt complex.' For he recalls being 'packed off to boarding school' from the age of five until that of eighteen. 'During those thirteen years I can certainly count on the fingers of one hand the times he visited me at school', and he remembers 'many, many occasions when I would come home for the school holidays and my parents were away...We rarely went on a family holiday. And even when we did, he hardly ever came swimming with us, or put his arm around us, or had any close contact.'[2]

The same remote-control autocracy followed him into adult life: 'My father was never a man for formal meetings. In fact, I don't recall attending a proper board meeting as such. His method was to call into his office those directors who were in the building – which is what he did on Monday 1 April 1968...In his laconic, to-the-point manner, he told us, "I'm leaving the country because of tax reasons and I must be out by 5 April. I'm appointing Bobby as the new chairman." So I became chairman of Butlin's on All Fools Day – and, as a City journalist once put it, I've been trying to see the joke ever since.'[3]

Bobby Butlin was then 34, while most of the senior men in the firm belonged to his father's generation. But none of them had much experience of making decisions, since 'the "Old Man" was the autocratic type of boss, giving us responsibility without authority'. Furthermore, in the mid-1960s the business was in trouble since the leisure industry was changing, and Fred Pontin was opening up package holidays abroad and self-catering at home. But his father used to argue, 'I built up this business. You've only been in it for five minutes. What makes you think you know what should be done?'

By 1972, the new management was succeeding in reconstructing the firm. An unsuccessful take-over bid meant that the Phonographic Equipment Company (now Associated Leisure) had by then $12\frac{1}{2}$ per cent of the shares, and Bobby Butlin found that his father, with his 7 per cent, had approached that firm to form a consortium to win back control. 'My father set out to try and oust me as chairman and managing director of Butlin's. Whether it was because I had not consulted him sufficiently, or because I had upset him over some matter, or because he had simply become bored in Jersey, I do not know.'

Hurt, and conscious that at any Extraordinary General Meeting called for the purpose of removing him, his father could depend on the loyal support of the small shareholders, Bobby resolved to dig in his heels 'and would probably have been forced to tell the shareholders how bad things were before he retired – which was the last thing I wanted to do. It looked as though we were heading for a major public row.' At the last minute the Rank Organisation made its take-over bid, which the directors recommended to the shareholders. Bobby Butlin remained as managing director, and 'the situation between my father and me eased considerably, and in the last few years of his life we became good friends.'[4]

But the jungle warfare of the boardroom was far in the future when Billy Butlin was prospecting the Lincolnshire coast in his Austin Seven.

Butlinism

> Stan Whittaker is forty-nine years old, and a Butlin camper type from way back. He met Bill, as a customer, in the early 'thirties at the Skegness Amusement Park. He and his wife were two of Bill's first campers in 1936. He worked hard for his money, did Stan. As a metallurgist at a Sheffield steel works his weekly pay packet bulged with £5 12s. 6d. if he could fit in the necessary shift work and week-end overtime. Butlin gave him a week's holiday, in those days, for £3 10s. 0d. In Stan's book, that was sheer commercial genius, anyway he enjoyed himself.
>
> Stan went back to Butlin camps year in, year out – and to week-end parties at the camps too. Every time he went to Butlin's there were even more people around him...He realized that he was in at the dawn of a new conception of holidays; in fact, almost a revolutionary new way of life. 'As a matter of fact, I had my own shrewd suspicions about this chap from the start,' Stan told me. 'And I'm grinding no axe when I say that if the history of my generation is ever written, Butlin's name is going to rank along with Sir Winston Churchill's, Marconi's and Sir Alexander Fleming's.'
>
> Stan had what he calls 'a little bit of brass' salted away for a rainy day; not much, but enough to keep the wolf from the door in an emergency; but after Bill first swung to success reckoned that his cash was not doing its best work in a bank. 'I drew it out, even cashed our National Savings, and bought 250 of Butlin's 5s. Ordinary shares which at that time, about 1940, stood at 13s. $6\frac{3}{4}$d.' he told me.
>
> Stan did not stop there. Over the years he carried on buying...He never for one moment considered selling. There was always this idea in his mind that it would be like parting with one of the family...The prices of the shares fluctuated, especially after the Bahamas episode, but Stan convinced himself that while Bill was at the helm everything would work out in the end. He was right. The Butlin share structure was altered in 1946 and the five-shilling ordinary share reduced to a shilling. In 1958 Stan's holding was worth £2,500.
>
> In the spring of 1962, he received a breakdown of his share interest. He held 50,000 one-shilling shares. Each of them was now worth nearly £1 each on the Stock Exchange. Stan Whittaker was a £50,000 man!
>
> (Rex North, *The Butlin Story*, Jarrolds, 1962)

Billy Butlin may have inspired both affection and resentment among those closest to him, but he certainly changed the British holiday and undoubtedly won the loyalties of hundreds of thousands of families, who not only returned year after year to a Butlin's camp, but attended winter re-unions and invested their savings in the firm. A new cult, Butlinism, came to mean, not simply holidaying in a Butlin camp, but the whole idea of holidaying *en masse*, paying a weekly fee and getting everything provided.

Almost all the characteristics we associate with Butlin camps: the catch-phrases, the obligatory conviviality, the chalet-patrol to enable parents to dance through the evenings while their babies slept, the techniques of mass-catering, existed in one or another of the 'pioneer' camps. The difference was that Butlin added to the formula the panache of his long experience as a showman and immense success as an operator of amusement parks, the glamour of the same kind of luxury that was found in the super cinemas of the 1930s, and the thrill of

I am

delighted

to know that my idea of Luxury Holiday Camps has had such a tremendous response, and that my ambition to provide the most wonderful of all holidays at a reasonable cost has been achieved.

W. E. Butlin

seeing entertainers and sporting celebrities whose names were household words. When his first camp was opened, Amy Johnson, a national heroine at the time, performed the ceremony, and after Len Hutton had scored 364 against the Australians, he was paid £100 to play cricket on the stage with a bat made from Skegness rock against the bowling of Gracie Fields. It was a recipe for success that Butlin had found through hard work and risk-taking shrewdness.

William Heygate Edmund Colborne Butlin, though he spoke with a West Country accent, was born in Cape Town in September 1899, where his father, son of a clergyman, had been sent as a 'remittance man'. As Butlin put it, his father was 'a typical country gentleman of his time. He was not trained for anything, and had never expected to work for his living.' His mother was the daughter of a baker who peddled gingerbread at the local West Country fairs. Her four brothers became travelling showmen, operating 'rides' or roundabouts on the fairground circuit.

It was thought best on both sides of the family that this contrasted couple should emigrate to South Africa, but while Mr Butlin was always in white as the local tennis champion, it was left to Mrs Butlin to run the business of importing, assembling and hiring out the new safety bicycles. Eventually she returned to Bristol and Billy travelled the rounds of summer fairs in her caravan, running a gingerbread stall. Later she married again and they emigrated once more to Canada. Billy's schooling was fragmentary and soon ended. It was while working at Eaton's Department Store in Toronto that in 1914 he went to the company's lakeside summer camp, 'which gave me the first real holidays I'd known.'[5] He joined the Canadian army at 15, lying about his age, served in France, survived the war, and returned to England in 1921, picking up the family connections at what was then called Dorney's Yard at Bedminster, Bristol, the off-season home of travelling showmen.

Starting with a portable hoop-la stall, his first day in the amusement business taught him how to bring in the customers by making it easier to win. 'On this day, as usual, the other stallholders hardly lost any prizes, but they only took £5–£6 each. I had lost £10 worth of prizes, but I had made a profit of £10. It was obvious who had done the better business. That day I discovered the benefit of small profits and quick returns – which is something I have practised successfully ever since.'[6]

The fairgrounds were controlled by families of 'riding masters' and the stallholders were at their mercy. When some began charging impossible rent for 'ground' at the fairs, Butlin rebelled, seeking out first smaller fairs and church fetes, and then the opportunities provided when Bertram Mills' circus at Olympia began introducing amusement stalls. But at the local fairs the crowds were beginning to dwindle. Butlin concluded that the cause was 'the charabanc, that early lumbering product of the motor age, the predecessor of today's luxury, air-conditioned, all mod-con coaches. With the arrival of the charabanc people were escaping from their often dismal surroundings to spend a day at the seaside. It occurred to me that it would be good business to follow them.'

In the 1926/27 season at Olympia a fellow stall-holder told him in the bar about Skegness, where there were a few summer stalls. He took the train through the flat Lincolnshire landscape to see the place, which in spite of John Hassall's famous railway poster of 1908 of the jolly fisherman leaping over the sands saying 'Skegness is so bracing' consisted of 'little more than two streets and a short promenade called the Grand Parade'. He resolved that a site opposite the area known then as The Jungle would be the place for a permanent amusement site. He learned that these sand-dunes belonged to the Earl of Scarborough and was told 'Oh, the Earl would never dream of letting the land for a fairground, even if the council gave consent.' A direct approach to the Earl enabled him to lease, for the summer, a hundred yard long strip of the dunes for £50, and he got rid of the sand by selling it at five shillings a lorry-load to builders.

He opened his amusement park at Skegness in 1927 and in the following year acquired a second site further along the coast at Mablethorpe. Stretching his credit to the limits he brought in the more spectacular rides like the Big Dipper or Figure Eight. It was Butlin who introduced the Dodgem Car to Britain in 1928, and he opened a chain of amusement parks at Hayling Island, Bognor, Felixstowe, Portsmouth, Bexhill and the Isle of Man. By 1933, before he entered the holiday camp industry, Butlin had arrived. A newspaper interview that year by Cedric Belfrage stressed the fact that he had a future:

> Big business has come into the English fair world in the person of Billy Butlin...From the start he was the perfect successful man in embryo, for while the old-fashioned showmen who set up their booths alongside him merely saw their business as a means of making a modest income, Butlin visualized it as the potential source of a magnate's fortune. Not for him the hand-to-mouth gipsy life, the crazy hooey and ballyhoo by which other showmen generally bluffed a willing public out of coppers. 'I worked on a fair profit basis, and always gave the public value for money spent,' 'To that I attribute my success.' He has 900 men in his permanent employ, and 2,000 during the six-months' summer season. He has his own workshops and specialists for designing ever-newer and more up-to-date rides and side-shows. By means of his special weekly carnivals at seaside resorts he has raised nearly £20,000 for charity. Five hundred thousand pounds of capital is involved in the various enterprises under his control, which earn him an annual profit of between £20,000 and £25,000.[7]

Butlin was ready for his next step, whose inception he described a hundred times in retrospect. It had been born, he used to explain, when as a travelling showman in the early 1920s, he had stayed in a boarding house on Barry Island: 'It was my first experience of such places and I was astounded at the way the guests were treated. We had to leave the premises after breakfast and were not encouraged to return until lunch-time. After lunch we were again made not welcome until dinner in the evening. When the weather was fine the routine became acceptable, but when it rained life became a misery...I felt sorry for myself, but I felt even sorrier for the families with young children as they trudged around wet and bedraggled, or forlornly filled in time in amusement arcades until they could return to their boarding houses.' He remembered Eaton's summer camp on Lake Ontario, and resolved 'One day I'll build a camp like that here in Britain, with the same happy atmosphere. But it will have more indoor facilities to allow for the British weather.' What he intended was 'a holiday centre for the great mass of middle-income families for whom no one seemed to be catering.'[8]

When he took the plunge into realizing this aim, he did so on a scale far larger than that of any previous holiday camp, except Cunningham's on the Isle of Man, which had taken many years to build. Butlin's Luxury Holiday Camp at Skegness was put up in a few months. He had £50,000 of his own capital, he borrowed £25,000 from the bank, and had many thousands of pounds worth of credit for building materials. He designed the camp himself, and most of the 300 men working on the site had been employed in his amusement parks in the summer. 'My plans were for a site to accommodate 1,000 people in 600 chalets with electricity and running water, dining and recreation halls, a theatre, a gymnasium, a rhododendron-bordered swimming pool with cascades at either end and a boating lake. In the landscaped grounds there were to be tennis courts, bowling and putting greens and cricket pitches. One major improvement on the camps then in existence was the modern sanitary arrangements, which included 250 bathrooms.'[9]

Work began on the empty site in October 1935 and the first 500 campers came on Easter Saturday 1936. Even for Butlin, overwhelmingly confident, it was a nerve-racking time. He was running out of money. On the understanding that payment would not be demanded until the summer he took a £500 half-

BOATING AND TENNIS, BUTLINS HOLIDAY CAMP, SKEGNESS,

page advertisement in the *Daily Express* 'offering holidays with three meals a day and free entertainment from 35 shillings to £3 a week, according to the time of the season. Within a few days more than ten thousand inquiries poured in.' They were booked for almost the entire season, with a thousand campers a week from June. 'Scraping together enough cash for a deposit,' Butlin told Peter Dacre, 'I bought a Rolls Royce on the "never" and esconced in this symbol of wealth I drove to see all my creditors. "I can't pay you just now," I explained, "because all my capital is tied up. But the camp is fully booked and your money is safe. I guarantee you will be paid during the summer." To this day I wonder what would have happened if I had called upon them in my Austin Seven.'[10]

His £100,000 gamble had paid off. By September 1,200 campers could be accommodated and in the following winter another £40,000 was spent, adding more facilities and preparing for 2,000 people a week in the second year, a figure which was ultimately increased to ten thousand. Even though the 'pioneer' camps anticipated many of the features of Butlin's, they were transformed by the sheer vastness of scale and the organizational needs that resulted from catering for such masses of people. W. J. Brown had claimed from his experience of the civil service camps that the limit for a 'rich and full corporate life' was 500 campers. Butlin found this to be true in the very first season and the Redcoats were invented to stimulate it artificially. Rex North explains that 'There was something missing. It was not easy to define, and for a time he was puzzled that he could not put his finger on it. Everything seemed to have settled down efficiently; the campers obviously took enthusiastically to the chalet

Morning 'physical jerks' at Skegness, 1939.

system, and they had all the facilities they could want. All they had to do was to go ahead, arrange their days as they wished and have the time of their lives; but they did no such thing. Bill watched them, as they moved about the camp and on the beaches; as they sat around the pool or ate in the dining-room; they were bored. Believe it or not – and Bill had to admit this to himself – they were bored stiff...He was mulling the problem over in his mind three days after the camp opened. These first campers had four days left – and they were gloomy, unhappy, and – in many cases – friendless.'

Butlin and his associates Frank Cusworth and Norman Bradford watched the long lines of bored faces. 'They thought about it, and decided that more colour had to be brought into the lives of campers. You can be very lonely in a big town without a friendly introduction or two – and a Butlin camp is quite a big town. Norman went to the microphone. He joked, laughed, and generally warmed the atmosphere. Friends became friendlier; strangers became friends. Five minutes later the room was noisy. The frightening gloom had lifted; the sun of enjoyment was shining on happy faces.' Butlin told him to devise a distinctive uniform, and next morning, in red blazer and white flannels, 'he leapt on to a platform and boomed a good-morning. It was answered with a sincere, thunderous reply that must have been heard everywhere in Skegness.'

'The experiment was socially significant. Obviously, holiday-makers desire comfort, variety, sun, sand, and sea; but on holiday, they are more relaxed if relieved of some thinking and organizing. Throughout the year, most of them work hard for a boss. One elementary reason for the success of a Butlin camp is that Big Boss Butlin is working for the holiday-maker by providing everything possible he can think up.' Butlin, so the story goes, assembled his staff to instruct them to 'muster under the flag of Norman Bradford – and in the same uniform. They would *not* attempt to regiment customers into some kind of fun factory. But they *would* lead, advise, explain, comfort, help out, and generally make themselves the closest thing to holiday angels on earth. The Butlin Redcoats had been born.'[11]

Butlin himself embroidered this story by explaining that Norman Bradford anticipated the practice of the Church of England by forty years by telling the assembled congregation 'Now I want everyone to turn to the person on your right, introduce yourself and shake hands.' After the initial embarrassment, people did so, and on further instruction did the same with the persons on their left. 'This time people did it with more gusto and friendliness. The ice had been broken.'[12]

The same two Butlin lieutenants devised the 'Come and join us' Salvation Army song routine of a follow-my-leader routine to lead campers out of the bar and the ballroom at closing time. It was an organizational problem solved, for as Butlin explained, 'What we needed was a painless, friendly way of emptying the bar which would not spoil the atmosphere and make people feel they were being bullied or turned out.' Similarly it was, as he recalled it, in that first season that 'One day, addressing campers from the stage, Norman Bradford shouted "Hi-di-Hi." and was greeted with a spontaneous answering roar of "Ho-di-Ho.".'

A Touch of Class in Clacton

> 'I am sure', said Councillor Green, 'that if we turned down this scheme and Mr Butlin went to the Ministry he would beat us. The position then would be that we would have antagonized a man who would probably be a good friend to the town...We must take Clacton as it was – catering for the masses; we will never get the elite.'
>
> (*Clacton Times and Gazette* 5 December, 1936)

Skegness had welcomed Butlin's enterprise. The demands of his camp may have initially overwhelmed the resources of its water undertaking in providing an adequate supply of drinking water, but this was resolved by sinking deeper wells. The important thing was that the resort which had never managed to attract the volume of visitors that might have been expected from the manufacturing towns of the East Midlands, was now beginning to draw them in. The London and North Eastern Railway, as successors to the Great Northern Railway, promoters of the famous poster, actually agreed to meet half the cost of Butlin's advertising for the Skegness camp. And when the local Chamber of Commerce proposed a Skegness Carnival, Butlin urged the traders, who subscribed about £50 each, that they should think bigger, underwrote the cost himself, bringing visitors from London, the Midlands and the North to the town in Carnival Week in 'the first of a long line of eye-catching, headline-making, publicity-bountiful stunts'.[13]

Butlin was good for Skegness. Would he be equally valuable for Clacton? He already had a site of 28 acres next to his amusement park there. He had the agreement of the same railway company to share the advertising. Millions of Londoners were only seventy miles away by train. Legislation for statutory holidays with pay was envisaged, and Butlin was ready with the very effective slogan 'Holidays with pay: Holidays with play: A week's holiday for a week's wage'. But Clacton's council was not altogether ready for Butlin, wondering how his proposed camp would affect the 'tone' of the resort and the incomes of its many ratepayers who catered for visitors.

Clacton-on-Sea was born as a holiday town in 1871, the year of earlier government legislation, the Bank Holiday Act. It was launched by Peter Schuyler Bruff, 'East Anglia's most colourful and successful civil engineer from the heroic age of railway building', who envisaged a 'limited high class development.' But 'the arrival of the railway in 1882 and a massive increase in the number of steam boat passengers began to tilt the delicate balance away from a select resort of substantial properties to a seaside town catering for day trippers and London excursionists. An exclusive and high class resort was to be developed instead at Frinton...'[14] By the 1930s councillors were divided as to whether the arrival of Butlin's holiday camp would lower or raise the 'tone' of Clacton. Already on the western fringe of the town a speculative developer Frank Stedman had set up Jaywick Sands, selling individual plots and chalets as holiday homes. It had many of the features associated with holiday camps, and at £50 for both plot and hut was very popular, enjoying a 'permanent carnival atmosphere'.[15]

When Butlin applied to build his camp at West Clacton, under the Town and Country Planning (General Interim Development) Order, 1933, the Bishop of Chelmsford wrote to urge the council to refuse their consent since, even at their best, 'holiday camps were not suitable things to be allowed in the neighbour-hood of a girls' school.' In the face of potential opposition, Butlin followed what was to become his usual course. 'He decided to stage one big outing at his Skegness camp for the Clacton authorities. He showed them every inch of the place, mesmerized them with facts and figures, bathed them in the atmosphere of lightheaded holiday fun, and plugged away relentlessly at the new paid holidays argument. The men of Clacton came, saw, and were conquered.'[16]

Not completely, however, for at the end of 1936 the council had a long and acrimonious discussion about the proposal. One councillor declared his conviction that 'the modern development was that people were going for their holidays in groups. It was the factory psychology. People lived in towns and worked in factories and were used to noise. They took the same sort of system in their holidays as they had in their ordinary everyday lives and that was the reason why these group holidays were proving so successful.' He thought the fears of the boarding house keepers were misplaced. The coming of holidays with pay meant that if the town was going to be successful it had to fit itself in with the demands made by the people of the country.

'There is a suggestion that Mr Butlin has nobbled some of the councillors,' said Councillor Ball. 'Well Mr Butlin is a very clever man.' Others complained that the rows and rows of chalets would be a disfigurement to Clacton. 'It would not be an improvement. It would be an abomination. The camp would have its own shops. Clacton would get nothing out of it. It would be a self-contained place.' Others claimed that the camp would not affect the boarding house keepers. 'In the summer the town has a population of 100,000. The camp would cater for 1,500. That was one and a half per cent of the total.' Councillor King, having seen Skegness, also believed that Butlin would bring 'a touch of class' to Clacton. 'It would also bring a new type of visitor much better than they had in the past. People using it would be paying £2.10s to £3 and they would be a decent class of people.' In the end the proposal was accepted by twelve votes to five.[17]

Butlin had no doubt that he would get his way and went ahead with preparations for setting up the camp at break-neck speed to open in 1938, which it did. To raise the £70,000 needed to build and equip the camp, he later explained, 'I decided to turn Butlins into a public company. The prospectus of Butlin's Limited was published on Monday, 8 February 1937 and five minutes after the list was opened the issue was over-subscribed.'[18] He kept control of the company, with £118,000 Ordinary Shares and £123,000 in cash, and became Managing Director.

The share issue was over-subscribed and the Clacton camp was over-booked from the start. The facilities, added to each winter until the war, were far better than those available to any ordinary holidaymaker in Clacton, and were

The swimming pool at Clacton.

Panoramic view of Butlin's Luxury Holiday Cam[p] every Holiday Sport and Entertainment has been plan[ned]

included in the price of bed and board. Parents were especially appreciative of the constant child supervision that was available to all. The Clacton camp boasted a vast 'Viennese' ballroom, as at Skegness, and a theatre where campers could see the current stars of radio, cinema, music hall and the world of sport. These included Gracie Fields, Florence Esmond, Elsie and Doris Waters, Will Fry, and the boxing idol, Len Harvey, who sparred with a boxing kangaroo. Campers danced to Lew Stone and his Band, or enjoyed the sounds of Mantovani and his Tipica Orchestra. And throughout the day there was free access to tennis or table-tennis, bowls or billiards, darts or dancing lessons.

This was so unlike the normal British holiday experience that it added more than 'a touch of class' to ordinary holiday expectations, and it won the permanent allegiance of many families, so that, beginning in the 1930s and interrupted by the war, they returned year after year in several generations to Butlin's at Clacton, and felt a sense of loss when that particular camp closed for the last time at the end of the 1983 season. 'It wouldn't be the same' they said, when offered an identical deal at another Butlin's holiday centre.

Skegness and Clacton were runaway successes. For the grand opening day at Clacton, Butlin hired a special train to bring every MP who had voted for

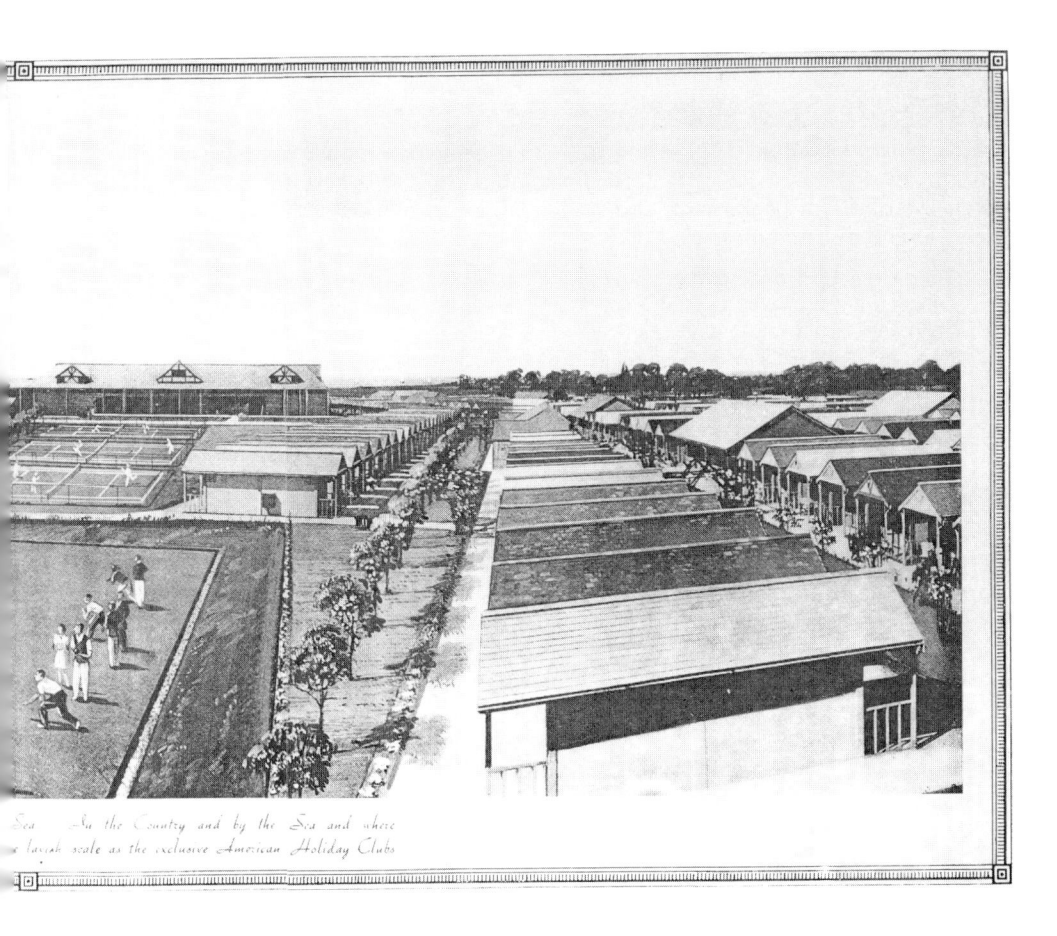

Sea ... In the Country and by the Sea and where ... lavish scale as the exclusive American Holiday Clubs

holidays with pay and show them what kind of holiday a week's wages could buy. At the same time he did not neglect the showground side of his business. He had won the concession for the amusement park at the British Empire Exhibition at Bellahouston Park, Glasgow. Rex North wrote, correctly, that 'No matter what the state of his business at any one moment, the Gov'nor has never been able to resist a massive nationwide promotion that calls not only for organisation on a grade scale, but the feeling for publicity that is born in every fairground busker.'[19] The vast Glasgow exhibition had several legacies for the Butlin camps. He had installed a miniature railway to take visitors around the park, operated by two scaled-down versions of the Flying Scot. The track and the engines, later converted from steam to diesel, served for decades at the camps and the exhibition theatre was rebuilt at Skegness in the summer of 1939.

Meanwhile, Butlin had been seeking out a third east coast site, and had located it near an 'exclusive' little seaside resort on the Yorkshire coast, Filey. He had barged his way into Skegness, a middle-class holiday place which had never prospered as its promoters had intended; he had out-Clactoned Clacton which had meant to be posh but hadn't made it. Now he meant to spoil unspoiled Filey where the Princess Royal took her children and their shrimping-nets for a marine nature ramble.

When Filey first entered the holiday industry, the local paper was called *The Filey Post and Visitors List*, telling who had arrived and where they were staying: 'In one issue Filey boasted an archbishop, four peers of the realm, seven members of parliament, and no less than 44 officers of the Army and Navy.' One old resident recalls how,

> As a small boy, I remember going to the station on Saturday mornings to watch the special trains arrive. They comprised one first class carriage which held the family and nanny, a third class carriage which contained the servants, a flat truck with the carriage, a cattle truck containing the horses for the carriage, and in the guards van were the hampers from the country estate containing food enough for the stay. The family would take over the whole of one of the Crescent houses, and the servants were accommodated in one of the many lodging-houses in the town.[20]

Long before Butlin this kind of seasonal removal had given way to apartment houses and tented camps. 'One of the forerunners in this mode of holiday was the firm of Reckitts of Hull, who annually gave all the young women in their employ a week in camp at Primrose Valley. They came in their hundreds as did boys from the "reformatory school" at Castle Howard. Towards the end of the 1930s tents gradually gave way to caravans and resulted in the sprawl of caravans which dominate the coastal scenery, not just of Filey, but almost the entire Yorkshire coast.' Nevertheless, when Butlin decided to buy a 240-acre site for his third camp, 'Filey's longstanding policy of anti-commercialism blocked all but one attempt by the fun merchants to cash in on the town's popularity.'[21] He adopted his usual and straightforward tactics for winning them over. He hired a special train and invited the members of the council, the Filey Traders Association and the Hotel and Boarding-House-Keepers Association to come to Skegness and see for themselves, and to meet their opposite numbers there to learn whether they had profited or lost from the arrival of the Butlin camp. 'Skegness reported in glowing terms of the increase in trade, and any opposition from the various organisations waned.'[22]

Butlin went ahead with the preparation of the camp the moment the 1938 holiday season had ended, and arranged with the London and North Eastern Railway for a special spur railway line to deliver campers to the site. The grand opening was promised for Whitsun 1940. But of course, war intervened. He recalled that 'Like Lord Beaverbrook, whose *Daily Express* had been proclaiming "There will be no war", I too was convinced there would be no war — and I told everybody so. My optimism was reflected by the campers themselves. Though a number of people such as government officials, reservists, school teachers and air-raid wardens had to cancel their holidays, we still had 6,000 visitors in the two camps when the war began on 3 September.'[23]

Butlin claimed that, driving between Clacton and Skegness that morning, he had no idea that the country was at war. But in the afternoon he had a visit from Admiral Buckley, as expected, asking how soon he could get rid of the campers. He paid back the campers' money and 'That Sunday evening comedian Izzy Bonn topped the bill at the camp concert. The following day Skegness was taken over by the Royal Navy and Clacton by the Army.'[24]

Camps at War

> War sends the current of purpose and activity flowing down to the lowest level of the herd, and to its most remote branches. All the activities of society are linked together as fast as possible to this central purpose of making a military offensive or a military defence, and the State becomes what in peacetime it has vainly struggled to become...The slack is taken up, the cross-currents fade out, and the nation moves lumberingly and slowly, but with ever accelerated speed and integration, towards that *peacefulness of being at war...*
>
> (Randolph Bourne, 'The State', in *Untimely Papers*, Huebsch, 1919)

As Britain moved lumbering and slowly into the Second World War, 'the complicated transport arrangements to evacuate nearly 4,000,000 mothers and children from vulnerable potential target areas around Britain began to slowly grind and click into place.'[25] The sudden official interest in camps in the late-1930s was as a result of disquiet at the Ministry of Health's reliance on home billeting as the solution to the evacuation problem. 'A large number of MPs representing the rural areas of East Anglia petitioned the Minister of Health to think seriously of building a series of large camps instead. One county council feared that householders would end up taking the "dregs of London".'[26]

Butlin and all the other camp operators knew that they had an asset of great importance for a nation at war: the ability to house and cater for a large and transient population. In the autumn of 1938 'top-ranking Service officers from Britain and France had made an inspection tour of the camps.'[27] Camping began as a military activity and it is not at all surprising that in the century of total war there has been an interchange of expertise and premises between welfare and warfare. We have seen how the Cunningham Camp was instantly pressed into service in the First World War, with Mr Cunningham in charge of catering for the interned aliens. He 'employed internees for all his own building projects,' his great-granddaughter explains, 'and in this way he was able to make improvements to his Holiday Camp for a fraction of the peacetime cost.'[28] Billy Butlin had similar good fortune in the Second World War when he was employed to build camps for the armed services which he did on condition that he could buy them back at the end of the war at three fifths of their original cost. As his biographer puts it, 'Bill Butlin wanted to help the country, and it so happened that the assistance he gave in camp-building eventually rebounded in his own favour.'[29]

On the eve of the war six hundred refugee German and Austrian Jewish boys were housed in the Dovercourt Bay holiday camp (where over forty years later the television series *Hi-di-Hi* was filmed). Six months later, enemy aliens were rounded up 'and many of them held for a time in Butlin's Holiday Camp at Clacton before being dispersed to the Isle of Man or overseas.'[30] Butlin recalled that 'At first it was intended to be a camp for prisoners-of-war, and barbed wire had immediately been put up around the perimeter. This had involved knocking down some chalets so that the wire could be stretched in a straight line. A row of floodlights were erected and these were kept on all night — beacons in an otherwise blacked-out countryside. There were loud protests from the citizens of Clacton, who rightly felt the lights made them a target for marauding German bombers ... Eventually it became a training centre for the Pioneer Corps.'[31]

Skegness became a naval training establishment, HMS Royal Arthur. In 1940 Ordinary Seaman Bill Young sent his Auntie Win a Butlin's letter-card of the place with the message 'Just a few hurried lines and some pictures to show you what this place does *not* look like...'[32] Butlin himself paid a visit and remarked, 'You can imagine my feelings as I walked round the camp to find that the dining-rooms, once called York, Gloucester and Kent, were now known as the Forecastle, Top and Quarterdeck Divisions. The Tyrolean Beer Garden, where many thousands had spent happy hours singing along with an accordion band, was now the Sick Bay waiting room and the Fortune Teller's Parlour was the dentist's clinic...'[33]

As with the other requisitioned camps up and down the coast, a deal had to be struck with the armed services for the use of Skegness and Clacton. Butlin did better than the small proprietors. 'The figure finally agreed was 25 per cent of our last year's profits, but it was not enough to pay the company's debenture holders. They received no dividends until after the war.'[34] Work on the Filey camp had begun in 1939 with the aim of opening at Whitsun 1940. Butlin was resigned to it remaining incomplete when the War Minister, Hore Belisha, sent for him and asked him to quote a price for completing it for the army. 'From him I learned that it cost the army £250 per occupant to build a camp. I estimated that I could do the job for £175 per head.'[35] His stipulation for the right to buy back the camp at the end of the war was, he thought, quite a gamble.

'But, if all went well, the deal meant that Butlin's would have a ready-made camp at a time when there would be great demand for holiday accommodation. It was also a good deal for the government. After the First World War the cost of demolishing the Service camps and rehabilitating the land was more than the price of building them. For that reason alone, it was later acknowledged that the arrangement was one of the best deals that the Service departments made in those hectic days of expansion.'[36] Harry Warner, 'my old friend', took over the task of completing the Filey camp for the RAF Regiment, but not before Butlin had devised the huge sunken parade ground which he envisaged as a future boating lake.

While Filey was being completed, Butlin was asked by the Admiralty to build 'another Skegness' on the south coast, a plan that was dropped – as the whole north coast of France fell to the German army – in favour of a site in North Wales at Pwllheli, which became HMS Glendower. Yet another camp was sought on the coast near Ayr, facing the Isle of Arran. This became HMS Scotia. Both these camps were built on the same 'buy-back' terms.

Meanwhile Butlin had been asked by the Minister of Supply to report on the reasons for low morale in hostels for women and girls working for ordnance factories. He went to Chorley in Lancashire, where there were 10,000 girls.

> Chorley impressed him – with disgust. He found it rather like an internment camp. There were rows of huts, naturally heavily camouflaged and surrounded by barbed wire. Obviously, it was there to keep out the unwanted. Equally obviously, Bill took one look at it, and at the girls, and realised at once that they felt like prisoners. This was the atmosphere of an internment camp.[37]

THE GOLDEN SANDS
HOLIDAY CAMP (RHYL) LTD.

TELEPHONE:
RHYL 706

TELEGRAMS:
GOLDEN SANDS, RHYL

RIGHT ON THE BEACH. AT THE
VERY GATEWAY TO THE HOLIDAY
WONDERLAND OF NORTH WALES

VORYD, RHYL.

Season 1940.

Dear Sir/Madam,

     Owing to prevailing conditions we regret that we shall not be able to issue our usual descriptive Brochure for the coming Season, but we are pleased to inform you that we intend to **carry on as usual,** and preparations are well in hand for the forthcoming holiday season.

     After an exceptionally long and severe winter with its added trials of War restrictions and Black-outs, a holiday in the sunshine at **"Golden Sands" will be more desirable than ever**—your cares and troubles will be quickly forgotten in the happy holiday atmosphere that pervades the whole camp. Jolly care-free companions and the delightfully invigorating air will give you a wonderful feeling of fitness to carry you through another winter.

     You will see by the attached scale of charges that we have not increased our terms for accommodation. We are unable so far ahead to fix a definite scale of charges for Board Residence but all meals will be available in the Cafe, and we hope later on to be in a position to quote terms for full board and accommodation.

     We fully appreciate that it may be difficult for you to fix a definite date for your holiday, but you may **book now with confidence** as in the event of your holiday having to be cancelled owing to the War or sickness your deposit will be refunded less a small booking fee.

     As **Rhyl is regarded as a safety area,** we anticipate **the demand for accommodation will be greater than ever** and we would advise you to make sure of your reservation by completing the enclosed application form and return to us **without delay.**

     We hope to have the pleasure of entertaining you during the coming season, and shall be pleased at any time to give you any further information you require.

Yours faithfully,

THE GOLDEN SANDS HOLIDAY CAMP (RHYL) LTD.

Some of the smaller
camps remained open.

Butlin's recommendations were very simple. 'Get rid of the barbed wire; invite some lads – and this he underlined – from a nearby camp over for dancing in the evening. Paint up the place, give them something of a holiday atmosphere when they are not working...He encouraged many things that now help to make his camps a success; dancing, whist drives, amateur theatricals,

71

variety shows, and so on. He also used, as he does now, gay paint, anything to brighten the places up. Morale most certainly improved.'[38]

By this time Britain actually was in that paradoxical *peacefulness of being at war*. The emergency services had learned how to cope with the bombing of the cities, and the blitz itself had tailed off into occasional nuisance raids. The shock of the fall of France and the imminence of invasion had passed. The Normandy landings and the horrors of flying bombs and rockets were still to come. The government itself was secretly sampling civilian morale and monitoring the effects of continuous overtime on industrial production.[39] In spite of increased taxation there was money around but very little to spend it on. People yearned for a holiday, and those with a network of rural or seaside relations and connections were able to manage it. Many coastal resorts on the south and east coasts were 'restricted areas', not easy of access for casual visitors. Some, like Clacton which were once 'reception areas' for evacuees, now had their own children evacuated. Not all the holiday camps had been requisitioned. Some small ones like Golden Sands on the North Wales coast, too small or too ill-provided for permanent occupation, remained open for 'week-end breaks' for their old customers.

Reg Tomes, who was brought up in one of the little 'private' camps at Withernsea on the Yorkshire coast in what is now North Humberside, recalls the paradoxical situation of being in a place which was both an evacuation area and a reception area: 'In 1939 my school was evacuated to Scarborough, but I didn't go, as my parents wished me to stay at home and assist them with our family's holiday camp, as far as a schoolboy could. One afternoon I saw a German bomber circle the lighthouse half a mile away and drop a bomb on Larder's caravan camp. A Mrs Read suffered a fractured arm and leg when the caravan she and her husband shared was flattened by the explosion. Mrs Read moved subsequently to the Kenwood Camp right behind my parents' home, as this was a chalet camp used for billeting soldiers and bombed-out people, as was our camp...Regularly, fresh people would arrive to dwell in our requisitioned timber holiday chalets, having been bombed-out of Hull, many still living there till 1960, when they were found council accommodation.'[40]

By 1943, the government was fully convinced that war workers needed holidays but was anxious that they should be 'Holidays at Home'. Butlin, after his success at the Ministry of Supply in changing the atmosphere of 'Emergency Hostels' into that of 'Residential Clubs', was asked to help a number of towns, like Gloucester, Leicester and Sheffield, in organizing holiday weeks, and as the owner of a variety of fairground rides which had been idle since the beginning of the war, brought them into use again.

> I asked to be relieved of my post in order to help the Holidays at Home project – something much nearer to my heart. I recruited my old fairground friends Billy and Charlie Manning and they formed three travelling fairs with forty-four rides between them. Among them were the galloping horses and switchback roundabouts – the latter with large decorated cars in the shape of animals, which had been so popular in the 1920s. I had always admired them and had an ambition to own one, but in those days I couldn't afford £12,000. Only the big showmen could pay that kind of money and, as a result, there were only ten or so in the country...When I was asked to help

> with the Holidays at Home, I remembered these rides. With Bob Lakin, I went to see the various owners and to my immense delight I was able to buy every one of them for between £200 and £500. My ambition had more than been achieved, for instead of having one, I had them all.[41]

From Holidays at Home, Butlin moved to the Directorate of Army Welfare Services running Leave Centres for the services in Belgium, as the military authorities were 'anxious to enlist Butlin's unique knowledge and flair' to run rest camps as 'miniature seaside camps, in fact, very much on the same lines as Skegness and Clacton before the war.'[42]

The war ended with Butlin in an impregnable position as 'King of the Holiday Camps'. He had held, with success, a series of honorary appointments concerned with both service and civilian morale. He was a familiar figure to cabinet ministers of the coalition government, to the chiefs of the armed forces, and throughout the world of entertainment. Impatiently awaiting the demobilization of the Skegness and Clacton camps from the navy and the army, he knew that he would have no difficulty in buying the three naval camps built to his specification at Filey, Pwllheli and Ayr. For a vast new seller's market in holidays was about to open.

Meanwhile, what had become of the pre-war government's hasty resolve to become directly involved in the provision of camps? As we have seen, this was presented partly as an educational matter, and it opened up parliamentary debate about the design and siting of camps, which spread into the world of architecture and planning. A total of fifty camps were to be built, as a result of the Camps Act, 1939. Those in England and Wales were to be entrusted to a new body, the National Camps Corporation Ltd. and those in Scotland by the existing Scottish Special Housing Association. By the middle of 1940 thirty-one camps had been built in England and Wales, and five in Scotland. They were expected to last for twenty years and each had six dormitories with classrooms attached, with kitchens, dining and assembly halls, staff accommodation and a sick bay.

In England and Wales they were let to local education authorities and used by 'individual or composite secondary or post-secondary schools.' Their population ebbed and flowed with the experience of bombing in the cities, but R. A. Butler as Minister of Education felt able to claim that 'the educational and physical advantages derived by the children...are beyond doubt.'[43] In Scotland they were used by elementary school children, particularly those who were hard to billet elsewhere, as the city education authorities felt 'it might savour of "class discrimination" if "luxury accommodation" was reserved for secondary education,' and there was 'a bitter and prolonged struggle over their administration.'[44] The SSHA ran the camps domestically and the education authorities educationally. 'The teaching and domestic staffs were quickly at each others' throats, making mutual accusations of laziness and dereliction of duty.'[45] After 1941 the child population steadily dwindled and in 1945 jurisdiction was transferred from the Department of Health to the Scottish Education Department which after the war handed them over to a new Scottish National Camps Association for use for outside studies in term time and for recreational use in vacations. The camps thus 'became a casualty in a political struggle, serving only to intensify the suspicion and lack of trust prevailing in relationships between central and local government in Scotland, all of this discreetly veiled from public view in the interest of fighting and winning a total war.'[46]

Reopening the Gates

> In those vast new wildernesses of glass and brick the sharp distinctions of the older kind of town, with its slums and mansions, or of the country, with its manor-houses and squalid cottages, no longer exist. There are wide gradations of income, but it is the same kind of life that is being lived at different levels, in labour-saving flats or council houses, along the concrete roads and in the naked democracy of the swimming-pools...
>
> (George Orwell, *The Lion and the Unicorn*, Secker and Warburg, 1941)

The end of the war brought a holiday explosion among the British. Not only had the pre-war holidays with pay legislation come into effect, so that five out of six earners had holiday pay, but the war had brought full employment for the first time, with a huge increase in the size of the work-force. It had also lowered the average age of marriage and had brought a baby boom. A new generation of young families were conscious that their children had never seen the sea.

Demobilization of four and a half million men conscripted into the armed services was phased over several years, with continual delays and postponements. De-requisitioning of seaside hotels, boarding-houses and holiday camps was similarly spread over the period of 1945 to 1947. Servicemen came home

Back into Civvy street with a holiday at Squires Gate.

with a gratuity and with little to spend it on. What more natural a celebration of the return to normal life than a holiday, especially when so many families were obliged to live with their in-laws and when food rationing was even more severe than it had been during the war itself? Paradoxically, a chalet at Butlin's was for many couples their first experience of domestic privacy.

In 1946, the first year of peace, the Ministry of Information conducted a campaign for 'Staggered Holidays' to spread the demand on holiday resorts over a longer season, and the Ministry of Agriculture campaigned among the young and active under the slogan 'Lend a Hand on the Land', to popularize working holidays on farms to help in the fruit, cereal and potato harvests. In the early post-war years agricultural camps attracted 200,000 city workers every year, and they continued to be popular all through the 1950s.

The peak year in the popularity of the traditional British seaside holiday resorts was reached as early as 1948, the year when one in twenty holiday-makers went to Butlin's and another 200,000 failed to get a booking. In 1947 the British Tourist and Holidays Board was asked to report on the demand for holidays and the accommodation required to meet this demand. The purpose of the report was to assist the preparation of development plans under the 1947 Town and Country Planning Act. The Board stressed that 'the bulk of our people are better off economically than they were in the past: they are better educated and their living conditions have improved. As a result they expect a much higher standard in holiday conditions than formerly. They are no longer satisfied with crowded accommodation, indifferent service and gloomy conditions. It is for

After the war, Skegness was demolished, but the message on this card (posted in 1948) says 'Hello, all. These bunks to sleep in remind me of the army. John has bagged the top one.'

this reason that there is a slackening in the demand for low-grade apartment and boarding house accommodation.' On the other hand they confirmed that 'The demand for holiday camps is increasing rapidly as is proved by the fact that most camps are already practically booked to capacity for 1949.'

Their report urged the declining resorts to win back holiday makers by giving them the facilities they sought in the camps: 'We stress that the demand is for the *type* of accommodation provided by holiday camps and holiday centres because we feel that resorts could attract some of the holiday camp adherents if they would give "all in" terms and set themselves out to cater for families. Such action might lessen the future demand for holiday camp accommodation'. They also stressed that 'There already exist a large number of holiday camps where extension of accommodation would be welcomed. Such a step would also lead to economy in running costs and a saving in materials and labour.'[47] In other words, despite the shortfall in supply, they were anxious not to allow the growing demand to lead planning authorities to sanction a growth of new holiday camps where none previously existed.

Interestingly enough, despite the growth of caravan sites, 'chalet parks' and 'holiday villages', virtually all the holiday camps existing in 1986 were already installed in 1946. They may have been completely rebuilt or greatly extended and their ownership may have changed several times, but with the major exception of Butlin's camps at Bognor, Minehead and Barry Island, all three in long-established resorts, the sites are those of the pioneering pre-war camps or of wartime service camps.

But there were some improvisers who siezed upon the new hunger for holidays in the spirit of earlier pioneers. One was Colonel Horace Fielder of Canvey Island in the Thames Estuary, landowner, councillor and magistrate. In 1951 he took the admiring C. H. Rolph for a tour: 'With an expanse of "dead-ripe" land and a peculiar genius for circumventing building restrictions by the use of unorthodox materials, he has laid out a holiday camp on 35 acres at Thorney Bay, with 160 furnished chalets and pitches for 1,000 tents and 90 caravans, accommodating, at the height of the season, about 7,000 people. Most of the buildings are of licence-free timber and corrugated asbestos sheeting, the doors were formerly table-tops in NAAFI canteens and the mattresses, blankets and equipment have been bought at government disposal board sales. The camp has main drainage, flush toilets, mains water, gas and electricity.' Chalets cost between two and three pounds a week for four people. Caravans could be pitched for £1 a week, tents for 10s, including all camp facilities, like hot baths. Meals were cooked on slot meter gas stoves for those who chose not to use the restaurant. To his surprise Rolph found that it was run with a staff of three, was clean, adequate and admirable. The campers 'love it, and they love "the Colonel" who has laid it all on – and who, having done so, leaves his guests to themselves. It is the latter detail, plus the improvised amenities of the camp, that distinguishes it from the geraniums-and-gingerbread holiday camps at which the middle classes pay 8 to 10 guineas a week to a kind of pageant master.'[48]

The comment is interesting since it shows how the distinction between 'pioneer' and 'commercial' camps survived the war.

CHAPTER
4 The Business of Fun

Leysdown-on-Sea attracted hustlers and cowboys and provided apprenticeships in mild crookery for generations of school leavers who, in the 1950s, 1960s and early 1970s, went 'down Leysdown' to work as cheap labour, cleaning the chalets in the holiday camps, serving in cafes and bars and minding stalls and machines in the fairground and amusement arcades. The holiday trade provided a myriad of opportunities for small business enterprises to start with little capital, and the regular flow of new clientele prevented the build-up of bad reputations: fiddles could be perpetrated all summer; prices could be exhorbitant; and high labour turnover prevented possible protest but spread bad practices. Some parents refused to let their sons and daughters go off in the summer to pick up bad ways. However, such seasonal employment also had the useful function of providing independence, some pocket money and the experience of a number of bosses, without any opprobrium resulting from having 'changed jobs too frequently'.

(R. E. Pahl, *Divisions of Labour*, Blackwell, 1984)

The post-war era has been one of mixed fortunes for the British holiday camp. New investors were drawn towards what must have seemed like the dawn of a Golden Age. By the early 1950s, with rationing and austerity ended, holiday camps became one of the symbols of the new society. The prospect of millions at play was an obvious social gain, but it was also very much a matter of business. It was not just the camp owners who saw it this way, but also the large workforce for whom the idea of a holiday camp as a place of fun seemed to offer something over and above the normal workplace. For the customers, the millions of campers, the attraction was more straightforward. Balance sheets and brooms were kept in the background, and enjoyment was all that mattered.

But the very idea of a Golden Age is notoriously fickle, and the reality of it all was sometimes rather different. Camp entrepreneurs were to find that, like any other business, competition in the trade was extremely sharp, and the market for their product was by no means as stable as first it had seemed. Workers drawn by the aura of fun were to find, as well, menial tasks and all the usual problems of wage labour in a large industry. And, while the customers were generally happy (filling the camps year after year, at least in the early period), for some one visit was to be more than enough.

Holiday camps have always been a world of bright images and strong feelings, seemingly larger than life but often really quite mundane. These contrasts and contradictions have caught the attention, in turn, of a different kind of 'participant', the literary observer, fascinated and bemused by the whole business and wanting to write about it. They reflected on what they saw, colouring the image that others already held, but also detecting nuances and, significantly, changes in the image itself.

New Faces

> In 1945, William Hoseason (the name is Scandinavian; he was a Shet-lander), then harbour master at Lowestoft, had the bright idea of renting out cruisers moored at Beccles as static holiday homes – static because fuel rationing meant their tanks were empty. He sold 200 holidays. This year the company, now run by his son, James Hoseason, will sell one million boating and self-catering holidays all over the UK and in France and Holland.
>
> (*East Anglian Daily Times*, 20 May, 1985)

The Lowestoft harbour master with a bright idea was not the only new face in the holiday industry. In many coastal areas there were wartime hutted camps built for the services, sold with relief by government departments to the site owners, since the alternative would be expensive demolition. These owners could either become holiday entrepreneurs, or sell the sites complete to people with this ambition. They found it advisable to bring the camps into use rapidly, for by the autumn of 1946 over a thousand camps in England and Wales had been occupied by nearly 40,000 homeless families as squatters.[1]

For the new holiday camp proprietors, it was a matter of make-do and mend. Building materials were available only by licence for essential purposes, but large quantities of war surplus beds, tables, chairs and catering equipment were being sold by auction, and the holiday seekers were prepared, like the pioneers of an earlier generation, to 'rough it' in return for a cheap holiday. Some of these camps, continually modified and improved, exist to this day. One such was the RAF camp at Skewjack, near Sennen in the far west of Cornwall, which is now Surf Village. Others, together with many of the pre-war pioneer camps, were taken over by new owners with access to capital for redevelopment, as the standard of accommodation and facilities sought by holidaymakers gradually rose. Warners and Hoseasons each bought several and completely rebuilt them.

But the major new face in the business was that of Fred Pontin. Born in 1906,

he left the Monoux Grammar School at Walthamstow at 15 to become an office boy on the Stock Exchange. Rejected by the services in 1939 because of his defective hearing, he spent the war years in the Orkney Islands, employed by the Admiralty to run catering and welfare services. He was then sent to Kidderminster to run a camp for 800 sheet-metal workers. It was an unhappy place and he soon found that he was the ninth manager in a single year. He moved to Bristol to take over industrial catering at a camp with an explosive mixture of employees of the aircraft factory and French workers who had come over to dismantle hutted camps for re-erection as temporary housing in the devastated town of Caen. The daily task of running the camp was so fraught with trouble and disputes, that Pontin concluded that there must be some less harassing and more rewarding way of earning a living. 'I asked myself "What does the public want that I can provide", and as my only experience was of the Stock Exchange and the money market and of large-scale catering, I decided on holiday camps which would at least be more cheerful and easier to run than the camps I was used to.'[2]

With the money he could raise and a £500 overdraft from Barclays Bank in Bristol, he bought the Brean Sands Holiday Camp near Burnham-on-Sea in Somerset. This was a pre-war camp which had been occupied by the American army whose last gesture on departure for the Normandy beaches was to drive its Whippet tanks into the buildings. He undertook a hasty patching-up and opened the camp for cut-price holidays in 1946. 'You'll ruin the business', Harry Warner told him. He formed a syndicate to raise the cash to buy further pre-war camps, like Osmington Bay near Weymouth, and in that same year, 1946, Pontin's Ltd was floated as a limited company. After the nationalization of the railways, the controlling interest in the LMS camp at Prestatyn had been held by Thomas Cook's, who sold to Pontin's for £650,000.

Many of the other owners of the pioneer camps had moved into other occupations during the period of wartime requisitioning, and found the com-

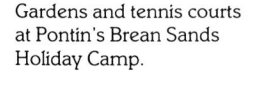

Gardens and tennis courts at Pontin's Brean Sands Holiday Camp.

pensation payments insufficient for the post-war task of modernizing their facilities, and happily sold to the better-capitalized large-scale firms. Others continued their pre-war business, feeling able to compete for their slice of the market because of their exclusiveness, their family atmosphere, or simply because they provided basic accommodation very cheaply. Mr H. G. King rebuilt and re-opened the Constitutional Holiday Camp at Hopton-on-Sea, stressing that 'there is absolutely no regimentation: you can do exactly as you please.' The Dodd family made the same claim for their pioneering Caister camp. Not until many years later was it to become Ladbroke's Supercentre, headquarters of another new face in the industry, Ladbroke Holidays Ltd, the 1972 offshoot of a gambling conglomerate. Tom Starbuck, formerly area manager of the Cash Betting Division, took over as general manager to find that his year spanned 'the extremes of mass catering in the summer, to satisfying the palates of American gourmets in the winter', on the very site where a visitor in 1914 took heart from the way 'the interchange of opinions amongst friends of different nationalities adds great interest to the discussions and debates on all the important questions of the day.'[3]

The Workers' Travel Association re-opened the Rogerson Hall Holiday Camp with its 'gleaming white buildings and smart rows of neat ultra-modern chalets'. Although there was dancing three nights a week, one regular visitor from the post-war years remembers that the programme of entertainments officially provided by members of staff known as Tom and Jerry was so inept that the five Griffiths Brothers, campers year by year, would take over completely.[4] The new face that finally took over at Rogerson Hall was that of Holimarine, who made it their Corton holiday village.

Nearby, the Civil Service camp at Corton was bought by Harry Warner, augmenting the existing Warner chain, with other camps at Hayling Island (where it all started), the Isle of Wight, Seaton and Dovercourt. The neighbouring Corton Beach camp was similarly re-opened after the war, eventually acquired by Hoseason's as part of their growing chain of self-catering camps. The pre-war impetus for 'non-commercial' holiday camps had run out of steam, partly because of the capital expenditure involved in upgrading the premises, and partly because of the entrepreneurial flair of the commercial operators. Subcommittees of the clerical unions and the retail co-operative societies starved their camp managers of funds for essential repairs, while Butlin embarked on extravagant and imaginative gestures. His wartime shrewdness in building service camps for repurchase had put him far ahead of his rivals in the new golden age.

Bobby Butlin remembers his first visit to one of his father's camps when, at Filey, a few weeks after the end of the war, the new generation of holiday makers were settled in one half of the camp while RAF recruits were still drilling in the other half. 'It was almost symbolic: the campers thronging in at one gate, with the airmen marching out at another.' A new firm, Butlin Properties Ltd was set up with a capital of over a million pounds to finance the repurchase of the Butlin camps. Filey was re-opened completely in 1946, as were the pre-war camps at Clacton and Skegness. In the following year the camps put up for the armed forces at Ayr and Pwllheli were opened for campers.

Butlin was determined to enter the world of post-war austerity with a grand

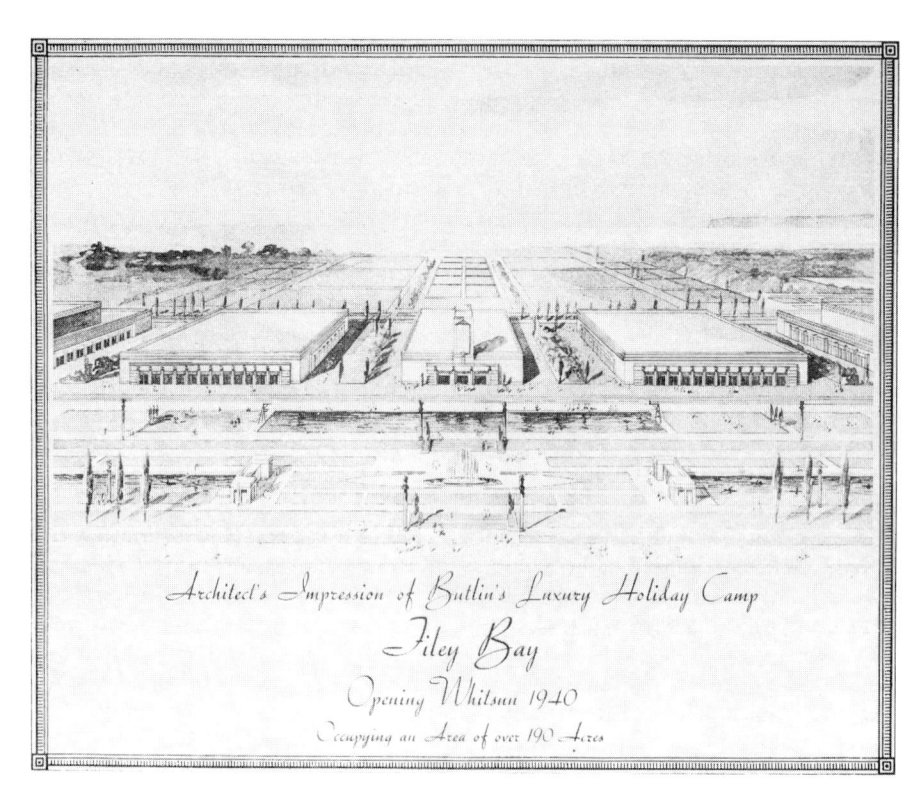

Architect's Impression of Butlin's Luxury Holiday Camp

Filey Bay

Opening Whitsun 1940

Occupying an Area of over 190 Acres

Planned to open in 1940, Butlin's Filey camp was finally 'demobbed' in 1946.

gesture. At a cost of £1,100 he brought the Yorkshire Pullman luxury train out of storage for a VIP trip to Filey.

> Then he wrote 400 invitations to the top names in politics, science, theatre, art, music and the London social world for a great colourful evening in the massive concert hall at Filey, where he had decided to put on an unthinkingly expensive production of Puccini's *La Bohème* by the famous San Carlo Opera Company...The show was a colossal success, and it played for a week to packed houses. Music-lovers, starved for six years of opera of this scope and brilliance, came from all over the country. William Butlin, a little short of days at school – and this through no fault of his own – had discovered that there is prestige in encouraging culture. So he tempted the Old Vic Company to Filey for a short season of Shakespearian plays. Again the customers turned up in thousands; again Bill was the person least surprised. Meanwhile, the San Carlo Opera Company was touring all the camps, and, at the same time, Bill was introducing ballet to them as well.[5]

None of the rival operators could hope to emulate him, but there was room for all in the expanding market of the late 1940s and early 1950s. They all met in the National Federation of Permanent Holiday Camps, while Butlin, Warner and Pontin were increasingly involved in the world of sport and the show-business charitable enterprises. Sir Fred Pontin once said to Butlin at one of these functions, 'You've taught me everything I know about holiday camps', and received the reply, 'Maybe, but not everything *I* know.' Pontin however knew the City better than to get involved in the next Butlin venture. After forming yet another new company, Butlin's Irish and Continental Holidays Ltd, to open Mosney Holiday Village north of Dublin, and having bought and sold at a profit two hotels in Bermuda, he was lured into setting up Butlin's (Bahamas) Ltd to build a vacation village for the American tourist trade on the island of Grand Bahama. In 1951 the firm went into liquidation and was compulsorily wound up. As Rex North put it, 'Like any other institution the City is not free of its own sharks who make a fine art out of carving in on the good name or reputation of bone-fide finance houses. Butlin learned the hard way...The result was that the City turned against him, and he was cut off like a wayward son for several years.'[6] He and a great many faithful ordinary share-holders who had followed him into the venture, lost their money.

Butlin relied on his personal popularity to help him weather the storm of criticism of the complicated interlocking finances of his various companies and the lack of information for shareholders. 'Certain shareholders and other City critics were vocal in their attacks on the board, and from 1951 Billy held the annual meetings at the holiday camps instead of in London. Much publicity attended this move, whereby 200 members were entertained for a weekend each year at the company's expense.'[7] While he remained in control of the firm, expansion was confined to Britain. Several chains of hotels were bought and the last three big holiday centres were built, at Bognor in 1960, Minehead in 1962 and Barry Island in 1966, with the aim of having a camp within 200 miles of every major centre of population in the country. Christmas opening and 'special week-ends' were introduced, to extend the season, some chalets were provided with private bathrooms to meet the rising standards of hotel accommodation elsewhere, but as we have seen, by the time Butlin retired, for tax-avoidance reasons, the firm, despite record bookings, was failing to keep abreast with changing holiday expectations.

Pontin meanwhile was pioneering the 'self-catering' holiday and under the slogan *Go Pontinental!* opened his first package holidays at Platamona Beach in Sardinia in 1963, following this with further continental holiday camps at Torremolinos and Majorca. But he, too, was to be ousted from his own firm by a take-over bid unsuccessfully resisted. Just as the betting firm of Ladbroke's had begun buying up camps and hotels in the early 1970s, so Joe Coral's betting shop group gained control of Pontin's in 1978. Both firms found themselves in trouble in 1980 over the gaming laws, and Pontin's was sold once again, this time to Bass Charrington.

In the same year, Ladbroke's managing director remarked that 'I envisage some independent sites coming on to the market and I foresee being able to increase the size of my circuit this coming winter. I am in an acquisitive frame of mind.'[8] A similar line of thinking was revealed a few years later by Warner's marketing director. 'We are very growth conscious and acquisitive' he said.[9] Warner's themselves had been taken over, along with the Mecca Leisure company, by Grand Metropolitan, whose other interests include the Watney brewery, Gilbey's gin and J and B whisky, Express Dairies and an international chain of hotels. It was reported in 1985 that 'The Hi-di-hi holiday camp in Dovercourt is to be sold off, as part of a multi-million pound deal along with ten other Warner camps and the entire Mecca empire. A management buy-out is being negotiated in which the two subsidiaries' directors may purchase the business.'[10]

Thus, in the course of a single lifetime the holiday camps movement has altered beyond recognition, from bell-tents put up by parties of enthusiasts in a rented field, to the boardroom warfare of rival groups of financiers. It is a trend which has made its mark behind the scenes, amongst the workforce as well as in the boardroom.

Working in Camp

I was called to the office of the steely Commandant.
'Why the hell are you here?' he yelled, almost before I was through the door.
'...Here?'
'Don't play bloody stupid with me. I know what you've been up to. Too many rough nights with that bit from drama school!...Why are you in this camp?'
'Er...to help people enjoy themselves?'
'*Exactly!*'
He threw a photograph across the desk. It had been taken by a wandering ballroom photographer and featured the King of Po-land. It also featured, well in the foreground, me; there was an expression of such cosmic sadness on my face that I saw his point.

(P. J. Kavanagh, *The Perfect Stranger*, Chatto and Windus, 1966)

The most interesting thing of all about the comedy series *Hi-di-hi*, and its immense popular success, is that it wasn't about campers at all, but about the staff. The holiday makers appeared in crowd scenes only, with mere walk-on parts in the drama of Maplin's which was mostly about the personal relationships of the staff, partly about staff relationships with an unseen management structure, and not at all about staff relationships with the campers.

Since the comparison between holiday camps and prison camps has so often been made, it is tempting to look at them in terms of the sociological theories about 'total institutions' – prisons, military establishments, asylums – developed by Erving Goffman and others.[11] These students of institutions stress the way in which inmates develop an underlife of their own in response to the official culture of the institution which aims to modify their original identity to fit that official culture. The sociologist Pradeep Bandyopadhyay has examined how camps, as places where strangers eat, drink, interact and sleep in a temporary closed institutional setting, can be fitted into this model, and concludes that the concept hardly applies since

Entry is voluntary; staff and campers are not structurally prone to conflict; they mutually exploit each other, with the campers being, for structural and temporal reasons, more vulnerable. Instead of rituals of degradation and loss of esteem, there are processes of elevation of status and roles; instead of imposed unpleasant work routines there are optional pleasurable 'fun' or play situations. Instead of maximizing organizational control over inmates, the campers are enabled to manipulate the organizational machinery within the limits of organizational survival and economic profitability; instead of an underlife exclusive of staff, the involvement of staff is essential to the culture of a holiday camp.[12]

In fact the various inmate roles which sociologists discover in the culture of penal institutions – Robin Hood, Robber Baron and so on – belong in the holiday camp, not to the inmates but to the various categories of the staff. This has to do with the sheer scale of the operation. The pioneer camps were run as family concerns, frequently by members of the same family with local friends helping out with the catering during the season. There was no demarcation of jobs. When the Coventry Co-operative Society appointed Harold Worthington to run its camp near Rhyl, he was designated Camp Steward because, it was explained to him, if the job was described as 'Manager' the appointee might think he was supposed to sit in an office all day – just managing. In fact he found that his job was that of magician, mind-reader, quiz master, sports organizer, pianist and, after hours, cesspool emptier and scenery painter.[13] How different is the role of the general manager of Butlin's Bognor camp who sees himself as 'the commodore of a cruise liner'! His one formal engagement of the week is to greet the new campers at the variety show on Saturday nights. The rest of his job is keeping control of a vast and complex operation run by a huge staff each member of which has expectations from the job which do not coincide with his:

> During the company's summer peak, there will be 6,050 beds full at Bognor, 1,200 of them self-catering, 300 bed-and-breakfast and 4,550 on full board. To look after this complement there will be 1,300 staff, 1,150 of whom live in, waiters, attendants, bed-makers, entertainers, redcoats, kitchen staff, maintenance men, administrative people, security men, a vast range of different occupations. More often than not, this staff will be on shiftwork. Breakfast, for instance, has two sittings, at 8.30 am and 9.30 am. On a Saturday, the game gets tougher than ever, as 6,000 customers leave and another 6,000 arrive.[14]

Caferteria staff at Golden Sands Holiday Camp.

Catering staff at Golden
Sands Holiday Camp,
1955.

Chalet maid at Butlin's
Filey camp, 1953.

The preoccupations of these varied grades of camp employees are not the same as those of the 'commodore', nor those of the holiday makers. They are, in the words of the *News of the World*, 'divided into rival tribes':

> *Jaffas* are the cafe workers who wear bright orange overalls and 'are always good for a squeeze'. *Chalet bikes* are the chambermaids – girls with the sexiest reputation. *Reds* are the Redcoats – despised by many because they attract girl campers, are showered with tips and free drinks, and believe they are a cut above the rest. An army of security men patrols the camp in an effort to stamp out the nightly rave-ups. They are nicknamed *scum*.[15]

The paper's intrepid investigator reported that 'Our revelations on the hi-de-high old time for staff came as no shock to Butlin bosses' who commented that, 'People are motivated to work here for a variety of reasons apart from nipping into a chalet with the nearest girl. There's a certain camaraderie about the place, a special atmosphere...But each one is fully briefed when he arrives and it's made clear that the first responsibility is to look after the guests' interests. We're all geared to providing top-class family holidays and that's our prime consideration.'[16] To the bleak eye of the sociologist however, the usual relationship of staff with campers was one of exploitation. 'Almost all staff have a low opinion of and disrespect for the bulk of campers. They are "suckers", paying so much money to get just what the staff were getting for almost free; and so easy to cadge drinks from, eager to spice the holiday with a "romance", crying out to be cheated.' On the other hand 'Those who were admired or respected among campers were those who demonstrated special skills on musical instruments or in acrobatic dancing, etc., or those who were deemed to be showing courage or moral rectitude – for example, an English woman with a blind Indian husband who quietly did everything to make his stay enjoyable, or the many families who wheeled around a disabled or paralysed member.'[17]

There was thus a clear demarcation in the eyes of the staff as to which of the customers was ripe for exploitation and which should be treated according to the official ethos of the camp. But if the customers were there to be exploited, so of course were the employers. Billy Butlin had come up the hard way in the rough, tough, world of fair-ground entertainment and was always convinced that his employees were fiddling. They reminisce about the way his hoopla stall attendants were issued with coats without pockets to prevent them from pocketing the change, or about his habit of turning up and scratching around in the sand under the tills in his amusement parks to pick up the pennies that 'happened' to have fallen for later retrieval. The comedian Charlie Drake, a Redcoat in the early 1950s loves to tell the tale of how he actually succeeded in swindling Butlin of a ten shilling note. The catering and restaurant trade is of course notorious for the institutionalized pilfering which is built into every level, and as its investigators remark, 'the enormous range of fiddles which we have found have a common feature: they are acts of dishonesty that the people involved do not consider to be dishonest.'[18] They also note how there are both 'core' workers who gravitate to the centre of operations and 'peripheral' workers who stay on the fringe: 'Core workers are both self-selected and management-selected. Beyond their basic wages they have to exploit the total rewards system. The enterprising worker, then, will build up his total rewards by tips, perks and fiddles. In turn, his initiative will be recognised, and management will put the pickings his way. Head waiters, head porters and chefs are typical "core"workers, each of them negotiating his own individual contract and making himself less and less dispensable as he colludes more and more thoroughly with management'.[19]

Apart from the small nucleus of permanent employees, staff are recruited for the summer season from May to September, with additional recruitment in the peak period. The catering trade has always been a low-pay, casual and non-unionized industry, and one in which there has for a long time been the habit of shifting in the summer months to live-in jobs at the seaside, as the catering workers' equivalent of a holiday. The advent of the holiday camp, with its access to all the usual facilities in off-duty hours, was an attractive variation on the usual range of catering and hotel work. 'The camp recruitment is thus confined to a largely self-selected category of workers who are geographically mobile, hold unsteady jobs and are not hampered from moving from one occupation and place to another. A very large proportion of camp staff are consequently young or, if old, single with little or no family attachment...Most are unskilled, used to living with strangers, and have usually developed the combination of casual openness to social intercourse and sharp suspicion and unsentimentality that life in mobile occupations requires. They feel little sense of loyalty towards the organisation that employs them and have few career hopes. Their commitment is wholly instrumental. Wages can nearly all be saved (board and lodging is free) and campers can be "conned" into providing drinks, snacks, petting and sex – and a job at the end of the season.'[20]

People queue for employment when the season begins. 'That night', noted Roy Kerridge when he came to the end of the Pentecostal week at Minehead, 'I saw some rough young men being turned away at the gate by the security guards, for the main Butlin season had started, and no seasonal workers would be admitted until the conference was over. The young men, some with bundles, sat on kerbstones on a freezing night, and wondered what to do. The police moved them on, which didn't help.'[21] Another observer explained that 'the camp at Bognor attracts its share of drifters, the educationally sub-normal, "trouble-makers" and those who are out-and-out unhappy.'[22] The turnover has always been very high. In the mid 1970s with a staff of about 500 people at their Blackpool camp, 'a Pontin's spokesman confirmed that the turnover of staff can be more than 1,500 during the season, usually about 25 weeks long.'[23]

To discourage 'floaters', the major companies operate a bonus scheme for all who stay for the agreed period of employment, and this becomes a source of bitter complaint. (For example 'while the convention is that those guilty of physical violence, drunkenness or molesting campers are to be immediately dismissed, the actual distribution of dismissals is associated with slack periods and periods when students are available for employment and are rare when the camp is full'). A chalet porter at Blackpool said that 'one of the biggest complaints concerns the bonus scheme. Obviously the majority of people dismissed are not suitable, but others – and I would say around 20 per cent – feel they have been sacked wrongly. They do not then, of course, receive the seasonal bonus from the company.' A kitchen worker there said 'I have worked for this company for some time. I cannot get work outside so I have to accept what I

All smiles for the punters at Ladbrokes' Caister Camp.

am paid. I think the wages are very low and I am against the bonus scheme. I know towards the end of the season people are scared of putting a foot wrong, me included, in case they are shown the door.'[24]

There is a hierarchy of pay and prestige among the seasonal and occasional employees at the holiday camp. At the top are the visiting celebrities, sporting stars, snooker and darts champions, TV personalities (including now, the cast of *Hi-de-hi*), entertainers, singers and musicians. Orchestras, bands and groups, great and small, are booked to meet the anticipated tastes of different generations of campers, from strict tempo dance music to hard rock. Butlin's used to hire annually touring repertory companies of actors who went the rounds of the camps giving half-hour potted Shakespeare performances, but the audience dwindled away in the 1960s.

Then there are the famous uniformed staff, Butlin's Redcoats, Pontin's Bluecoats and Warner's Greencoats. They used to be aspirant entertainers themselves, and they still recite the litany of names of those who soared to fame and fortune as Redcoats in the past. Today they are chosen for displaying the kind of personality and patience that suits their function of keeping everybody happy, but they still include people who hope that on those evenings when entertainment is provided by campers and staff rather than by professionals, they will carry off the acclaim and prizes as a launch on a show-biz career. In 1977 Yvonne Roberts found that 'Most of the 40 or so Reds at Bognor are ex-Butlin holiday-makers who see the job either as a quick and temporary route to "a lot of talent", as a way to meet the stars or quite simply as a calling. "Everybody wants to be a Redcoat," says Ken, a wages clerk in the winter "because the blazer gives you the authority to be the kind of person you really are." '[25] By 1985, when Julie Simmons followed around a trio of Redcoats at Skegness for the BBC, she found, not only that they were far fewer in number than in the days when they were *the* public face of the holiday camp industry, but that they tended to be young people escaping from the dole, and, with no preliminary training at all, rising to the occasion with previously unexploited skills to be patient as Uncles and Aunties in supervising children's activities and in putting on an extrovert approach to the adult guests. 'They're part of a generation of young people who don't expect security; they just think: "At least its a job for five months." One week they were on the dole, the next they were doing a show onstage like old troupers.'[26]

But just as the ordinary staff resent the Redcoats, so the Redcoats resent the professional entertainers. Sue Ann Scott, a Greencoat at the Dovercourt Warner's camp, says 'I work about a 72-hour week and pick up £55. I get my accommodation and food and only need money for drinks in the evening but it isn't much. The band pick up £150 each which isn't fair. We get a bonus at the end of the season of £150. I don't think I'd do this sort of work next year, it really is hard work. It's given me a lot of confidence, I can go up and talk to anyone now.'[27] She was in charge of the Wagtails (the children between three and nine) and in fact a number of successful teachers we have met have told us that they owed their bright, breezy and compelling teaching style, not to their teacher-training but to their experience in this kind of job in camp during their vacations as students.

But not many of the enormous number of people who belonged to the post-war generations of students were lucky enough to pick up the uniformed jobs. They were usually at the bottom of the hierarchy, and were seldom given the jobs where contact with the public brought tips and favours. They were peripheral as the tough old hands of the catering trade had, quite naturally, collared the strategically most favourable situations. One who did get employed as a Redcoat was the poet Patrick Kavanagh, sent to Butlin's from the sixth form of a Catholic boarding school as his father wanted to counteract his cultural snobbism. He was sent to preside over the Viennese Ballroom although he hardly knew how to dance and had scarcely met any girls. He fell victim to an increasing melancholy as the weeks went by. 'Most evenings I got through by talking to the drummer of the Squadronaires, whose gloom was so immense it made me feel almost hearty.' His misery grew with each week's repetition of the same occurrences with a new bunch of campers: 'Every Saturday night there was a fancy-dress ball in which the campers paraded in costumes new to them but very familiar to us. It was always won, as far as I remember, by the man who clad himself entirely in enamel chamber-pots: the King of Po-land. Thus garbed he clanked round the edges of the floor all evening, alone...'[28]

For others the experience of working in camp filled the same function as military service had done for an earlier generation in introducing them to a wider spectrum of their own contemporaries. Jim Dumsday, lucky enough to get a job behind the bar at Filey in 1967 told us 'I got £6 a week plus board and it seemed a fortune. I also had my eyes opened, as a fairly reflective and reserved youth, to a variety of different lifestyles. There were some amazing contrasts between the lads down from the Fairs Week who only needed one phrase of comprehensible English ('Gi'us a Snakebite, Jimmy') and the Bryl-creamed boys of the juvenile ballroom dancing fortnight at the end of the

The Dining Hall, Butlin's Holiday Camp, Clacton-on-Sea. 'Empire'

season.' Several of our informants, in seeking holiday work, had been warned off Butlin's because of the immense pressure of work involved in the double-sittings for meals, when the first sitting had to be fed and eased out of the huge dining rooms as quickly as possible to make room for the next batch of hungry campers. 'You remember Wesker's play *The Kitchen*? It was like that multiplied by ten.' Shirley Stewart started in the 1950s as a washer-up in a small camp near Sandown in the Isle of Wight, moving on in the following year to the Constitutional Camp at Hopton, which with its 850 guests all singing the camp song at mealtimes, seemed big at the time. Most of the catering and domestic workers were local women brought in by bus from Yarmouth and the atmosphere was good. At the same time Della Chapman was a waitress at the New Pakefield Camp near Lowestoft and found the atmosphere far friendlier than in the camps of the big operators. Her problem was in fending off the attentions of the male staff.

The cultural shock experienced by most students whose first taste of the world of work was gained in Butlin's, was remembered by everyone who spoke to us about their jobs there as students. 'We had absorbed at school the usual ethic about honesty and fair play, and suddenly found we were in a jungle', said one, and another spoke of the ruthlessness of the security guards, which was excused by the need to ferret out illicit campers who had been smuggled into camp as visitors and obtained the keys of empty chalets. Brian Edwards, as a Clacton boy, knew Butlin's from childhood. He used to earn tips from campers 'parsling' as it was called: bringing their luggage from the station in his barrow.

But even he was shocked by his week-end job as a student as a laundry-boy on 'change-over day' when the chalets had to be cleaned and the linen changed as one army of campers left and another moved in. 'I was astonished at the unscrupulousness of the other workers, and the endless arguments not just with the supervisors but between the members of the staff.' His wife Lynn worked in the restaurant and couldn't believe the endless and cut-throat competition she saw between the other waitresses. In the 1960s, as an eighteen-year old kitchen porter, the first thing Roger Milne saw in a huge maggot-strewn kitchen, was the cook bribing the public health inspector to stay out.[29]

These of course are features of the hotel and catering trades at a much grander level than that of the holiday camp. Hardened workers take them for granted. They only surprised the newcomers who expected that everything would be fun in Funland.

Elusive Campers

> The original concept of our business was a recognition that by far the largest percentage of people would holiday in the UK. When the weather is uncertain, people want to have plenty to do at a price they can budget for themselves. These were the fundamental facts in creating the company and I personally don't see that any of these has changed. Proof of our formula's success is that 25 per cent of the population holidayed at Butlin's at some time in their lives.
>
> (R. F. Butlin, Managing Director, Butlin's Holidays, 1981)

Searching for the typical holiday camp customer, we were wary of popular (and generally unflattering) stereotypes. Instead, if there is an overriding impression it is one of people who had made a rational choice among the variety of holidays offered in an intensely competitive market and had concluded that their best buy was a holiday camp. Just as there are families with a tradition of going every year to Walberswick, Porthcurno or Portree, and where part of the private ritual that cements family relationships is the annual return to repeat last year's experiences, so there are families where the ritual question 'Where shall we go this summer' meets the response from the children, 'Let's go back to...' In any given year 40 per cent of the population do not go away for a holiday at all,[30] but those who do are very strongly influenced by the desire to reinforce the bonds of family life.

Arthur and Jane Foster went for years to Wallis's camp near Scarborough (now a Ladbroke Supercentre). He's a retired electrical engineer with three children, now married themselves, and he remembers family holidays in the 1930s. 'My parents used to go for farm holidays near the East Yorkshire coast, and emphasised, quite unconsciously I'm sure, what they were sacrificing for the sake of us children. We went for bracing walks in the countryside and along the cliffs, but what we really yearned for were the occasional trips into town at Scarborough or Whitby. When they yielded to our desire to push our pennies into the slot machines at the amusement parks it was the high point of the holiday for us, but they thought it terrible. One day I fed my last penny into the

Millions of family albums have their snapshots like this.

Families like the Renshaws return annually to the same camp.

fruit machine at Whitby, and either because the machine had gone wrong or because I had struck the right moment, it kept on spilling out money. I stuffed the pockets of my khaki shorts with the pennies that kept on spilling out, and still came away with handfuls. This embarrassed my mother and father when we met them outside. They thought I must have stolen the money. And even when I convinced them of the truth, I was made to feel that just by winning I had betrayed every moral principle they stood for. Icily they agreed that we should all spend these undeserved gains on the rides in the amusement park, and this was the high spot of my childhood. Years later, when I was a parent, I resolved that the holiday ("for which your mother and I made sacrifices all the year round, etcetera") should be built around what the children wanted, rather than around what we thought they ought to want. That's why we went back to Wallis's year after year, and it's why we sometimes come back here with the grandchildren. We aren't tied to the place but we do notice that the accommodation has got a lot better from the days when six of us all crowded into one little chalet. My wife has never gone in for the Glamorous Grandmother competition, though I'm sure she would win it every time.'[31]

Richard Page is the senior administrative officer at a London college of further education. He has never been dragooned into a Knobbly Knees competition, but for years has been going with his family to Butlin's Minehead camp. 'I'm sure that when the children are older', he says, 'my wife and I will try something totally different for ourselves, but we have found the place that suits us. We have been, in the past, to Butlin's at Bognor and at Pwllheli, and we once went to Pontin's camp at Brixham and to Warner's South Bay camp, also at Brixham. We simply found that Minehead gave us everything we wanted while the children have been growing up, while for us there has been swimming, skating and acres of full-size billiard tables. We go for the all-in tariff and have nothing at all to worry about for the whole holiday, though in fact we tend to ration the

'The best thing about a holiday camp is that it is a holiday for the wife . . . I danced with her every evening.'

time the children can spend on the rides. There's so much of everything there.'[32]

Like sport, popular music, or any other aspect of the mass entertainment industry, the holiday camp trade has its seedy underside. It has also had occasional outbreaks of food poisoning which led to the hasty closure of some camps and a rapid transfer of occupants.[33] But most of the regular customers we have met felt that they were getting their money's worth. If they wanted a superior cuisine or a more sophisticated style of entertainment they would go somewhere else. But what they value most is the happiness of their children or the reinforcement of their own conjugal relationships. It is different for the young and single but, as an earlier investigator found, certain views were 'frequently expressed and showed little individual variation'. One husband remarked to Pradeep Bandyopadhyay that 'The best thing about a holiday camp is that it is a holiday for the wife. When we went camping or stayed with relations it was not much of a change for her, was it? Now we are really together, none of us has to work, and we can do things together. I dance with her every evening. She is a woman, you know.' And a wife responded with a similar view: 'I like holiday camps. It is like having a second honeymoon. Arthur and I went to a little place in Wales when we were married. This is the only time I am with him for everything. This morning we had breakfast together – I have never had bacon and eggs with him in the whole year. We have such different hours: I just barely see him before tea, and then I usually have the children to look after.'[34]

The same thing was said to us with a certain regularity, so we asked whether this was a characteristic of any kind of holiday, not simply one in a holiday camp. The kind of answer we received was that holiday camps were different in two ways. The first was that the programme of activities for children was very much appreciated by their parents. Nearly everyone felt that it was good for them and their offspring to be relieved of each other's company. The second was that many people actually prefer the impersonal service of meals in the setting of large-scale catering, or self-service in a cafeteria system, to the role-playing exercise involved in being waited on. 'I've been a waitress myself, and I know it's just a matter of putting on an act. But it is for the customer too.' But since many campers had stressed that, unlike a holiday in a caravan or individual holiday bungalow, the great advantage of a holiday camp was that it removed the burden of domestic tasks, what explained the growth in popularity of self-catering? (This accounted for 12 percent of holidays in 1951, but 43 per cent by 1972.[35])

Some people, like Mr Page and his wife, stayed with a full board tariff precisely because to them this made it a real holiday. Others weighed up the cost and picked the tariff that fitted their budget. 'It doesn't bother us all that much. There are take-away food shops in or just outside the camp if you want a quick meal. As we have a car we take supplies along with us.' Margaret Partridge, whose husband is a farmer, has a long-standing loyalty to Pontin's, staying at their Prestatyn camp in the 1960s as a young married couple, moving to another camp in the 1970s just because there was 'something for everyone' when three generations of the family went there together, and finally moving out of the camp scene altogether to more expensive and less regimented holidays provided by the same firm.

Mrs Margaret Jones and her husband who works for the Post Office first went to a holiday camp in 1969 when their oldest child was one year old. 'It was a Warner's camp, at Minster on the Isle of Sheppey and only held about 500 people. It had waiter service though I prefer the way they do it now, with cafeteria service. We went there for a couple of years, but the camp closed down. We've been to a lot of the camps run by the different firms since then, but that was the one I liked best. It was very basic: just a wooden hut compared with the luxury chalets you get nowadays, but everyone joined in to make it enjoyable. You had to make your own amusements and I think that's what I liked about it. It was organised, but the kids all played together – football and cricket and joint things like that. You played with your own children. I've never laughed so much in my life as on Sports Day at Minster. We've been to some other Warner's camps. We went to Dovercourt twice and liked it. And we've been to Butlin's at Clacton and Bognor and Barry Island. But I think the Butlin's camps are just too big. It's like going to another town. You feel lost, and it's quite an achievement to find your chalet. And all that queueing up all day when the children were small for the slides and swings. With most of the other camps you all get roped in for the amusements, but with Butlin's it's like being in a theatre with row after row of you all sitting back. Then it ends and everything stops.'

As veterans who have sampled many camps, Mr and Mrs Jones have been very aware of the changing needs of their children as they grow up. They now appreciate a camp which provides a late disco for their teenage daughter, and they have moved to self-catering partly because you can book later for vacancies in self-catering accommodation but mainly because it is so much cheaper for a big family. They have been to hotels and 'actually hated it' because the children couldn't run about and do what they liked and because 'In a hotel you stay apart, but in a place like this you're close and easily associate with each other.' They favour Pontin's, and find Bluecoats more willing to enter into the spirit of the holiday than Redcoats. (One Bluecoat came to visit them after the season was over.)

They weigh up the cost of holidays carefully, which is why they decided on self-catering, and have settled into a pattern of holidays through the year which gives them best value and most suits the whole family. 'We go away every Christmas to Pontin's at Hemsby in Norfolk, in spite of the cold.' Mr Jones works in the Post Office until Christmas Eve, and they find that this provides the best kind of winter holiday for them. In May they go for a cheap five-day short break, with a group of about sixteen friends from work, and in the summer they now go for two 'midweek breaks for four days' so as to get two holidays for the price of one. They have also been on "bargain week-ends" organized by the union branch.

The Jones family and their friends have thus, with a discriminating choice, adopted the habit of using holiday camps throughout the year in the same way as wealthier people would use a country cottage or second home. Did they think that holiday camps had a future? 'Probably not,' Margaret Jones replied, 'because they are getting so expensive. A few of our friends have dropped out and go abroad now. It's *my* decision to go abroad next year, but if the children have their way, we'll go back to the camp.'[36]

But there are, of course, people who are in love with the very idea of the holiday camp as it used to be. The record for attendance is claimed by 'wealthy company executive' John Hilton who claims to have spent 200 weeks of the past 35 years of his life in holiday camps and to have spent £40,000 there. He says, 'I don't care if people think I'm mad, but I went to all the foreign tourist traps when I was younger. Compared with the British holiday camp, they are all second rate.' His parents took him to Butlin's at Filey when he was seven, and his most memorable moment was when Billy Butlin bought him a pint when he was fourteen. His wife was appalled when he took her there for their honeymoon. 'But in the end I found I loved it. Friends tell me of their holidays in Italy or Yugoslavia and seem amazed that I'm content with a couple of months at a holiday camp every year.' They have been to all the Butlin camps and Mr Hilton's favourite is Pwllheli where he has been at least twenty times. 'But much as I love it now, I must say I miss the hi-de-hi, ho-de-ho, wakey-wakey announcements over the loudspeakers in the early days.'[37]

Hi-De-Hi Reflected

> What is happening at the Victoria Palace is less a drama than a social phenomenon: the ideal reviewer would be somebody from *New Society* seated on the stage and watching the audience...
>
> (Chris Dunkley, reviewing the stage show of *Hi-de-Hi*, *Financial Times*, 28 December, 1983)

In any given year the proportion of holidays spent in Britain in holiday centres or camps is far smaller than the percentage spent in the homes of friends or relatives, in hotels, motels or guest houses, or in rented holiday homes or caravans. But the image and imagery of the holiday camp is deeply rooted in

British experience, partly because vast numbers of people have been to one at some time in their lives, or have been on day visits for the entertainment, or have worked at one in one capacity or another. In the post-war generations of students, many found their first summer job in a holiday camp. In the overcrowded world of popular entertainment, apart from all those stars who recall how they began as Butlin Redcoats (Charlie Drake, Cliff Richard, Des O'Connor, Dave Allen, Roy Hudd, Jimmy Tarbuck...the list is endless) there are thousands of lesser names thankful for the summer engagement with bed and board thrown in.

But until the BBC television series *Hi-de-Hi*, with its audience of about ten million viewers, it could hardly be said that popular art, literature or drama had provided a worthy reflection of its original. There was a pre-war murder story, *Death at the Holiday Camp*, which seems to have sunk without trace. John Creasey added to his fifty-five thrillers about The Toff, a novel where his hero signs on as a Redcoat at Pwllheli:

> They met at the end of the counter, and the girl led him along passages between glass-walled offices. Dozens of people were busy in these, typewriters were clicking, comptometers working, people stood or sat at telephones...
> 'Here we are,' said the girl, and tapped on a door which was already open. 'Dick, here's someone to see you...'
> 'Oh, the new chum,' said Middleton, who was in charge of Redcoats. He didn't get up; he didn't look enthusiastic or, for that matter, hostile.
> There were a dozen chairs around the walls. Rollison sat down. Two men Redcoats came in within two minutes, nodded, put something on the desk, and went out. A girl, wearing a red coat, appeared, dropped a sheaf of paper on Middleton's desk, and went off, casting a glance at Rollison.
> Middleton finished what he was writing.
> 'Sorry,' he said, casually. 'Well, now you're here, you'd better start learning the ropes. 'You've been to Filey I'm told'.
> 'For a little while.'
> 'We aren't the same as Filey,' said Middleton. 'Not in our internal organisation, anyway. For the first day or two, you'd better take it easy. Let me give you a tip – don't start throwing your weight about...'
> Rollison looked out of the window and saw a group of thirty or forty young children. 'Uncle Pi' Wray walked along the road leading towards the bridge which Rollison could see in the distance. The children followed him – all shapes and sizes, tinies and early teenagers.
> 'Amazing what he can do with kids,' said Middleton. His admiration sounded reluctant. 'I'll bet you won't be able to compete with him. Kids drive me crazy...'[38]

The author of *The Toff at Butlins* gave an impression of easy and informal efficiency behind the scenes. The girl Redcoat who smiled at him 'looked as if she had walked off the cover of the pamphlet; she was the Cover Girl come to life.' Paula Deal, in her first encounter in Reception had an equally pleasant impression, reported in her book *Nurse at Butlins*:

> 'How do you do. I'm Stella Freeman,' replied this tall, elegant girl, dressed very smartly in a cream pleated skirt, scarlet blazer, and white high-heeled shoes. Her blonde hair was beautifully styled in the newest *bouffant*

creation. She had bright blue, twinkling eyes, delicately made up, and a wonderful smile. She held out her hand in welcome.[39]

Everything about her account is similarly brighter than life, from the buildings 'shining with gay fresh paint' to the 'really wonderful people' on the staff. Even the platoon of Beatniks 'did not take offence when the Redcoats occasionally good-humouredly made odd remarks about their attire.' They would have had short shrift in *Billy Bunter at Butlins*, also published in 1961, one of the last of the incredible number of 'yarns' about Bunter and the Famous Five from Greyfriars School written by Frank Richards. At Skegness they find that

> There might be moments when, amid swarms of teenagers, a few might prove a little too braced by the bracing air and get a little out of hand. That was where the Redcoats came in. The Redcoats were officials whose duty it was to keep order in the Camp, tactfully but firmly subduing any undue exuberance: but so far as the Greyfriars fellows could see, they never had any trouble. Good-humour reigned supreme.[40]

The artless tale revolves around the theft by a pickpocket of an expensive-looking wallet with the monogram 'WB' from a 'portly gentleman' with 'pleasant blue eyes, very kindly in expression, but very keen', who of course, is Billy Butlin, and its appropriation in all innocence by another WB, the 'Fat Owl of the

Remove', Billy Bunter. Copies of the book were sent that Christmas to all the children who had joined the Butlin Beaver Club at the camps in the previous summer.

Cynical readers could well have concluded that all these books were products of the Butlin publicity machine. They would not feel this about Timothy Lea's *Confessions from a Holiday Camp* which was a sequel to the same author's *Confessions of a Window Cleaner* and *Confessions of a Driving Instructor*. The hero has a sexual encounter on almost every page of his adventures as a Holiday Host at Melody Bay Holiday Camp, for as his Mum says knowingly, 'Well we all know what goes on at holiday camps, don't we?' This was the kind of innuendo that Butlin himself tried to counter for years. He used to complain angrily about an 'insidious form of criticism that was thrown at us for years, particularly in the more straight-laced Thirties. Holiday camps, it was alleged, were nothing more than hives of immorality. This kind of lip-smacking gossip was put about, again by people who had never visited the camps, or by such competitors as hotels and boarding houses, wanting to give us a bad reputation.'[41]

Timothy Lea, however, introduces us to a completely recognizable camp geography:

> Melody Bay Holiday Camp is situated on the edge of town and surrounded by a high wire fence. This is presumably there to keep people out. The first impression is one of a lot of mock-tudor chalets laid out in orderly lines along paths with names like 'Laughter Lane' and 'Happiness Row'. From the bus I can see tennis courts and putting greens and a couple of large buildings that look like aircraft hangars (I later find out that they were aircraft hangers before their true potential was realised). The camp is approached by the coast road and a wide expanse of almost empty beach stretches away opposite the main entrance. This entrance is vaguely reminiscent of those Hollywood studios I have seen pictures of. Gold topped wrought iron gates, a commissionaire type bod, and an inscription carved in the stonework. The difference is that this does not say 'Ars gratia artis' but 'Let good fellowship be your guide, and Laughter your companion', Sir Giles Slat, founder of Funfrall Enterprises, who, I imagine, has quite a lot to laugh about.[42]

The novel's hero, Timmy, far from getting the sack for his sexual athleticism, is summoned to Funfrall House, for an interview with Sir Giles himself, who explains to him the new venture for which he has been selected as a potential staff candidate:

> 'Holiday Camps were developed to cater for a simple basic need: that of providing an affordable escape from the dark satanic mills for those who had not previously envisaged a bucket and spade as other than implements required to wrest combustibles from an open cast mine. With increasing affluence and greater freedom of movement between the classes, so the seaside holiday became the rule rather than the exception and horizons extended even beyond the three mile limit which borders these shores. What so far we seem to have ignored, in this country at least, is the changing moral climate. The expression of love and affection between adult human beings is no longer solely the prerogative of those united by bonds of marriage. Whilst not wishing to undermine the bedrock — I use the word

advisedly – upon which such strong family-orientated enterprises as Melody Bay were built, we believe that there exists the opportunity to create a new kind of pleasure resort for the emancipated seventies.'

'They're getting a bit old, aren't they?' I interject.

'I referred,' grits Sir Giles, 'to the nineteen-seventies. We envisage a holiday village where responsible adults can celebrate the new found sexual freedom of the age in which we live, without blanching before the cold cynosure of antediluvian morals.'...

'I think I've got the idea,' I pant earnestly. 'You think that with everybody going on coach tours of the Balkans, Holiday Camps are on the way out. Therefore you want to introduce somewhere like those frog places where they all live in each other's mud huts and run around in grass skirts with strings of cocoa beans round their necks.' A long silence follows my remarks.[43]

Needless to say, Sir Giles is broaching the idea that our hero should be his agent on Isla de Amor, 'Love Island, Funfrall's new Mediterranean experience for the mature holiday maker.' Beneath an exterior of soft pornography, the pseudonymous author of the Timothy Lea novels brings out aspects of the functions of holidays which are seldom discussed by other fictional, or factual, recorders of the holiday camp experience.

It was paradoxical that in the very decade when Sir Billy Butlin was embarking on his ill-fated Grand Bahama venture and when Sir Fred Pontin was urging his customers to 'go Pontinental', as well as upgrading their accommodation at home, other entrepreneurs, like Club Méditerranée and its many imitators, were exploiting the lure of the primitive and uninhibited. Orwell's 'naked democracy of the swimming pool' was offered in sun-bleached straw huts consciously imitating those of the sex-happy Trobrianders. Lacking pockets or handbags, they were obliged to hand in their cash on arrival, changing it for a string of beads as currency. This was a persuasive formula for holidays in the 1950s, and even in the 1980s, when Laurie Taylor tried to read between the lines of the holiday brochures for those good times in a programme intended to 'bring sophistication to a market which has suffered from a reputation of rowdiness and bad behaviour' he found that the promotors were much more shy in explaining their chosen market than was Sir Giles Slat:

> Nowhere, of course, is there any open talk of the sexual possibilities – all this half naked romping is presented as 'fun' and 'sport'. But the key euphemisms seem to be 'like-minded' and 'active'.[44]

Back in the pioneering days of holiday camps, these words had a completely innocent connotation. But many veteran campers have told us that the attraction of holiday camps for them, when they were in their teens, was precisely that, in their first holiday away from the family, parents would tolerate their going away with a group of other girls or other boys to one of the well-known camps, in a way that they would never countenance for an individual. Once there they were, of course, in and out of each other's chalets, and it was a function of the Chalet Patrols, not merely to listen for crying babies, but to ensure that the right people of the right sex were sleeping in the right places.

Acutely sensitive on this issue, the big operators began to decline bookings from groups of 'singles' and to stress in their advertising and booking literature that they were catering for families and couples. In 1968 Butlin's began the conversion of the large chalets previously used by parties of teenagers, into self-catering units. But the picture of holiday camp life in Timothy Lea's book was confirmed in a feature from the *News of the World* in the 1980s (which Butlin's had the good grace to reproduce in their *Students' Guide* for 1985) where a member of the Bognor staff is reported as saying that 'Any night there's something sexy going on in half the chalets on camp. Staff with holiday-makers, holiday-makers with holiday-makers and staff with staff. *That's what it's all about at Butlin's, isn't it?*'[45]

No such scandals obtruded into the film *Holiday Camp*, made in 1947 from a story by Butlin's friend Godfrey Winn, with an all-star cast. This portmanteau film interwove tales of a murderer and his victim, a bereaved spinster mourning her lost love, confidence tricksters, romantic love, and a cockney couple, played by Kathleen Harrison and Jack Warner, creating their patronizing portrait of working-class heroes which became the television series *The Huggetts*. When the film turns up on television every two years or so, it is seen as a quaint period piece.

By far the most successful evocation of the atmosphere of the holiday camp has been *Hi-de-Hi*, as the response of its audience shows. Its authors, Jimmy Perry and David Croft, shrewdly selected the year 1959 as the golden age of the holiday camp, where the vogue for nostalgia and actual reminiscences effort-lessly blend. The story-line is unimportant, superb characterization is every-thing. Everybody recognizes Paul Shane's Ted Bovis, the tough and shrewd stand-up comic, Ruth Madoc's Gladys Pugh, the chief Yellowcoat who falls for the entertainments manager and Su Pollard's Peggy the chalet maid who yearns to become a Yellowcoat. Joe Maplin, the boss of the Maplin holiday camp empire is never seen, though his presence at the other end of the telephone is felt by his staff and there is always the threat of an unannounced visit. He is clearly modelled on Billy Butlin, though Sir Fred Pontin recognizes elements of himself in the absent looming figure. There is even a faction among viewers who see him as Harry Warner, as the series is filmed at Warner's Dovercourt centre. There the management report a boom in bookings as a result of *Hi-de-Hi*, and 1950s evenings are staged among the entertainments programme, to recreate the 'authentic' atmosphere of the television show. There are even viewers for whom the high points of each episode are the few seconds of 'genuine' old film used as backgrounds for the credit titles at the end.

Nostalgia for the golden age of the holiday camp takes other forms. There are avid collectors of holiday camp picture postcards. One dealer in these explains that the camp operators 'knew a thing or two about free advertising. These postcards always depict the nicer aspects of holiday camps and therefore lure the initiated into the sometimes good, sometimes grotty camps. I know: I've been to both types.' There is also a Magic Circle of collectors of Butlin's Badges. It's organizer explains that 'Badges were originally introduced as a form of proof that the persons wearing them were in fact bona fide guests of a particular Camp. Variations as to both design and colour for any one Camp during the year were an attempt to ensure that the badges were not mis-used. Where one or two designs were used, then colour variations were introduced to both, again with the purpose of off-setting any abuse. No records were ever maintained as

'No records were ever maintained as to the badges, numbers thereof, produced by the Company over the years.'

to the badges, numbers thereof, produced by the Company over the years. From the badges collected over the years a pattern emerges from which many assumptions can be drawn. It is believed that the total collection of badges, starting from 1936 through to 1967, totals in the region of 1,750.'[46]

It must have irritated the other holiday camp entrepreneurs that, even among collectors of badges, ephemera and souvenirs, everyone was interested only in Butlin's. The same is true of travel journalists and authors of books about the British way of life. Perhaps the rivals should have been relieved at having escaped the observation of the literary intelligentsia, whose verdict is always scathing. They were, of course, always there in the rain, when as Nicholas Wollaston observed at Skegness in 1965, 'During the long hours between bar opening times the big public rooms were like the waiting-room of a railway terminus, full of people waiting for a train to take them on a holiday – except that now they were all waiting for it to take them home again.' He loathed the Viennese Beer Garden where 'a sham water-wheel splashed weakly in a cement trough, and dusty cockatoos swung from the ceiling.' He despised Ye Old Pig and Whistle where 'hundreds of cards with funny jokes written on them twisted slowly on strings' and he pitied the elderly campers in the Tudor Bar, who 'yawned under a gigantic plaster tree, or giggled at the plight of a real pigeon that had flown in and was battering itself among the saucy little lattice windows above them.' Even the indoor swimming pool 'lay under a jungle of synthetic greenery.' For Wollaston, 'This obsession with the bogus and the dangling may have served to disguise the architecture of the buildings, and certainly the rain that in places dripped through the roof added authenticity to the picturesque settings, but it was disappointing to find that so few modern ideas of design had been adopted. The Festival of Britain might never have happened.'[47]

His conclusion was 'That nine thousand holiday-makers appeared to be enjoying it only showed how bleak their other lives must have been; though sometimes at the sight of the women hurrying from one bingo hall to another and of the men standing outside the betting shop feebly whistling the tune of the nearest transistor radio, I wondered how happy they were. Butlin's told them loudly that they were having fun, and they believed it. If they had stopped to think, they might have begun to wonder, but the whole point of Butlin's was that it was a holiday from thinking.'[48]

When Paul Theroux visited Butlin's at Minehead on a cold, windy and overcast day in 1983 he found its barrack-like buildings and forbidding fences like a prison. 'A prison look was also an army camp look, and just as depressing. This one was the more scary for being brightly painted. It had been tacked together out of plywood and tin panels in primary colours. I had not seen flimsier buildings in England...But the more I saw of Butlin's the more it resembled English life; it was England without work. Leisure had been overtaken by fatigue and dull-wittedness; electronic games were easier than sports, and eating junk food had become another recreation...If it had a futuristic feel it was the deadened imagination and the zombie-like attitude of the strolling people, condemned to a week or two of fun under cloudy skies.'[49]

People familiar with neither have often, half seriously, compared holiday camps with concentration camps. The Rev. Wilf Curtis, who was camp chaplain at Butlin's Filey camp for thirty years, likes to tell the tale of the time he was sitting with some fishermen on the cliff top. 'The little lifeboat went out and it went towards Butlin's and we couldn't see any sign of trouble out there at all, and in the quietness which followed one old fisherman said, "Happen someone's escaped from Butlins".'[50] And Kenneth Lindley, in his study of Britain's seaside architecture, complains of Butlin's Clacton camp that it was 'cut off from the seafront by a tall iron rail pallisade surmounted by barbed wire, and the view of the camp from the promenade could easily be mistaken for a film set for a prisoner-of-war epic.'[51]

One of the things that appalled outside observers of the Butlin-style, every-thing-provided holiday camp, was that campers need not leave the site at all between arrival and departure. They were hermetic institutions, all too reminis-cent of the Gulag Archipelago. As one of Solzhenitsyn's characters remarks, 'Forget the outside world. Life has different laws in here. This is Campland, an invisible country. It's not in the geography books, or the psychology books or the history books.'[52]

The Camp is indeed a universal symbol of the twentieth century, along with barbed wire and the Unknown Political Prisoner. Concentration camps were a British invention, devised during the Anglo-Boer War for concentrating Afrikaner women and children in one supervised place, where vast numbers died. It is a rational, efficient solution to the problems of providing for basic physical human needs: sleeping, feeding and defecating at minimal cost. This is why every twentieth-century nation state has had its camps, whether for its armies or its victims. 'Strength Through Joy' was emblazoned over the gates of the Nazi camps for indoctrinating the young. 'Labour Makes Freedom' was the message on those of the extermination camps.

It touches upon a very insular, insentive and misanthropic nerve, even to make the comparison with Butlin's first camp where he put up a sign on the reception block with the Shakespearean slogan 'Our True Intent is all for Your Delight.' It remained there to greet the wartime conscripts, and it was combined with the ethos of the English public school. 'Bill had divided the camp into four Houses, largely because he had learned that even when they were relaxing the English, as a nation love to be in competition for something. So each House was duly given the opportunity to fight for honours...'[53] It invites comparison with another application of the public school ethos which was happening at the same time, in a penal setting.

At the end of the last century there was widespread agreement among the people closest to the prison system with Peter Kropotkin's dictum that 'prisons are the universities of crime', and in 1895 it was decided to separate young offenders from hardened criminals, first at Bedford jail and then at Borstal prison outside Rochester. By the late-1920s, through a lucky accident, there was both an enlightened Borstal governor, Col. W. W. Llewellin and a visionary prison commissioner, Sir Alexander Patterson. They were influenced by Ameri-can experiments in developing self-governing institutions for young offenders, which filtered into British experience through the publicity given to Homer Lane's 'Little Commonwealth' in Dorset. If the idea of a prison without bars was attractive, still more desirable if it was not a prison at all, but a camp, and even more so if it was a camp set up and built by the boys who were to live there. In

1930 a farm was bought at Lowdham, near Nottingham, and sixty carefully-selected boys marched one hundred and thirty-two miles to pitch their tents and to begin the building of a permanent camp. It was seen as an exciting venture both by the boys and by the outside world and was followed in 1935 by a further such venture. Staff and boys were assembled at Stafford prison. 'With a very small but growing circle we were a happy party tuned up to a high endeavour for the adventure ahead.'[54] They marched across England to build the North Sea Camp on the shore of the Wash north of Boston, and the purpose of the camp was to build a bank for the enclosure of a large area of marshland for reclamation.

> On May 31st, a perfect summer day, we marched into the Camp, and settled ourselves down in tents. A central hut contained dining-hall, kitchen and offices, was being erected by contract, and we had to erect the remainder of the huts. We marched in with 20 lads, and the next four months were occupied in building up our spirit, our numbers and our huts. Huts somewhat of the Army pattern, but with double walls and roofs of asbestos and match-boarding, have been erected, to house and sleep 120 lads.[55]

The layout, the buildings, the programme of sporting activities and sailing expeditions, were precisely those of a holiday camp, and the same was true of the next of these ventures, Hollesley Bay in Suffolk. Unlike the bleak North Sea camp site, this was actually adjacent to a holiday camp site on the sea shore. The site was a 1400-acre fruit and vegetable farm, previously used by the London County Council for training unemployed young men in horticulture.

'I liked the buildings,' wrote one inmate 'because they were more unlike a jail than any place could be.' He found himself in one of the new houses, 'These were modern camp-style buildings, one-storey structures of timber, corrugated iron, and plasterboard interiors...very comfortable, with a billiard-room, games-room, wireless-room and thermostatic showers. The dining-hall and dormitories were centrally heated.' This appreciative camper was Brendan Behan, who had been arrested in Liverpool in 1939 as a sixteen-year-old IRA terrorist with a caseful of explosives. His book *Borstal Boy* is in fact a hymn of praise for Hollesley Bay and the people who ran it. The flavour of the book and of the institution can be seen from another passage:

> It was announced in the first week of April that we were to have an Eisteddfod in May. The Eisteddfod had nothing to do with Wales or any place else, for the matter of that, only ourselves. The Old Man told us the history of it when he made the announcement. He founded our place, one of the first open Borstals in 1938, with fifty fellows from Camp Hill on the Isle of Wight. They walked to our place, from where they came ashore: all the way from Hampshire across the country, camping out on the way. The Old Man had boasted to the Prison Commissioners that he would not lose a single man in the transaction, and he didn't...
>
> All the fellows in the dining-hall cheered this announcement because they looked forward to an extra day's holiday from hard graft and also because most of the time we liked the Old Man – the Squire, as he was also called.
>
> There was to be, at this Eisteddfod, a boxing tournament, a cross-country race, plays in the evening, a concert, prizes for gardening and handicrafts,

Seventh Day Adventists at Butlin's, Bognor.

and an essay competition on the subject, 'My Home Town', One hundred Player's was the prize and that, I said in my own mind, is my hundred Player's.[56]

It could have been any of the holiday camps of the 1930s. It could even have been Butlin's except that Hollesley Bay had no perimeter fence. Perhaps, though, the dour recorders of the British scene are at their best when describing those special events that the camps seek to attract to extend the use of the premises beyond the twenty to twenty-five weeks of the holiday season. Ladbroke's specialize in conferences, Pontins, helped by the smaller size and geographical spread of their sites, were hosts in 1985 to dozens, 'They vary,' the director explained to *Marketing* magazine, 'from an electronic organ festival to snooker coaching weeks, to retirement planning courses. They can be very profitable, provided you get it right. You can have an antiques week at the centre for 400–600. It wouldn't work at one for 8,000.'[57] For Butlin's, consequently, the events have to be really big. Roy Kerridge attended the General Conference of the Assemblies of God, when 7,136 Pentecostalists were staying at the Minehead camp:

> We all crowded into Lula's gloomy little chalet for tea and biscuits, in a seedy corner of the camp reserved for self-catering customers. Lula shared these cramped council-flat conditions with the two other girls. 'It's like a prison here,' said Lula, 'I'm ever so sleepy, 'cos we got up for the morning meeting at six-thirty, and we have to sleep three in a bed. The other bed there is full of dead fleas.' 'You should complain and they'll move you,' said the blowzy pastor's widow who had just dropped in. 'My complaint is the meter men. They just barge in to empty the meter without knocking.' 'Our meter's broken, and we've got no electricity at all,' said one of the boys. 'What's more, the lavatory don't flush, and we have to empty buckets down. The lady next door's got a mouse – she makes enough fuss about it, you'd think it was a rat. Her roof's leaking, she says. Or is it the tap?'[58]

Jacquie Hughes also complained about her bedroom. 'I was too long for the bed, and during the night the door rattled. A camper filled me in. Every winter the doors swell, so every summer they're shaved down a bit, and after a few seasons...' She was at the Barry Island Butlin's along with 5,000 other people for the 1950s Music Festival – an instant sell-out, and she remembers that

> Late at night, at the end of every party, the Gaiety Ballroom is deserted, all the fittings cruelly highlighted; cracked chipboard ceiling, rows of orange upholstered seating complete with ciggy burns, hundreds of fag ends, glasses, burger boxes and wooden forks strewn all over. Two grey-coated cleaners 'doing' the rows, the rain is pouring through the roof by one of the big fruit machines. Even after drinking and bopping until the small hours, early next morning everyone is out and about freshened up and respectfully subdued for a Sunday.[59]

At least the morning after was cheerful too, when Ian Walker went to the original Skegness Butlin's in 1983: 'The sun had got its hat on by morning and Butlin's was transformed. Children in the paddling pool and you didn't notice that the blue and yellow paint was cracked and peeling. On the fairground the dodgem cars, so shiny and orange, looked delectable as that first taste of ice cream. Sparks fell like yellow rain. Please can we do it again Dad?...'[60]

That is what Billy Butlin wanted every child to ask. But the grisly picture from the professional observers of other people's pleasures explains why Butlin's have been spending £1.6 million with a firm of advertising agents 'to overcome some of the negative images'.

Changing the Image

> The world is woefully obscure about this camping racket...One thinks its visitors live in the rain; another wonders whether they are being washed out by the sea; another doubts if there be anything to eat but bread and cheese and so on.
>
> ('The cheapest holiday in the world', article in *The Tourist*, 1899)

All through the history of holiday camps, their proprietors have been anxious to change the way they were perceived by the public. Joseph Cunningham patiently pointed out that there was a world of difference between a camping holiday and a holiday *camp*, and that his young men were given three cooked meals a day in a setting as luxurious as a hotel. When W. J. Brown started the civil service camp at Corton he felt obliged to stress that his campers were not expected to share the chores or to 'rough it' in tents.

The word Camp itself soon became an embarrassment rather than an attraction. From its beginning in the 1930s, NALGO used the word Centre to describe its camps for local government officers, and all the other operators have long since made the same change in nomenclature in their publicity, even though, just like the public they cater for, they invariably use the word Camp in conversation. When he began his enterprise Billy Butlin, who saw all previous camps as 'primitive affairs', used the word Luxury in the names of his camps at Skegness and Clacton, to make clear that he was introducing new standards of accommodation and catering, as indeed he was.

As long ago as 1947 Butlin's circularized previous visitors urging them to book again, in a letter with the heading 'Holiday Villages by the Sea' which included the statement that the holiday camp title was being dropped in favour of 'holiday villages'.[61] In the following year when Butlin opened the centre at Mosney in Ireland (disposed of in 1982) it was given this proposed change of name, though it was the only one where the policy was carried out. Years later he recalled, 'You notice I called it a Holiday Village, not a Camp — and this reflected something that had been in my mind for some time. I had always visualized my camps as self-contained villages, but I started with the name Camp in 1936 and it was difficult to change it in Britain. Starting anew in Ireland, I was able to go back to the drawing board. And to help eliminate the old-style image I began to tone down some of the more strident aspects of the original camps.'[62]

But, to a far greater extent than any of the rival firms, Butlin's were trapped by their own public image. Rival firms and the smaller operators took advantage of this to stress that there was no regimentation in *their* camps. The publicity for the Prestatyn camp in 1946 addressed its campers thus: 'Now...don't — please don't — get the idea that you've GOT TO BE GAY at Prestatyn. You can take part in the fun or if you choose, be a spectator — whatever attracts you. No compulsion. No chivvying you to do this or that. Nor should there be; you are the guest — and it's *your* Holiday.'[63] To this day, as you travel through the holiday camp belt between Yarmouth and Lowestoft, Potter's Holiday Club proudly announces itself to be unlike all its neighbours in being 'Privately Owned, Family Run'.

The famous 'Wakey, wakey' morning cry from Radio Butlin was first introduced to meet the necessities of mass catering in two sittings, and it was reported in 1959 that 'Regimentation is not exactly the word for the hearty hospitality dispensed through the broadcasting system and by the blazer brigade of hosts and hostesses. The old "Wakey, wakey" regime has been toned down.'[64] But it was not until 1979 in fact that the last 'Wakey, wakey' call was broadcast to campers: 'With a colourful ceremony, probably including an 8 am. loudspeaker rendering of the Last Post, the holiday firm is abandoning its most famous link with the past.'[65]

The other big operators, were, as Pontin's marketing manager put it, 'lumbered with people's original perception of holiday camps being, for want of a better word, "over-organised" ' but at the same time were able, since their camps were smaller, to shift more readily than Butlin's to self-catering, presenting this as 'freedom'. When Bobby Butlin took over from his father, he introduced the slogan 'Butlin Land is Freedom Land' in response. Hurriedly, he began the introduction of self-catering and the effort to extend the season. 'Before 1968, Pwllheli for example had been trying to feed 12,000 people three meals a day with seasonal fluctuations; in all camps at no time before 1968 were more than two or three weeks fully occupied. There were more beds then and less than three-quarters of the business that we do now. Here the move into self-catering was a blessing in disguise. Conversion meant losing beds, and if the season were stretched out longer, business would increase: a marvellous coincidence between social trends and economic pressures.'[66]

The public image of their activities has preoccupied the management of

Butlin's for decades. As long ago as 1961 it was reported that 'Butlin's are consciously raising their sights for the kind of people they want to attract.'[67] The same aspiration is repeated every year, but the process of change has regularly involved following the formulae of their major rivals, in acquiring smaller sites with other names. 'One of Butlin's first diversifications was into buying up smaller caravan and chalet sites, some marketed as the Leisure Holiday Parks and others featuring in the Freshfields venture which has taken Butlin's into camping and boating holidays. There has been a successful expansion into the French canals.'[68] This policy involves a complete rejection of Billy Butlin's recipe for success and an adoption of the methods of some of the surviving 'pioneer camps'. Down the road from the closed Butlin holiday centre at Filey is the Butlin-owned Primrose Valley caravan park. 'The Valley accommodates 6,000 visitors in 200 modern chalets and 1,100 caravans — 150 of them owned by Butlin's, who also act as letting agents for other owners.'[69] This is precisely the arrangement that has been followed since the 1930s as we have seen, in humble camps like Golden Sands or Robin Hood, outside Rhyl.

Questions of social class and of social snobbery are major preoccupations in the holiday industry in Britain. Here Butlin's have been the victims of their own populist image. For contrary to the usual assumptions, their pre-war clientele was predominantly middle-class and it remained so in the early post-war years. In 1947 'it was calculated that a mere 5 per cent of the visitors was working class,'[70] and 'until the mid-1950s, holiday camps tended to attract middle class rather than working class visitors.'[71] In 1961 Butlin's defined their market as 'the middle income group'.[72] By 1983, Paul Theroux, who thought that Butlin's at Minehead was cheap, asked a Redcoat what sort of jobs the visitors did. He laughed:

> 'Are you joking, sunshine?' he said
> I said no, I wasn't.
> He said, 'Half the men here are unemployed. That's the beauty of Butlin's — you can pay for it with your dole money.'[73]

Two years later Martyn Harris found Butlin's at Bognor dear. He talked to a Jamaican who came to Britain in 1945 and has a good job as a buyer for an office equipment firm. 'He has a white wife, but no children because, he says, they wouldn't be accepted by "the other side". They have been coming to Butlin's for 14 years, mainly for the ballroom dancing, meeting the same couples every year.' For Harris,

> It's the first clue as to why people come to Butlin's these days. It is not a cheap holiday after all — about £400 a week for a family of four on half board in high season, which is probably no cheaper than Spain or Greece. But there are quite a few couples of mixed race about, and lots of families with handicapped children and quite a few shy groups of Chinese. Butlin's is big and anonymous enough to give an illusion of integration. A place to escape the curious glances over the breakfast table of a small hotel, or the claustrophobia of a package tour. But what about all the rest, who are they? "The blue collar worker from Dagenham with a wife on the check-out in Sainsbury's and two kids aged six and eleven," is Number Two's succinct definition of the average guest.[74]

This is not, however, the stereotype that the management wants to promote, and apart from spending £1.6 million with advertising consultants to 'overcome some of the negative images' it was reported in the winter of 1985 to be 'spending £15 million in a further shedding of its traditional holiday camp image and a bid for higher-spending customers. Even the Butlin name is being played down, but not phased out.[75] Bob Webb, the managing director explained that 'It would be a mistake to lose the name of Butlin's, but because of the way the market is going you have to identify something different...There is a huge market of middle-class people who want a well-organised activity holiday. That is what we are providing.'[76] Not only the image, but the camps themselves are to be 'changed beyond recognition'.

CHAPTER
5 Holidays by Design

 Governmental encouragement of holidays with pay is bound to raise some problems of great interest and not a little difficulty for the planner. Where will all these millions want to spend their annual holiday?...Probably the main solution of the problem lies in the provision of holiday camps, both by the sea and in the country, and the proper organisation, placing and arrangement of such camps presents an important planning problem.

(*Journal of the Town Planning Institute*, January 1939)

Holiday camps, by their very nature, lent themselves to a rigorous process of design and planning. Accommodating large numbers of people in a restricted area could hardly be left to chance. Some of the pioneer camps thrived on a measure of spontaneity and informality. But for the mass camps the tidy rows of sleeping cabins and carefully-located entertainment buildings marked the imprint of the drawing board, not to mention the regulations and bye-laws of local authorities anxious to safeguard public health and to minimize the impact of such large developments on a fragile environment.

For the proprietors and investors good design was a prudent means of maximizing the efficiency and competitiveness of the new camps. These were substantial investments that required the same degree of forethought that might have gone into, say, a factory or a hospital. At the same time, the great attraction for local authorities was that here at last was a chance to control the use of land. In some ways akin to new villages the mass camps offered rare opportunities for comprehensive planning of a kind. Far better, certainly, than allowing further coastal development on an individualistic basis that was harder to control and unruly in appearance. Geometry, order, regulation and perhaps even beauty in design were qualities that could win for holiday camps the promise of respectability and public favour. In reality, the new camps did not always match up to expectations but in theory at least they were conceived in a context of intended good design and planning.

Breaking New Ground

> Most architects have discovered holiday camps comparatively recently, and far too many of them are condescending in their approach to a subject on which their opinions are certainly not unchallengeable...How many architects have actually spent a holiday at a camp?
>
> (Unattributed article: 'Do you want neon lights and chromium at your camp?' *Holiday Camp Review*, August 1939).

By the end of the 1930s the design and layout of holiday camps was on the agenda of architects and planners alike. Published articles in the professional journals could look both backwards and forwards. In looking backwards there was already a recent but growing portfolio of experience from which to draw. Studies were made of carefully-designed camps, reflecting the state of what was very much a new art as well as providing alternative models for new developments.

Looking ahead, there was a widening recognition that the demand for this type of development had barely started. Professional attention was drawn to two trends. The first was a long-term transformation in patterns of holiday-making. Thus an article in 1939 for town planners advised its readers that holidays with pay were the thing of the future and planners had an important job to do if the new demands were to be met in a sensible way. An estimate of the likely increase was that the numbers enjoying annual holidays would double to twenty million over the coming four years.[1] The second trend to which professionals were alerted, namely, that of the provision of evacuation camps, was more immediate. In one sense this was of less general interest since the Camps Act largely removed this type of camp from the control of statutory planning. Yet, in another sense, there were important lessons to be taken from what amounted to an enormous planning exercise.

There was agreement, then, that holiday camps in one form or another were on the increase and that this presented an exciting challenge to professionals with an interest in development. Questions were asked as to suitable locations for new camps, their appropriate scale and layout, their detailed design.

On the first of these points, that of location, guidance of a very general nature was at hand in the form of a Ministry of Health circular. Against a background of concern about coastal encroachment the advice was to restrict new holiday camps to specified areas.

> There will no doubt be a demand for such camps, even in areas far removed from the regular holiday resorts, and the demand will have to be met within reason. The Planning Authority should consider, therefore, whether it is practicable to specify areas in which on grounds of amenity the erection of camps should be prohibited, leaving them to come elsewhere

with consent, or whether the requirement of consent generally is sufficient by itself. If the first method is adopted it will clearly be essential that the land remaining available for camps should be land suitable for the purpose of a camp and should have ready access to the sea.[2]

Other than recognizing that most camps would need to be located near the sea, ensuing discussions stressed the more negative rather than positive aspects of location. The first concern was to preclude new developments from specified stretches of coastline. The advice of the influential Council for the Preservation of Rural England was that five types of land should be avoided.[3] Camps should not be located on high quality farmland; they should not consume level sites which may alternatively be used for playing fields or for access to safe bathing beaches; they should avoid remaining stretches of unspoilt coastline; likewise, mountain and moorland areas should be preserved; and they should not be allowed to impact on common land. Bearing in mind the enormous damage done to natural coastlines in the previous twenty years or so this type of restrictive approach was understandable.

Less palatable, perhaps, was the kind of advice that appeared in the *Journal of the Town Planning Institute*, urging the separation of campers from other users of the coast and countryside. Ideal locations were those with 'a degree of isolation' and where each 'camp should have an ample area of land, as a well-equipped camp containing a large recreation area [that] will probably keep within its boundaries the bulk of holiday-makers, thus leaving the country free for nature lovers and the less gregariously minded.'[4]

Writing in the same year, the architect Gordon Stephenson took a different approach, making a case for more integration with a camp's surroundings.[5] On practical grounds, the goal of isolation had to be tempered by a need to be within reach of services. At the same time, on environmental grounds, the countryside around the site – full of interest for rambles and walks – was seen to have great influence on the life of the camp. It was assumed that visitors should be encouraged to use the countryside rather than to spend their whole vacation within the camp compounds.

The town planner and landscape architect, Thomas Adams, urged that more thought should be given to sites not necessarily on the coast but nearer to the main cities. Some of these might well be provided by large firms for their employees. He compared the limited evidence of holiday camps in Britain with their more extensive occurrence in North America. As an example of what he had in mind he referred to Dayton Park, Ohio, where families or groups of young people could be accommodated in artistically-designed log cabins in landscaped surroundings. Well-designed camps in Britain would be not only of immediate social benefit but would also help to protect the remaining countryside from the type of shoddy development that was becoming commonplace.[6]

The message of Adams was that careful planning was essential. Reflecting this approach, a sensitive environmental lobby viewed with concern the anticipated impact of a whole network of new Government evacuation camps on inland sites, which were likely to remain as holiday centres after the war. There was little scope for debate about location, but views were expressed about detailed siting and design. In presenting the scheme to the House of Commons, the Minister of Health was quick to point out that he had consulted closely with the Council for the Preservation of Rural England, and that Mr. Percy Thomas, a past president of the Royal Institute of British Architects, had been appointed to the board of the Camps Corporation. He commended MPs to visit the exhibition at the Housing Centre, where the state of the art in camp design was on display.[7]

The assurances of the Minister were not enough to quell the doubts of members on both sides of the house. Typical of these doubts were those of the Opposition spokesman who, while welcoming the idea of the camps as a social experiment, warned that 'we have also to ensure, if we possibly can, that they will not be an eyesore in the British country. There are to be 30 camps at once, and a great number more later on, if the experiment succeeds. If they are wrongly sited, if they are hideous in construction, if their design is ugly and if they are painted in colours which disfigure the landscape for miles around, as many buildings do – everybody knows it – then by this Bill we shall do much to debauch the diminishing stretches of British countryside that will remain.'[8]

Government camps were exceptional because of the scale of the operation and because local authorities had little say in the form they took. Elsewhere, though, accepted practice was gradually evolving. Once a location was determined, what was to be the most appropriate scale and layout? The architects Max Lock and Judith Ledeboer (commissioned to design the camp for Lambeth Borough Council) were very specific in their guidelines. The ideal site would be about 50 acres in extent, with half the land used for buildings and half for playing-fields. They were thinking in terms of accommodating about 350 campers – 'the maximum number that a good manager can get to know on any sort of personal basis in a week.'[9]

The new commercial camps were very much larger than Lock and Ledeboer's ideal, and yet other architects shared a similar interest in creating not simply camps but communities. Frank Bennett wrote a series of articles in *The Builder* in 1939 on the design and planning of holiday camps.[10] For him 'camps are small, self-contained communities, rather like temporary villages where recreation-rooms and the swimming-pool take the place of "pub" and village-hall, and perhaps even of a church.'[11] Fellow architects were encouraged to respond to what amounted to a new challenge and 'an opportunity to do something pleasing, amusing or even daring with the difficulties of a layout.'[12]

Technically, the agreed task was to combine the three basic functions of a camp – administration, social amenities and sleeping accommodation – to best effect. As well as fostering a sense of community, 'best effect' also reflected concern for what was referred to as the hygienic arrangement of buildings. This, in turn, embraced two aspects, physical hygiene (relating to fresh air, light and adequate services) and mental hygiene (to do with peace of mind in a well-designed environment).[13]

In another series of articles (effectively amounting to a manual for architects) the authors approached the question of layout with a twofold division into covered and open-air accommodation.[14] Over a period of eight weeks the articles proceeded to offer very detailed and practical advice concerning the arrangement and design of the various components within these categories. For the uninitiated, a profile was drawn of what holiday campers actually did – how and when they arrived, their preference for individual tables in the dining room

and for the tendency for most people to rush to meals the moment they were announced (and so the need to provide ample corridors), the popularity of ballrooms and how much space should be allowed for each couple, and the popularity of swimming, billiards and a licensed club-room. It was recognized that most architects would have had no prior experience in this area of work but that it was a form of development that could be expected to grow.

Apart from certain basic features in common, layouts understandably differed according to site variations, the size of the camp and architectural preferences. The Rogerson Hall Holiday Camp, for instance (as noted in Chapter 2), attracted attention because of the way that sleeping accommodation was grouped in unified blocks and this, for some, represented a great advance on the rows of

The observation tower,
Prestatyn.

individual chalets found in most speculative holiday camps. A nearby camp on
the East Coast offered a contrast to Rogerson Hall, accommodating 1500
campers in much smaller chalet groupings.[15]

As well as location and layout, holiday camps, the ultimate in escapism, were
an obvious opportunity to indulge in fanciful architecture. It was an opportunity
that was frequently spurned and many of the early examples were little better in
design than military camps — dull rows of buildings using functional materials.
An interesting exception is that of Prestatyn Holiday Camp, designed by William
Hamlyn (the architect to the LMS Railway), and opened in 1939.[16]

From the point of arrival, entering beneath a tall structure with the words
'Prestatyn Holiday Camp: The Chalet Village By The Sea' across the road,

117

visitors discovered an environment that was designed to impress. Within the gates they found themselves in a landscaped square known as Sun Court. On either side were large modern buildings, painted white and with the detailing that marked them as unmistakeable products of the 1930s. Names of the camp routes, like Atlantic Drive, Ocean Way and Admiral's Walk added to the distinctive flavour of marine architecture used in the main buildings.

To the east of Sun Court was the dining room, a massive structure that could seat the whole of the camp's 1750 visitors at a single sitting, not to mention space for an orchestra to play at mealtimes. On the other side of Sun Court was the ballroom and concert hall with maple floor, large enough to hold 600 couples or a seated audience to watch performances.

Beyond Sun Court the focal point was the camp swimming pool, surrounded by an elevated terrace paved with coloured concrete slabs with fittings for umbrellas. Overlooking the pool was a control tower used by judges of pool competitions, and by visitors who climbed the 60 feet to look across the sea. The tower, in turn, adjoined a ship-shaped structure used for deck games and known as the Prestatyn Clipper.

The chalets, too, were distinctive, planned around courts rather than in rows, and with shared washrooms in the centre of each court. Family chalets were grouped together in a part of the camp known as Penguin Haven, with easy access to a children's play area. There was also a laundry where 'lady visitors may wash and iron simple garments'.[17]

Making Plans

> Most planning of holidays in the future will be to the advantage of everyone. But planning should not mean control and direction. The essence of a holiday is liberty.
>
> (Elizabeth Brunner, *Holiday Making and the Holiday Trades*, 1945).

Prestatyn was a showpiece and yet by no means the only exemplar of a well-designed holiday camp. At the end of the 1930s, though, the general impres-

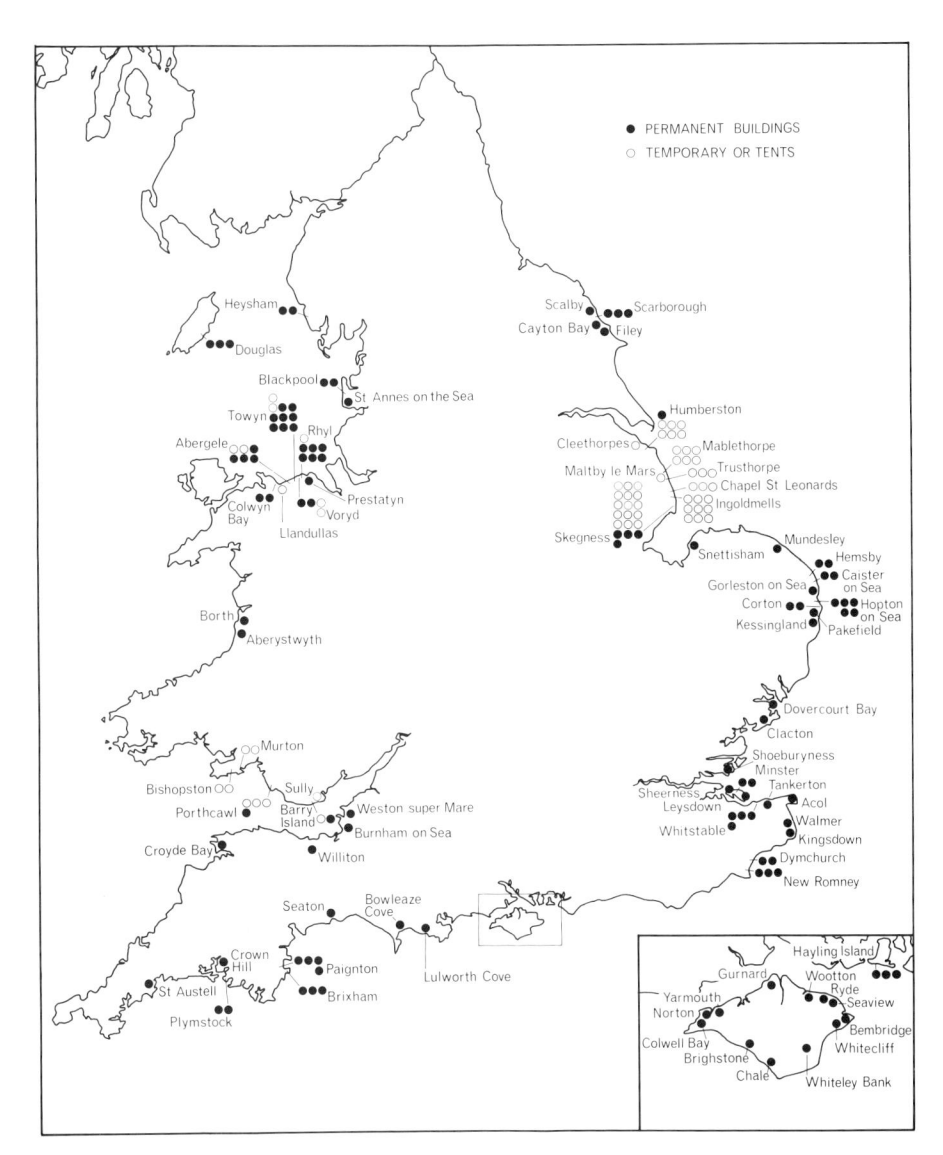

● PERMANENT BUILDINGS
○ TEMPORARY OR TENTS

Heysham
Douglas
Blackpool
St Annes on the Sea
Towyn
Abergele
Rhyl
Colwyn Bay
Prestatyn
Voryd
Llandullas
Borth
Aberystwyth
Murton
Bishopston
Sully
Porthcawl
Barry Island
Weston super Mare
Croyde Bay
Burnham on Sea
Williton
Seaton
Bowleaze Cove
Lulworth Cove
Crown Hill
Paignton
St Austell
Brixham
Plymstock

Scalby
Scarborough
Cayton Bay
Filey
Humberston
Cleethorpes
Mablethorpe
Maltby le Mars
Trusthorpe
Chapel St Leonards
Ingoldmells
Skegness
Snettisham
Mundesley
Hemsby
Caister on Sea
Gorleston on Sea
Corton
Hopton on Sea
Kessingland
Pakefield
Dovercourt Bay
Clacton
Shoeburyness
Minster
Tankerton
Sheerness
Leysdown
Acol
Whitstable
Walmer
Kingsdown
Dymchurch
New Romney

Hayling Island
Gurnard
Wootton
Ryde
Yarmouth
Norton
Seaview
Colwell Bay
Bembridge
Brighstone
Whitecliff
Chale
Whiteley Bank

Holiday camp sites in England and Wales, 1939.

sion of camps and of their impact on the coastline was coloured less by the Prestatyns than by their poorly-planned and scattered counterparts. Preservationists heard the arguments for camps as a means of containing crowds and holiday development, but they compared this with the reality of many ill-sited camps of shoddy design. Rows of utilitarian huts on bleak sites enclosed by cheap fencing were becoming all too familiar and a far cry from the rather spectacular liner designs, the dazzling white buildings and the Hollywood image of a few of the larger camps.

The Lincolnshire coastline, for instance – a popular venue for holiday-makers

AERIAL VIEW, BUTLIN'S LUXURY HOLIDAY CAMP, PWLLHELI

Planners and preservationists were concerned about the impact of new camps on the coastline.

from the Midlands — was something of a microcosm of the huge range of camps at that time. When civil servants surveyed this stretch of coast in 1942 they recorded no less than fifty-one camps with a capacity for nearly 32,000 visitors at any one time.[18] At one extreme, the range included the prestigious Butlin's camp at Skegness, 92 acres in extent and accommodating between four and five thousand visitors. Smaller but also noteworthy of its kind was the Derbyshire Miners Holiday Centre (also at Skegness). In contrast, most of the Lincolnshire camps did little to enhance their reputation. Often they consisted of a few huts and caravans with clubroom and minimal facilities, located side-by-side along a relentlessly flat coastline. Wallace's Holiday Camp, for example, was described as a small, second-rate camp with a small timber recreation and dining room, and with most of the accommodation under canvas. By all accounts it was fairly typical, and as the Ministry's surveyors moved from Chester's Site to Huckle's Site to Ely's Site and on to Keeton's Site they recorded a bleak scene. 'In most of these camps the owner possesses a few trailers, caravans or tents for hire during the season, the remaining part of the site being available for campers with their own accommodation. The result is an unsightly mess of temporary and moveable dwellings and tents.'[19]

Comparable observations were made in other counties, and when J. A. Steers made his own coastal survey in the following year he was able to reinforce the picture of extremes that impressed the civil servants.[20] Certainly there was no shortage of examples of the 'unplanned and haphazard' holiday camp that Steers regarded as a 'serious menace'. On balance, though, Steers reflected a

Rows of huts at the Holiday Camp, Seaton, Devon.

growing view in Ministry circles that, provided they were properly planned, holiday camps offered an opportunity that had to be grasped. There seemed to be no better way of coping with the anticipated growth in visitor use of the coastline in the years ahead.

For Steers the Butlin camps offered a shining example. He compared each of them with a cruising liner, complete within themselves. 'They are not eyesores, and they do fill a great need. It is not everyone who wishes to stay in one of these camps, but a great number of people are obviously satisfied, and, in general, the movement is to be encouraged.'[21] Moreover, it was not just the large commercial camps which attracted praise. Trade unions and other associations had also earnt a reputation for careful planning. Steers observed that usually these camps incorporated decently-built huts laid out in some sort of ordered arrangement. 'Provided the huts are well kept, and, what is more important, are perfectly sited, these camps fulfil very useful purposes.'[22]

For outsiders, concerned about environmental impact, the proviso that camps should be 'perfectly sited' was all-important. It was acknowledged that the Council for the Preservation of Rural England had an important role in determining suitability of sites, but there were also reservations amongst civil servants as to whether this body was capable of taking a broad-enough view. A difficulty noted was that branches of the Council were often largely composed of 'mere preservationists'.[23]

In fact, the Council responded in the constructive spirit that was called for, recognizing that demands for coastal land could not be stemmed but could be

121

channelled to suitable areas. Yet, to achieve a balance between the new social pressures and the enduring qualities of the coast, there was an urgent need for the exercise of greater national powers. Holiday camps were identified as one feature of the changing coastal scene, 'the necessity of (which) is not denied; the question with which the Committee are concerned is how they shall be designed and where they shall be sited, and how the essential characteristics of the coast and the adjoining landscape shall be saved from being destroyed in the process, as they unquestionably will if national control is lacking.'[24]

Yet even with greater national control questions were raised which would not easily be resolved. It was pointed out that the right use of land was not necessarily the same thing as land suitability. There would be instances where land might not be suitable for development in itself, yet where the demand for a holiday camp might be so strong that it ought to be built. The strength of demand was seen to depend on such factors as where there was a large concentration of working-class population within reach, and how much time and money holiday-makers were prepared to spend in travelling to a camp. Anticipating a flood of visitors to the coast in the first warm weather following the end of the war, officials in the Ministry of Town and Country Planning warned that there was 'obviously some urgency about holiday camps'.[25]

During the war years, then, a consensus emerged that holiday camps would feature in post-war coastal developments and that they would need to be planned. Equally, it was not anticipated that they would require special legislation but would, instead, be dealt with under general measures affecting all forms of development. But should the role of planning be simply to guide and coordinate or should it be a developmental process as well? There were those in the early 1940s who contemplated whether it might not be appropriate for the State itself to build and manage the post-war camps. The idea of nationalized holiday camps – in the belief that this would provide the best means of meeting social demands while at the same time safeguarding the environment – was by no means without foundation.

It was an issue that had already been discussed in the context of the Camps Bill in 1939.[26] Although that was an emergency measure the very process of State intervention was enough to stimulate thoughts of a longer-term involvement. Apart from a general expression of ideology, the prospect of State camps appealed to Labour politicians for a variety of reasons. For a start, the record of commercial camps left a lot to be desired on environmental grounds and were commonly a source of local nuisance. In social terms the rates they charged led to the exclusion of the majority of lower-grade manual workers. Perhaps, though, these were the lucky ones as another view was that 'nearly all [the camps] are organised with a view to making the visitors spend their money in a senseless way'.[27] With State holiday camps there would be the opportunity to pursue what came to be a popular socialist ideal in the 1940s, that of social mix. It was not a question of establishing camps simply for those most in need. 'I think it better for ordinary folk that when on holidays they should mix with people of diverse social experience. I think that is better all the way round. It makes for better social understanding.'[28]

A more common view was to accept the idea of holiday camps but to draw the line at State ownership. It was a tolerant yet sometimes a grudging view.

'There are camps to which people want to go where there is not a moment of peace morning, noon and night, and where you get neither rest nor sleep, and you live on the edge of your nerves, but people apparently are willing to pay to do it. If it is their idea of a holiday, and this is a free country, I have no objection to such camps being provided, but not at Government expense.'[29]

In 1942 the issue was debated again amongst civil servants in the Ministry of Works and Planning, though a moderate approach was counselled at that time.[30] It was questioned whether any State organization should be set up to establish camps or assist in their establishment on a non-commercial basis, or even more widely to be responsible for the provision of holiday accommodation. The view at that time was that, unless there was a sharp change in governmental policy, the planning authorities should apply a coordinating function but should not be the owners or developers of camps.

A year later, fresh from his survey of the entire coastline, the view of J. A. Steers was quite different. 'My own personal view is that I believe a strong case exists for the State itself to experiment in this form of enterprise.'[31] On a more localized basis (and for different reasons to those of Steers) there were local authorities with plans for municipal camps. The Borough of Margate was one such authority, drawn somewhat reluctantly into this form of intervention in the belief that in this way they could safeguard the interests of local suppliers and minimize the impact on boarding-house keepers.[32]

But for all the heady talk of nationalizing camps along with the mines and railways, little came of the idea in practical terms. The Labour Party manifesto for the 1950 General Election contained a proposal for a holidays council to promote more holiday centres with reasonably priced accommodation for families, but this was never implemented. In general it was left to the county councils to deal with holiday camps as part of their coastal and countryside policies under the 1947 Town and Country Planning Act. There was little that could be done about existing sites, although even there all new development had now to win the approval of the planning authority. Elsewhere, proposals for fresh sites could be assessed against environmental and other local considerations.

In an attempt to boost the quality of new post-war development (and, in consequence, public acceptance of holiday camps) the Workers Travel Association organized an architectural competition in 1946.[33] Entrants were invited to design either an inland or a coastal camp, in the case of the latter for about 500 people on a 20-acre coastal site. Stress was put on designing a camp that would meet not only various functional requirements but which would also not intrude upon the surrounding landscape. The sponsors were correct in their tacit recognition that acceptance of camps would depend more on their external impact than on what actually went on within the compound.

It was hoped that the entries would express new ideas in holiday camp design. What was called for was 'straightforward and economical planning and ease of working, combined with a certain lightness and gaiety of treatment suitable for a summer holiday centre'.[34] The assessors, however, found the results disappointing. A total of sixty-four schemes was less than expected, and the general level of the designs was not considered to be high. Many of the entrants were criticized for relying on single-storey sleeping quarters, which had the effect of creating a clutter of buildings. The winning design for the coastal site made use of two-storey blocks and was praised for its orientation of buildings, though it was not in other ways particularly remarkable. As a proto-type of post-war camps it is doubtful whether this type of concept – small in scale and conceived at a time when building materials were scarce – was particularly influential.

Another attempt to plan for the expected increase in demand came through the work of the Post-War Holidays Group.[35] Originally formed in 1938 by the National Council for Social Service (and known then as the Holidays with Pay Group), their main concern was to ensure that the process was properly planned and that the State accepted its share of responsibility. Various organiza-tions were represented in the group, including the Camping Club of Great Britain, the Cooperative Holidays Association and the Workers' Travel Associ-ation. In their review of what resources were available and what could be done, holiday camps were high on the agenda.

The Holidays Group conducted its own survey of holiday preferences in 1946 and concluded in general that most people were looking for organized holidays, with greater comforts than they experienced at home, and with plenty of company and entertainment. Holiday camps featured high in the popularity stakes, and the group noted that there was every sign that the popularity of camps would continue to increase. It was a trend they wished to encourage, not least of all because of the relief offered to women (freed from shopping and cooking) and because of the wider benefits of communal life. But the group also concluded that commercial camps alone would not be enough to meet the scale of the demand or some of the special needs that could be expected.[36]

To meet the shortfall, the group proposed the rapid conversion of a wide variety of government properties used in the war but by then redundant. Apart from the purpose-built evacuation camps, they had in mind industrial and rural hostels built to meet special labour needs in the war, and a range of army, navy and air force establishments. After conversion, the government would retain control of the camps, and would be urged to raise standards through, for example, offering a higher quality of popular entertainment than was common-place in the commercial camps.

The management of these camps might be transferred to voluntary organiza-tions, but it remained a sensitive political proposal. Its sensitivity was not lessened by another of the group's recommendations – that a new government department should be established to provide and maintain holiday accommo-dation. As the group itself acknowledged, 'the mere fact that the camps would be Government property touches the tender spots of self-respect and indepen-dence. To go to them would set one at a disadvantage with one's neighbours, who went to lodgings or a boarding-house, or to a commercial Holiday Camp. The Holiday Camp idea has, as we have said, some advantages over boarding-houses or lodgings, but the fear of being 'pauperised' is very vivid.'[37]

In the event, State holiday camps were not to feature in the new collective edifice of post-war Britain. This was due in part to the fact that the anticipated flood of camp developments failed to materialize. Certainly there were some new holiday camps after 1945 but the emphasis was on consolidating and upgrading what was already there. While several counties recorded clusters of camps – in West Sussex, for instance, there are currently nine – other coastal authorities attracted none.

It may not have been a flood of new developments, but when any did occur the local impact was, invariably, considerable, and mixed feelings were aroused. The example of just one of these, the arrival of a new Butlin's camp at Bognor Regis, is illustrative.

Butlin's Comes to Bognor

> I am sure that if Sir Christopher Wren had been available, Billy Butlin would have hired him to draw up the plans of his new holiday camp.
> I think that (the writer) is wrong in imagining that Sir Christopher Wren would have allowed himself to be 'hired' by Mr. Butlin. Both aesthetically and architecturally there is a great deal of difference between Butlin's holiday camp and St. Paul's Cathedral.
>
> (Correspondence in *The Bognor Regis Post*, November, 1959)

There can be few sights more depressing than an English seaside resort which has seen better days. Bognor Regis in the 1950s was just such a place – a small town with a regal name but little else. Trippers arriving by coach made their way along the front, past the isolated Rex Ballroom, to sit in the shelter of a breakwater on the beach or to visit the funfair and amusement stalls behind. The funfair belonged to Billy Butlin.

Butlin had in fact been in town since 1930, owning a large chunk of seaside frontage and building his reputation as a showman. The trippers may have been happy enough, but for years the local council had worried not only about the effect on the reputation of the resort of this brash and somewhat seedy complex but also about its blighting effect on future development. Thinking ahead, the local authority had acquired in 1946 a site, 39 acres in extent, immediately to the east of the fairground, with a view to developing it for housing. Though unable to buy the Butlin site, the two sites together at least opened the possibility of some form of comprehensive redevelopment. This is, in fact, what happened with, in 1957, the announcement of plans for a massive new holiday camp on the east of this land, with the prospect of further development along the sea-front to the west.

From 1957, with the plans in the open, the pattern of events is cast in a familiar mould. Bognor presented its own circumstances, but the scenario of big business in a small town had already been seen in earlier Butlin centres like Skegness, Filey and Clacton. First there was the initial reaction to news of the scheme, with opinions ranged for and against, and murmurs of underhand dealings. Characteristically, Butlin would intervene himself in an attempt to press his own case and dispel unsavoury rumours. Then, with the building of the camp, localized complaints about noise and loss of amenity were invariably overwhelmed by economic arguments about the benefits for the town, and by the sheer volume of campers who would return year after year.

Typically, then, the announcement of the scheme was greeted with enthusiasm by the town's business community and, so it seemed, by the majority of residents. 'Momentous news', the local press called it: 'The door to prosperity has been opened thanks to some astute bargaining by the Bognor Regis Council.'[38] The source of enthusiasm is not hard to find.

For one thing, the prospect of an initial investment of £2 million for a town of this size, desperately in need of regeneration, was attractive to most. In the construction stage, there was a promise of employing 500 workers, most of them drawn locally. As well as improving employment opportunities, builders' merchants and shopkeepers were quick to see the immediate benefits for them. And when the camp was built, employment levels were expected to stabilize at around 400 in the winter, rising to 1200 in the summer season. Some 40,000 to 50,000 campers could be expected each year, and estimates were made as to what they would spend in the town – between 50p and £3 per person. Food would be bought locally if possible, with claims that the camp would be ordering whole fields of cabbages and potatoes from farmers nearby.[39] In its impact, it all added up to a great deal more than the resort's existing stock-in-trade of day trippers and a legacy of mediocre hotels and boarding houses.

Nor were the benefits of the scheme simply financial. Butlin himself, attending a public meeting in the Rex Ballroom, assured ratepayers that they would gain in other ways too. The camp's theatre, ballroom and indoor swimming pool would be available to the town out of season, and celebrity entertainments from the camp could be booked for the town's Esplanade Theatre at special low prices. Those concerned about the appearance of the place were assured that the promenade in front of the camp would be 'something worth seeing'.[40]

In turn, the council was well-pleased with the deal. Butlin handed over his fairground site to the local authority at no cost, in return for a lease on the council's own 39-acre site to the east. On this, the location for the camp, he agreed to pay ground rent in addition to an estimated annual rates bill of £12,000. It was seen to be sound business but, as well as that, the council chairman affirmed that 'we can at last clear away from our town altogether the unsightly funfairs, the vulgar catchpenny stalls, the candy floss and popcorn stands. In a comparatively short space of time we can expect the paper hat and Bingo brigade to have disappeared through lack of encouragement.'[41]

There seemed to be no limit to the regenerative effects of the holiday camp. Alongside the camp, on the site of the down-at-heel funfair, a vision was forming of tall buildings and freeways, the futurist dream of local authorities from Bognor to Birmingham in that period. 'Tall, modern buildings in the style of Basil Spence, Corbusier or the many other gifted architects practising today are what I hope to see. Nothing pseudo, nothing shoddy. We must not tolerate drab brick boxes. This is our chance to have beautiful architecture reflecting our day and age, and we must seize it with firm hands. Fine hotels, luxury flats, a solarium, shops, theatres and conference halls, and civic buildings can and should arise, fronted by a broad, impressive seaway.'[42]

In such a heady atmosphere, the claim of a local newspaper that 'the feeling of almost everyone that the coming of the camp will be the finest thing that has ever happened to Bognor'[43] is perhaps understandable. When the council approved the scheme the vote was seventeen in favour and only one against. It was a single voice of dissent in the council chamber, but an expression of wider doubts and a growing sense of unease in the town at large. Once the initial excitement had subsided, questions were raised on a variety of fronts. Would

Butlin's be all that it promised, or had the web of make-believe that characterized the very appeal of these camps distorted the basis for rational judgement?

The dissenting councillor urged a little more thought as to what the long-term effects would be on the resort which still proudly bore the name of 'Regis'. 'Is it money we should be after or a town to live in? – not a town for which one has to apologise and about which people will say: Bognor, let me see, Bognor is where Butlin's is.'[44]

Far from seeing the last of the 'paper hat and Bingo parade', as the optimistic council chairman anticipated, residents living in Felpham, close to the site, feared the very reverse. 'Hundreds of people walking about with fish-and-chips'[45] is how one person saw it, while for another the nightmare was 'the thought of the noise if they have loudspeakers crying "wakey wakey" and jollying people along.'[46] Perhaps a more cutting criticism was that of urging caution in dealing with someone whose reputation was not necessarily all it had been made out to be. Reference was made to Butlin's ill-fated venture to establish a holiday camp in the Bahamas, with the implied warning that the same could happen to Bognor.[47]

The public inquiry into the case for planning permission was largely a parade of affirmation and support, but a small band of objectors spoke out against the way the development would spoil the character of their town. They pointed out that many people had come to retire in Bognor, while others commuted to London. It was argued that a holiday camp on this scale would drive many of these people away, and the town would no longer be able to attract those in search of a quiet life.[48] A press report included the view that successful resorts managed very well without a holiday camp.[49] There were also more practical objections to do with the loss of the coach park for visitors, with the obstruction of a footpath across the site, and the threat to bird life on the marshy ground.

In spite of the outcome of the inquiry in favour of the camp, disaffection with the prospect continued to surface. An exchange of letters, for instance, in the local press in September and October, 1959, showed that the detailed plans fell a long way short of many people's expectations. A former alderman of Wembley Borough Council, then living in Felpham, wrote to complain of the incongruous building materials and inappropriate design: 'I cannot imagine a more unsatisfactory contrast than that between the charm of Felpham village and the violent domination of this charm by a concrete-block and green-asbestos conglomeration.'[50] In a subsequent edition, a retired army major was less circumspect: 'The drawings remind me of the war-time hutted camps which the R.E.s constructed. We required no architects to lay these out...The Bognor scheme is, however, infinitely worse than any Army camp, because the huts are two storeys high, and these ghastly monstrosities will dwarf the surrounding bungalows. The canteen and recreational buildings are similar to temporary aircraft hangars.'[51]

Individual letters were followed, in turn, by a joint campaign at the end of 1959, designed to thwart the scheme even at this late stage before building started. Amenity was one well-aired issue, but now ratepayers were warned that, far from benefiting the town financially, they may well find themselves subsidizing the camp. Figures were produced to show that the council would have been better advised to have thought in terms of encouraging the develop-

Two-storey sleeping accommodation at Butlin's Bognor camp.

ment of the site instead for high-quality flats and hotels. The party that stood to gain most was not, in the view of the campaign, the town but Billy Butlin.

Public anxiety was aroused, and in February 1960 Butlin agreed to answer his critics at a meeting in the Rex Ballroom. Nearly 1,000 ratepayers attended. 'The ballroom and balconies at the Rex were packed, and many people had to stand. Dozens were turned away because there was no room. Many came to criticise. Yet within minutes Mr. Butlin had won the hearts of everyone...Any critics of the camp were easily tamed by the quietly spoken millionaire king of the holiday camps.'[52]

According to his biographer, Rex Norton, this was a familiar routine – meeting the 'Awkward Squad' at a public meeting and winning them over with a mixture of sincerity and showmanship. Before this he would already have secured the support of councillors and local businessmen: 'Little men in little towns who have been struggling for years find themselves big because they are part of the Big Butlin enterprise.'[53]

In the summer of 1960, just a few months after the meeting to oppose it the camp was opened, with about three thousand visitors arriving on the first day. By the time it was fully completed it could accommodate as many as eight thousand campers at any one time. It was billed, with some justification, as the biggest and the best, and Bognor – popularly renamed 'Butlin Regis' – was never to be the same again.

Twenty-four years after the opening of Skegness, the new camp was a product of experience. As Norah Butlin claimed, it was 'the first time my husband has had a chance to build a camp in the way he wants it.'[54]

It was tailor-made for the holiday-maker of the 1960s, and yet was it really so different to one of the first mass camps of the 1930s? A journalist who had previously visited the Butlin camp at Clacton thought they were almost indistinguishable. 'There was the same sweet-factory architecture with toy soldiers on cream walls; the same decor in the bars and cafes festooned like Christmas trees; the same chalets in two-tiered rows of orange and green...Butlin Camps – like international airports or Hilton Hotels – would probably seem the same at Spitzbergen or Honolulu.'[55] True enough, Butlin had found a winning formula, and Bognor was simply another outlet for the collective dream and fantasy of thousands.

The End of an Era

> The other reaction, far more general and far less articulate, and on that account generally ignored by students of environmental perception, was acceptance of the situation, a readiness to take whatever pleasures were made available in an increasingly urbanised environment. A lingering romantic tradition, popular in the academic and upper-class world, finds little of value in that acceptance and laments the crowded holiday highways, the crowded ball parks, the crowded beaches, the meretricious forms of recreation. But what some of us call crowds, others call people, and many enjoy these pastimes not as surrogates for the vanished agrarian experience, but as something entirely new and rewarding.
>
> (J. B. Jackson, *Discovering the Vernacular Landscape*, Yale, 1984)

The Bognor episode was not typical of the planning problems posed by holiday camps. Consolidation and modernization was, more commonly, the order of the day, with decline and closure a new item for the agenda.

A survey in 1984 revealed that at the county level holiday camps were not normally seen as presenting particular problems and that their control was encompassed within broader policies.[56] Most counties have stretches of coastline where no large-scale development is permitted and other areas where development can be contained. In the County of Avon, for instance, where there is one existing holiday camp the Structure Plan restricts the development of further camps to the vicinity of Weston-super-Mare. Developers are advised that any permissions would be subject to strict environmental controls in an attempt to strike a balance between the need to support the local tourist economy and the need to limit the environmental impact of such developments. Similarly, in the County of Cleveland, where there are no existing camps, the possibility of future developments is entertained at suitable locations outside the limits of what is defined as the county's Heritage Coast.

Most of the details of development control are now the responsibility of the District Councils but here, too, holiday camps are unlikely to feature as a specific item on the policy agenda. In this respect the response of the Borough of Christchurch in Dorset is typical. Although no written policy exists, any planning application relating to a holiday camp would be treated on its individual merits. Important criteria would be the effect on the amenity of surrounding residential development, the provision of public infrastructure, and the distance of the proposed camp from shops and beaches.

In one unusual case, in the very centre of Hastings, the arrival of a new camp, far from presenting problems, proved to be something of a salvation for the local authority.[57] The origins of the scheme date back to the 1930s, when the then Hastings Corporation opened an ambitious open-air swimming complex by the sea. Proclaimed as Europe's finest bathing pool, it boasted changing-rooms for 1000 bathers and terraces for 2500 spectators. In the post-war period the viability of this enterprise was called into question, and the municipality was relieved to find a local buyer with plans to convert the complex into a holiday camp. A large part of the pool was filled in, and the cubicles became chalets, all designed to offer 'carefree holidays at a reasonable price'.

Occasionally, where holiday camps have posed particular problems, a local authority has chosen to intervene beyond the level of broad policy statements. Norfolk, for example, inherited from the pre-1947 period its full share of holiday camps – one at Paston, two at Caister-on-Sea, and others at Hopton, Flegg-burgh and Great Yarmouth. In the 1960s an attempt was made to concentrate all these developments. The East Coast Plan proposed two new holiday towns to be built at Hemsby and Sea Palling, but the proposals were never carried out. A more successful example of intervention is that of Cleethorpes Borough Council which now owns and manages an unusual form of holiday camp known as The Humberston Fitties.[58]

In its origins The Fitties is a colourful example of inter-war plotland develop-ment, where ex-army huts from the First World War were supplemented by a motley of makeshift holiday homes. It was totally unplanned and in this period just 'grew and grew, haphazard, casual, delightful and probably most unhygie-nic'. After the Second World War the local authorities, Lindsey County Council and Grimsby Rural District Council were determined to bring the area under some form of control. As the landowner, the Rural District Council prepared a new layout and progressively introduced a drainage scheme and new roads. From 1958 caravans were permitted alongside the existing holiday chalets and a camp manager was appointed. Private companies were invited to provide shops and entertainments and as many as 6,000 people can be accommodated at the camp at any one time.

What is illustrated at The Fitties is that for local authorities holiday camps are undoubtedly easier to control than more individualistic forms of development. With its mixture of caravans and chalets it also exemplifies a problem of defining precisely what constitutes a holiday camp. This is, to a large extent, a recent problem reflecting changes both in traditional holiday camps and in caravan sites. On the one hand, holiday camps have incorporated a growing proportion of self-catering accommodation. At the same time, caravan and camping sites have often been transformed through the addition of clubrooms, shops and permanent buildings.

In Cornwall, for instance, there are no traditional large-scale holiday camps. Since 1945, though, there has been a very rapid growth in self-catering tourism and the development of a number of large chalet and caravan sites. In recent years many of these have been acquired by national companies such as Haven Leisure, Freshfields and Ladbrokes who then, typically, refurbish and upgrade the sites so that they resemble some of the traditional camps which have, in turn, moved towards self-catering.

Substantial investment is the key to meeting modern demands.[59] An example of this is St. Mary's Bay Holiday Centre in Kent, a site that started life as a holiday camp in the pioneering days of 1932. During the 1930s, 120 stone-built chalets were installed, and the central facilities included a waitress-service restaurant (with black tie evening meals) and nightly entertainment. After the war the site changed hands several times, and with no fresh investment decay set in. Most of the original chalets were demolished, and caravans were brought in to fill the gaps. The vision of the 1930s fast faded, until in 1979 new owners invested heavily in regenerating the site. Against a background of new landscap-ing, caravans are arranged around 'village greens' and there are plans for modern chalets and an all-season sports centre. It is a business enterprise, in which marketing and investment in the new-style holiday camp go hand in hand. In the words of the owner, 'I see a gradual change away from caravans in the next three to eight years to a more luxurious type of accommodation with many more on-site activities and a longer season...'[60]

In many ways this kind of change is encouraged by local authorities and, in planning terms, it is perhaps less the growth of holiday camps which have created the greatest problems so much as instances of their subsequent decline. Although total closures have been limited in number the local impact in these cases is considerable. And as these few camps are dismantled, the very process

Increasingly holiday camps came to resemble chalet and caravan parks . . .

of taking away the chalets and chandeliers calls into question just what it is that is disappearing.

At the end of 1983, two of the largest camps – Butlin's at Filey and at Clacton, both dating from the 1930s – closed their gates for the last time. Was this (as many thought at the time) the end of an era, or was it simply a rationalization of a massive business enterprise, not unlike the restructuring process taking place elsewhere in the British economy in the early-1980s? Undoubtedly, there was an element of both in what had happened.

In one sense, it was a clear indication of the end of an era. These camps had been opened in the days when paid holidays were hailed as a social innovation, when a week away from home was an adventure in itself, and when expectations were very different. The Lloyd loom chairs and the once-sparkling white terraces showed signs of wear, but so too did the total image. There is an obvious symbolism in the auctioning and physical removal of the colourful furnishings and paraphernalia that had been enjoyed by millions over the years.

At the same time, closure was also about sound business economics. Designed for thousands, high labour and running costs called for the camps to operate at or near capacity visitor levels, week after week throughout the season. With changing patterns of holidaymaking this could no longer be assured, and a corporate decision was taken to reduce the number of camps in the Butlin enterprise from eight to six. It was an investment decision, framed by wider considerations than nostalgia or local impact.

For those who were left behind to deal with the consequences, however, the effects of the decision were far-reaching. In both Clacton and, even more so on account of its isolation, at Filey, the closures inevitably created repercussions in the local economy. When a major camp had opened, the entrepreneurs had

and vice versa.

been quick to spell out the local benefits that would be enjoyed as a result of the massive investment, the purchases from traders and new jobs to run the camp, and the spending potential of thousands of visitors each week. Now, the process was reversed, with the loss of permanent and seasonal jobs, and a reduction in local incomes and expenditure. What was more, these empty encampments created a real threat to the environment and coastal landscape. For the local planners at Clacton and Filey, closure of these two holiday camps has posed problems far greater than those experienced when the camps were opened.

Filey and Clacton lay, like beached ocean liners, the victims of their own giantism. Filey, from an original maximum of 5000 visitors had been enlarged to accommodate 10,950, with a staff of up to 1,200 at the height of the season. It had paid £344,000 in rates to Scarborough Council, about 2 per cent of the borough's rate income. The local trading interests who had been so appalled when Billy Butlin first came to Filey, were even more appalled when Bobby Butlin announced 'this painful decision' with deep regret. 'It will be a body-blow for Filey' said the mayor, and the chairman of the Chamber of Trade was 'stunned, and absolutely staggered'.[61] So were those regular campers who had returned year after year, although one 'highly disillusioned' visitor, Roy Wood-cock, recalled 'peeling paintwork behind a brash exterior; a general air of having seen better days. Whole sections of chalets – and this in the height of the season – seemed abandoned; broken railings on balconies; dripping guttering and paintwork...A major niggle facing the self-catering camper – and these are surely the people who now provide the bulk of the company's revenue – is the fact that the camp was just not designed for families arriving by car. Makeshift car parks, that left vehicles covered in thick white dust after a windy day, left one

EAST ESSEX
GAZETTE

FRIDAY, OCTOBER 21, 1983   17p

BUTLIN'S CLOSURE SHOCK

● Butlin's Clacton holiday centre.

Call to council to buy site

THE SHOCK news that Butlin's holiday centre in Clacton is to close has left the town reeling – but hopes are high that some good will come from the decision.

Initial talks have already been held between the company and Tendring Council officers, who are anxious to ensure the best possible use is made of the 45-acre site.

A spokesman for Butlin's said yesterday that no decision had been taken about the future of the site, but it was "very unlikely" that Butlin's or any other Rank company would be running the site "at least for the next two or three years."

by IRENE KETTLE and CLARE RICHARDSON

but there was no hope of keeping the camp open, as it could not bring in the return necessary on the major modernisation investment required. In fact, it had not made a profit in the last three years.

Mr Met Butlin said it was

Bobbie Butlin announces his 'painful' decision

by IRENE KETTLE

BUTLIN'S chairman Mr Bobbie Butlin announced his "painful" decision to close the Clacton centre on Tuesday morning.

In a lengthy statement he revealed that 60 full-time jobs would be lost because the 45-acre site opened in 1938 was no longer viable. It had not made a profit for the past three years.

He said the Butlin's centre at Filey, Yorkshire, would also close immediately.

Almost 100 permanent staff and 841 seasonal workers were employed at Clacton's centre which could cater for 6,000 holidaymakers a week. A spokesman

take this painful decision and the affect that the closure will have on the staff of both centres and on the local community".

Mr Butlin said he hoped the closures would enable the company, which is part of the Rank organisation, to invest more in its other holiday centres.

Butlin's have already received bookings for Christmas and next summer, and have issued an emergency telephone number for inquiries. A spokesman said all holidaymakers would be notified about the closure and if possible offered alternative holidays. The number is 0243 826622.

Staff at the centre were sent

● Bobbie Butlin "deeply regrets."

Jeeves suggested opening a theme park on the site which, she claims, would boost the town's ailing industry. She criticised council

struggling with heavy cases over what seemed like a 200-yard assault course. Hardly an encouraging start...'[62]

Scarborough looked for a purchaser who would redevelop the site as a tourist attraction. A businessman who had previously sought permission to build a theme park at the former NALGO camp at Cayton Bay was approached. So was Don Robinson, chairman of Hull City Football Club, who, however, had already joined forces with Sir Fred Pontin to develop Marineland at Scarborough as 'Britain's first water theme park'. Finally, in 1985, a purchaser was found. Trevor Guy, a Harrogate property developer and demolition contractor, bought the site and announced his intention of building luxury bungalows for holiday letting, and adding a conference centre with a helicopter pad for visiting oilmen to the existing amusement park.[63]

At Clacton, catering for a maximum of 6,000 visitors, with a seasonal staff of 950, and providing £216,548 in annual rates to Tendring District Council, there were the same expressions of shock and disappointment. Butlin's had already held secret meetings with the Council to discuss other uses for the 45-acre site,

By Direction of the Proprietor
Websters
Specialist Auctioneers & Valuers

will sell by Public Auction in Three Separate Sales upon the Premises

THE ENTIRE CONTENTS OF ATLAS LEISURE PARK, FORMERLY BUTLINS HOLIDAY CAMP, WEST ROAD, CLACTON, ESSEX

FIRST AUCTION
WEDNESDAY, 22nd MAY, 1985 COMMENCING AT 10.30 a.m.

FURNISHINGS AND EQUIPMENT OF TWO SALOON BARS, 2,000 COVER RESTAURANT, TWO THEATRES, BALLROOM AND OFFICE COMPLEX

A very vast amount of seating accommodation inc. 750 matching good quality heavy framed modern dining chairs, assorted parcels of ditto totalling 1,500, 2,300 stacking chairs, fully upholstered Lounge Chairs. 130 x 84in. x 30in. and 200 48in. x 30in. Formica topped dining tables, excellent range of saloon tabling, coffee tables etc.

A very fine 19th Century 78in. PIER GLASS mirror in carved giltwood surround, Victorian ditto, set of 5ft. circular bevel edged ditto, a collection of Western Saddles, harness, tack, animal trophys, wall plaques and parapharnalia. 48 x 36in. circular 7 branch ceiling lights, set of 8 decorated Ceramic Spanish style ditto, reproduction Victorian hanging lights, selection of brass wall lights, various sets of contemporary lighting.

A 43ft. run of recently installed self-service Cafeteria Counter fitted electric heated cabinet and refrigeration, Stilh, stainless steel tables, counter top oven, hot-pie cabinets, sandwich counters, 70in. Craig-Nichol refrigerated serve-over counter, optics and stands, bar accessories, 180 doz beer mugs, galvanised racking.

1,600 tip-up Theatre Seats in Maron Velour, 240 similar in red vinyl. Fumeo x 1000 Cinema Projector, Fumeo H1 3000 ditto, stage equipment inc: Rank Strand SP 60/3 Theatre lighting system, back drop and curtain installation, flood lighting, automatic electronic bingo caller, table Tennis Tables, playground equipmennt.

250 bedroom Chests of Drawers, 200 white laminated wardrobes, 480 single and 170 double divans.

Office Furniture to inc. Desk, chairs, filing cabinets, stationery ditto, 10 Safes, 50 compartment Deposit Safe.

Viewing: Two days prior 9.00 a.m.-5.00 p.m. Monday and Tuesday, 20th & 21st May, 1985 and morning of sale only.

SECOND AUCTION
Wednesday, 5th June, 1985, 10.30 a.m.

Contents of Two Saloon Bars, Ballroom incl. 39 matching Crystal Glass Chandeliers, main Kitchens, contents of 500 Chalets, and stores.

THIRD AUCTION
Wednesday, 19th June, 1985, 10.30 a.m.

Carpeting, bar fixtures, fire extinguishers, hose reels, four wheel camp trolleys, mobile bulk rubbish bins, cardboard bailing machine and all other salvageable fixtures.

Catalogues Price £1.00 (£1.20 posted) from the Auctioneers Offices, 13 Great Colman Street, Ipswich. Tel: (0473) 57491/3.

The end of the road of the Clacton Butlin's camp.

but the news came 'like a bombshell' to the permanent staff who had no warning of the closure. Councillors attacked Butlin's for not having modernized the camp. 'They have creamed off the income from the town and left us stranded.'[64] Approached by the Council for help in retaining the site for tourist use, the East Anglian Tourist Board reported that it was in such poor condition that 'prospective buyers could well be put off. The whole place is in a really poor state of repair'.[65] But a buyer was found, Amusement Enterprises Ltd, who renamed the site as Atlas Park and announced the intention of developing a 'spectacular' theme park offering 'the best of all rides' and attracting up to 20,000 visitors a day.[66] It opened in the summer of 1984 but closed at the end of the season making its 100 employees redundant. In the summer of 1985 three huge auction sales were held to dispose of the mountains of furniture, catering equipment, bar and theatre furniture and sports goods inherited from Butlin's. Cut glass chandeliers, Wild West saddles and animal trophies, ceramic Spanish-style ceiling lights and automatic electronic bingo callers all came under the hammer. Finally, the Inland Revenue applied to wind up Amusement

Enterprises. 'The application was adjourned to give the company time to sell Clacton's biggest white elephant.'[67]

It was Butlin's faith in the economies of scale that led to the economic problems of his successors. Huge investments in improvements fail to show up in such vast camps, and an enormous advertising campaign is needed to fill them to anything like capacity in the 1980s. W. J. Brown used to claim that 'no camp should accommodate more than 500 people'. When we asked Fred Pontin his views on the economic size of camps, he replied 'You break even with 500 beds', even though the firm that bears his name has camps ranging in size from 250 to 4,000. The typical size of Warner's camps is 500 to 600. 'Warner, God bless him, decided that small was beautiful' says the firm's marketing director.[68]

All that Glitters

> Dedicated to the sole purpose of enjoyment, with all the resources of modern science and almost unlimited capital, the result could be something to dull even the vision of Kublai Khan. Unfortunately the average holiday camp possesses none of these qualities and stands half-way between the sophisticated conceits of the eighteenth century and the unselfconscious 'pop art' of the traditional fairground.
>
> (Kenneth Lindley, *Coastline*, Hutchinson, 1967)

As architectural monuments to the mid-twentieth century, will the passing of holiday camps (disappearing through renovation no less than through closures) be mourned? Undoubtedly, in design terms, holiday camps have always offered a unique opportunity to indulge in what has been referred to in Chapter 1 as 'the functional disguised as the fantastic'. This was the essence of the very first holiday camp, Cunningham's in the Isle of Man, where visitors were greeted amidst potted palms and marble, and went on to enjoy a strange patchwork of styles – minarets and mock-Tudor, romantic and neo-classical. Prestatyn, too (it has been noted) captured something of the glamour of the great ocean liners and their associated imagery of luxury and romance. People came to escape the commonplace, and the setting was a key ingredient in these worlds of make-believe. There was nowhere better for eccentric architecture to flourish than the holiday camp.

And to an extent it did. In his exploration of changing cultural patterns, Richard Hoggart sees camp architecture akin to that of colourful fairgrounds. The 'lovely stylised horses' and the 'fantastic mechanical organs' of the old fairgrounds have almost gone, but 'new materials are adapted to the old demands for a huge complication and exotic involution of colour, noise and movement. The same demands are met in the large holiday camps; if you look closely at the great public halls there, you may see the steel girders and bare corrugations of the roofs: but you will have to peer through a welter of artificial trees, imitation half-timbering, great dazzling chandeliers'.[69] It is, again, a synthesis of the functional with the fantastic.

Enter the gates of any large holiday camp, and these two elements of design, the functional and the fantastic, are there to be disentangled. The balance is not

From the 1930s the new camps offered a taste of luxury.

always a happy one. Sometimes it is the functional which dominates, the whole camp design reflecting utilitarian goals, with beauty or eccentricity very much in the background. Orderly rows of buildings and drab materials do little to lift the soul. In other cases the balance changes, and it is the fantastic which has caught the designer's imagination, to be seen in large colourful signs, in fantasy adventure worlds for children and exotic South Pacific terraces.

But perhaps above all, it is glitter and all that this stands for which the designers most frequently seek to create – glittering wallpaper, glittering chandeliers, glittering cocktail bars, all the perfect backcloth to the glittering cabaret and glittering lights of Las Vegas or Acapulco. The cult of glitter is itself bound up with two related themes in design and popular taste which Dick Hebidge has noted in the period from 1935 to 1962.[70] One is that of Americanization, the import of forms from a culture that was well ahead at the time in the art of consumption as compared with its European counterparts. Neon signs, milk bars and soda-fountains, jazz and juke-boxes were all symbols of a material age that in Britain, at least, had barely dawned but which, in artificial settings like a holiday camp, could at least create an illusion. The other theme noted by Hebidge is that of streamlining, a new design form that, like Americanization, carried its own meaning of change, of progress, of the future. Pressed steel, chromium and plastic could now be bent and curved into sleek and continuous shapes – perhaps to make a cocktail bar where campers could sip their drinks and taste a world of modernity and easy-living, far removed from their everyday lives.

To the critical eye, this is Hoggart's world of 'shiny barbarism...the ceaseless exploitation of a hollow brightness'.[71] It is also akin to George Orwell's view of milk bars – 'a kind of atmosphere about these places. Everything slick and shiny and streamlined: mirrors, enamel and chromium plate whichever direction you look in'.[72] Pioneer campers thought it had nothing to do with holiday camps as they knew them, these new worlds of 'neon lights and chromium...Contrary to the seeming belief of many architects, lavish use of concrete and chromium in odd geometrical forms do not impress thinking people'.[73] Yet for others, like Kenneth Lindley, the disappointing thing about camp design was that it did not go far enough, making 'no significant contribution to either the landscape or to the architecture of entertainment and their effect upon the immediate surroundings is to be measured in 'side-by-side' bicycles and 'kiss-me-quick' hats'.[74]

For some, then, the cult of the fantastic has not gone far enough, while for others all bounds of reasonable taste have been exceeded. That there has been a cult at all is perhaps easier to understand. Different periods in the era of the holiday camp have made their own demands. Glitter and an illusion of extravagance have a continuing appeal. In the 1930s the world of the new holiday camp offered a bright contrast with one's everyday experience of limited material well-being and common expectations. After the Second World War it was the sheer relief from the strains of war, coupled with the attraction of escaping from peacetime austerity (even though the post-war camps themselves survived on ration books). Then, from the late 1950s the bright lights were less a reaction to the world outside, and more a reflection of a new-found affluence. The camps could hardly allow themselves to fall behind, and popular images from television, pop music and consumption were incorporated, sup-

Every night is party night

'A foil to the realities of Britain in recession'.

plementing if not replacing the more sedate sense of liner luxury on which many of them had been based. Glitter had now really come of age. In the 1970s and 1980s some see again the camps serving as a foil to the realities of Britain in recession. Whatever the reason, a review of current publicity material (with its colour photos of exotic cocktails and cabarets, glittering ballrooms and flashing disco lights) endorses the continuity of what has proved to be, to some extent, a timeless theme in the British holiday camp.

6 Popular Places

There were only two of us from Langton's Mill at the Kosy Holiday Kamp – unless you count Mabel Arkwright. But we don't, usually. Apart from poor old Mabel's spotty face, there's her owlishness – always got her head in some book and peering like mad.

Anyway, June and I knew we were in for a smashing time the moment we set eyes on the place...three dance halls, two sunbathing parades, lots of milk bars – just the job!

(Richard Hoggart, on popular fiction in a 'candy-floss world', in *The Uses of Literacy*, Pelican 1958).

When future social historians review what has happened in the twentieth century, one feature that will undoubtedly attract their attention is the impact of what is commonly referred to as *mass society*. It is not that social life was previously characterized by individuality and freedom of action. Far from it. But it is undoubtedly the case that in the present century the lives of individuals and patterns of community have themselves become increasingly enmeshed within wider networks of influence and control.

The pace of change has quickened. In single generations we have witnessed the growing impact of national and international media systems, a steady erosion of traditional regional differences, and the packaging of food and culture, education and architecture so that everything is transferable and recognizable from one end of the country to the other. Centralization and control are nothing new, but in the twentieth century technological developments have strengthened the hand of the centralists. A version of the mass society has come of age.

Against this tide of change, individuals have sought to protect islands of freedom where what are often seen as the old values can be nurtured. It is a moral issue, a conflict of fundamental values and of material change, that permeates all aspects of modern life. Moral philosophers will extract the essence of this conflict, but for the social historian the evidence and personification of the conflict can also be found in specific features of twentieth-century life. It is this context which provides a basis for assessing holiday camps. They are of interest in themselves yet they can also be seen as an exemplar of broader processes and conflicts to do with new patterns of leisure and holiday-making, and with radical changes in popular culture.

In themselves, we must weigh up the arguments for and against holiday camps. Were they a source of social opportunity, enabling millions to participate in activities that had previously been denied? Or were the camps symptomatic of more general trends, reducing choice for the individual and imposing the uniformity of a mass society?

And then, standing beyond the camp gates, what can holiday camps tell us about the wider debate of the individual in a mass society? Has the twentieth century been an unmitigated story of individual values eroded to the point, perhaps, of near-extinction? Or is the rhetoric worse than the reality, in the sense that there are compelling arguments in favour of modern trends as well as against?

The Leisure Utopia

> The modern civilised man's idea of pleasure is already partly attained in the more magnificent dance halls, movie palaces, hotels, restaurants and luxury liners. On a pleasure cruise or in a Lyons Corner House one already gets something more than a glimpse of this future paradise.
>
> (George Orwell, 'Pleasure Spots', in *Collected Essays*, Vol. 4, first published in 1946, Penguin 1970).

The fantasy world of holiday camps (creating places where indulgence is a virtue) lends itself to a long-standing utopian tradition of leisure at the centre of life. Mediaeval peasants, who knew only work and poverty, escaped in their minds to that golden land 'of such joy and endless bliss...[where] Every man may drink his fill, and needn't sweat to pay the bill'.[1] Undoubtedly there is a bill at a holiday camp, but for one or two weeks a year 'joy and endless bliss' are there for the taking.

Fantasy is invariably rooted in material reality and holiday camps are no exception. In their case, the source of a twentieth-century dream has its origins in the new patterns of work in nineteenth-century industrial society. Social historians have demonstrated the radical changes that took place in family and social life as a result of the transformation from the basically agrarian to an urban-based industrial society. In all this, work assumed not simply a more dominant role on account of the great number of hours it demanded, but it also gave rise to its own ethic to legitimate the sacrifices required. 'Honest labour' became a mainstay of the new system, and social as well as economic institutions were directed to the promotion of productivity. A reliable, available labour force was a key component of the whole production process.

But the machines turned day and night, and the work was, at best, dull and, at worst, dangerous. Some visionaries responded, not by condemning work as such, but by seeking to redefine it. True dignity of labour could only be achieved, they argued, by reconstituting society so that work itself would become rewarding and enjoyable. Others sought instead (or in some cases as well as a redefinition of work) to reduce the amount of work and to improve working conditions. Reformers achieved gradual success in whittling away at the number of hours worked, and in the space that was freed leisure emerges. If not exactly with a life of its own, this expanding space generates its own distinctive patterns of activity.

The proportion of leisure time, and the availability of resources to use it, becomes an increasing factor thoughout the nineteenth century and has continued to the present day. What to do with this time has become a question of growing social importance. In spite of its inherent attractiveness, and the fact that it has been the dream of generations, leisure is now seen to pose its own problems. Not the least of these problems is the fact that leisure in this sense is the space left by work, and is subject to the same structural pressures and constraints as work itself. Leisure, in spite of its promise of escapism, remains solidly a part of industrial society.

The Holiday Habit

What came to be known as the 'holiday habit'[2] started in a modest enough way. Although pre-industrial societies enjoyed frequent festival days, these were characteristically centred around one's village or nearby market town. Going out for the day in large numbers was uncommon before precious hours were freed from work and, at the same time, the new railways in the middle of the nineteenth century made it their business to cater for trippers 'en masse'. Links were forged between the industrial towns and coastal resorts which had previously served only a privileged few.

A day at the seaside became one of the more colourful features of Victorian life, in stark contrast to the drab and harsh routines that marked the rest of the calendar. On Sundays (in the face of strong opposition from sabbatarians) and on odd days, the more fortunate workers and their families bought excursion tickets to Blackpool and Brighton, Scarborough and Southend. At the time of the 1851 census, Brighton was by far the largest of the resorts and the London trains brought 5000 or more visitors on a sunny holiday.[3]

Even these, though, were small beginnings. Opportunities to get away from it all increased with the widening practice of the free Saturday afternoon (a less inhibited time for recreation than the jealously-guarded sabbath) and from 1871 with the August Bank Holiday.[4] This latter was the most popular of all, and by the end of the century absenteeism was common on the day or two immediately after the Bank Holiday. Staying by the sea for a few days, if not for the whole week had now become more than a dream.

But with few exceptions a holiday away from home was a product of hard saving for the rest of the year. While some firms proved willing to concede time (sometimes, as in Wakes weeks, for their own direct benefit in overhauling the factory machines), the idea of paying employees while they were on holiday by the sea remained limited.

The quantitative change in holiday-making occurs in the years after 1918. More people were now spending a week or more away from home, the figure totalling an estimated 15 million in 1937 (the highest inter-war figures and in advance of national legislation for paid holidays). The view of the T.U.C. was that this was very much a post-1918 surge. 'The holiday habit is one that has grown since the war...It is an increasing factor in working-class life [and] most people now are appreciating the necessity for a complete change of surroundings.'[5] In 1938 the Holidays with Pay Act rationalized and encouraged this growing habit, normally on the basis of entitlement to a week's paid leave together with public holidays.

The Second World War intervened before the full benefits of the 1938 Act to promote paid holidays could be enjoyed, but with the ending of the war the annual exodus from the towns was renewed with a vengeance. Wartime hardships coupled with the austerity of peacetime stimulated millions to seek relief through a week or two away from home. To add to the incentive, much of Britain's coastline had been forbidden territory in the war years and for many youngsters a trip to Brighton or Clacton offered their first glimpse of the sea. By the summer of 1949, the number of holiday-makers in search of a seaside venue had reached some 30 million people. A well-publicized estimate was that this total would rise to 45 million in succeeding years.[6]

In the face of this upsurge, there was a growing body of opinion that more was needed in the way of planning. Additional accommodation was urgently needed and the reputed landladies' device of converting billiard tables and baths into makeshift beds could not be tolerated indefinitely. The call was for organization and leadership. As one commentator noted, as early as 1938, 'There is a great need for organised holidays. The people now for the first time getting holidays with pay are used to a routine job, and their recreation is of the mass-organised kind. More camps are necessary where amusements are provided all the time.'[7]

Little wonder, then, that holidays found their way onto the post-war political agenda. It was not just a question of the numbers involved but the growing importance that holidays were assuming in people's lives. Already, in the late-1940s, holidays were regarded as something of a cult.[8] In their 1945 Election Manifesto the Labour Party (although subsequently to usher in what is widely recalled as an austerity programme) encouraged thoughts of opportunities for more people to enjoy their leisure. Ernest Bevin saw holiday camps as playing an important role, and shared with Sir Stafford Cripps the idea that they should be used to attract foreign visitors to spend their holidays in Britain.[9]

The general pattern of the immediate post-war years has continued with a vengeance since then, with more people enjoying more holidays and with the whole business of holidays occupying a larger share of the nation's economy and social priorities. A paid week's holiday was soon replaced by longer periods. Whereas in 1951 some 61 per cent of manual labourers were entitled to two weeks holiday with pay, by 1955 this had increased to 96 per cent.[10] Since then, longer periods (three, four or five weeks) have become standard practice.

A further development has been that of taking more than one holiday in a year, with about 20 per cent of the adult population enjoying two or more

Enjoying the seaside 'en masse': Hastings in 1935.

holidays in 1983.[11] Taken together, the pattern that has emerged over the years is in striking contrast to that which existed when all that most people could hope for was a day out.

The growth of commercial camps in the period from the late-1930s can undoubtedly be explained as part of this general growth of holiday-making. At precisely that time when the demand for holidays increases most rapidly (15 million in 1937, compared with 30 million in 1949) the new camps seized their opportunity. It is sometimes noted that Butlin's opened at Skegness in the year when holiday-making figures were higher than ever before, and a time when talk of legislation for paid holidays assured investors of continuing trends. These figures are telling, yet, in isolation they do not provide a full explanation for the appeal of the new holiday camps. Locational factors are also important and so, too, was the scale of the operation in terms of investment and organization.

It is no accident that (unlike some of the pioneer camps) the new mass camps were all sited on the coast. James Walvin has provided an illustrative and well-evidenced record of the appeal of the sea for holiday-makers.[12] From its elitist use in the eighteenth century the seaside then becomes the focus for mass excursions and, later, for holidays. The alleged health-giving qualities of sea air, salt water and estuarial mud may in itself have been enough to draw the urban crowds. But, in addition, resorts lured their visitors with the colourful promise of fun for all. Bracing air was one thing, but all the better if it could be offered along with piers and promenades, Punch and Judy Shows and donkey rides on the sands, German Bands and photographers to capture and revive memories of the excitement and jollity of it all in the long winter months. Advertisements in railway stations and in popular newspapers provided a simple but enduring message, linking the seaside with health, family fun and an enticing hint of romance.

Successive writers have reinforced and contributed to a popular folklore and

Punch and Judy shows on the sands.

nostalgia for brief escapes to the sea. None better (in recalling and drawing out the meaning of it all) than Richard Hoggart with his images of charabanc trips from Leeds to Scarborough:

> The 'charas' go rolling out and across the moors for the sea, past the road-houses which turn up their noses at coach-parties, to one the driver knows where there is coffee and biscuits or perhaps a full egg and bacon breakfast. Then on to a substantial lunch on arrival, and after that a fanning-out in groups. But rarely far from one another, because they know their part of the tour and their bit of beach, where they feel at home...They have a nice walk past the shops; perhaps a drink; a sit in the deck-chair eating an ice-cream or sucking mint humbugs; a great deal of loud laughter...The driver knowing exactly what is expected of him as he steers his warm, fuggy and singing community back to the town...[13]

Hoggart's picture of a day at the sea will strike a chord in us all. It has for long been a national pastime to make a seaside trip. More than that, says Hoggart, it was one of those acts in traditional working-class life where one 'makes a splash...a short-lived splash, but a good one, because most of the rest of life is humdrum and regulated. One needs sometimes to make a gesture, even though finances do not reasonably permit it'.[14]

With its widespread and ingrown appeal, it is little wonder that most holidays in this country have traditionally been taken by the seaside, the figure remaining to this day as high as 75 per cent.[15] What is more, although the south and south-west coasts enjoy the best climates, resorts in all parts of the country continue to attract their own regional population catchments. It is being by the sea which counts for most, and visitors are seemingly undeterred by cold winds and rough seas. 'Skegness is so bracing', claim the resort's publicists, finding virtue in what might otherwise seem an unlikely stretch of coastline for a holiday camp mecca. A map of modern camps bears out, not simply the appeal of the coast, but also the persistence of locations away from the sunny south.

In explaining the timing and location of mass camps, in addition to the general increase of holidaymaking and the specific attraction of the sea, there is a third factor to consider. Even by the 1930s holidaymaking was already a sizeable industry and, in purely investment terms, the Butlin concept was a measured response to what was possible. The whole concept represents an attempt to capitalize on what had by then become unmistakeable trends in demand. If the State was reluctant to play a greater role than that of facilitator (passing legislation, for instance, to increase paid holidays or to empower local authorities to advertise the attractions of their resorts) then the way was open for the private sector to take the initiative.

Hitherto, the holiday industry was little more than a conglomeration of small businesses, buttressed by municipal investment to provide an infrastructure. Seaside landladies and hoteliers, entertainers, shopkeepers and stallholders contrived each year to keep the show on the road. The numbers of each could be very considerable. In Blackpool (which in 1931 could accommodate half a million visitors in a single night) there were nearly 4000 lodging and boarding-house keepers.[16] As an indication of the number of shopkeepers whose livelihood depended on the holiday trade, in Brighton in 1937 there were nearly twice as many shops as a town of that size would normally support.[17] With few exceptions, it was all a 'highly individualistic' process.[18]

It was also, arguably, an inefficient process, evolving in a modest way in Victorian times but ill-fitted for the scale of mid-twentieth-century holidaymaking. J. A. R. Pimlott, mindful no doubt of the telling message of music-hall jokes and seaside postcards, agrees that there must be 'substance in the evergreen complaints of high prices, poor food, incivility, congestion and dreary appointments'.[19] All this was attributed to a variety of reasons – to the problems of seasonal variations, to amateur and untrained personnel, and a lack of capital and failure to modernize. Damage and decay in the wartime years had done nothing to enhance the appearance and quality of the typical seaside resort.

Against this background, what the new camps could do was to offer a professional package. The whole range of services and attractions, traditionally provided by numerous agencies, were now brought within a single organization. Economies of scale, a principle for long applied to manufacturing production, proved to be no less applicable to the holiday industry. Heavy investment was attracted to holidays by the prospect of a high rate of return. It was a proposition that was well borne out in the early years. Butlin's first camp, at Skegness, was opened in 1938. Within a year it showed a trading profit increase of some 50 per cent and a dividend of 20 per cent on ordinary shares.[20]

Ralph Glasser endorses the point, seeing the 1930s as the great watershed in the holiday industry, with holiday camps providing the first commercial understanding of how to present a mass-produced package. The holiday camp idea flourished commercially – 'it could hardly do otherwise, competing with a tradition of Dickensian boarding houses, seaside rock, fish and chips, and lights-out-at-eleven'.[21]

In 1939, commercial camps were catering for an estimated 30,000 visitors a week, a figure which increased sharply with the opening of new large scale camps after 1945. The British Tourist and Holidays Board reported in 1949 on the concern in traditional resorts over the growing competition from holiday camps. In that year it was estimated that the camps could accommodate 70,000 visitors weekly, or a total of 1.2 million in an average season.[22] Holiday camps were already accounting for 7 per cent of the annual holiday trade, and this was only the start of an upward trend. Already, by the end of the 1940s, it was a far cry from the modest scale of provision that characterized the traditional sources of accommodation and entertainment, including the pioneer camps themselves with their tents and wooden dining-cum-general activities room, and a general air of informality and simple pleasures. The holiday habit had become a mass one and the new camps were, at the very least, a response to this.

Fantasia

From the outset, commercial camps, in responding to the holiday habit, sought to transport their visitors from a world of everyday drudgery to a make-believe setting. Images were compressed and interwoven to create a world that was everywhere yet nowhere. Hawaian bars and Viennese coffee lounges, Hollywood Terraces and South Sea pools, de luxe Grand Hotel ballrooms and sundecks named after Atlantic Liners – all could be part of a day's experience.

Holiday camps were about far more than increases in per capita incomes and statutory leave. They were about dreams, stimulating the popular imagination and sensing the enormity of the concepts behind it all. If a new age of leisure was dawning, the camp entrepreneurs did their best to see that the first light would be theirs. Forget the coming of war, the austerity of peacetime. Enter the gates of a world of fun and perhaps, one day, it might become the same outside too.

Fanciful and far-fetched though it all was, the idea of an age of leisure did indeed evolve at this time, offering a rationale of sorts for the rise of the holiday camp. Leisure incorporates holidaymaking but it goes well beyond that, encompassing new ways of thinking about work as well as play.[23] A privileged class had for long based its lifestyle on leisure pursuits. Now, in the second half of the twentieth century, it seemed to be the turn of the hitherto less privileged. It is an exaggerated but not unrepresentative view that in every industrial society, what was class phenomenon in the nineteenth century became a mass phenomenon in the twentieth century.[24]

Holiday camps can be seen as both a reflection of growing leisure opportunities, and also, perhaps, as a microcosm of what society in general might be like in an age of leisure. In the popular utopia, food and drink are plentiful, there is constant entertainment, and chores are done by others. A vision of abundance, it is not perhaps so very different to the utopian dream of the mediaeval peasant.

Already by the early 1930s (several years before Butlin's campers arrived at Skegness) social observers were heralding the advent of mass leisure. In a survey of life and labour in London, the otherwise-restrained authors were able to conclude that 'all the forces at work are combining to shift the main centre of interest of a worker's life more and more from his daily work to his daily leisure.'[25] They saw a trend under way where higher incomes (over and above

147

Successive generations of campers have been drawn into a world of commercial glamour.

what was needed for necessities) would enable the greater time that was freed from work to be used for a whole range of leisure activities.

Taking a broader historical sweep, J. L. Hammond believed that modern England, compared with that of a century before, was already a leisured society.[26] A fundamental revolution had taken place. For that we had technology to thank, and it was continuing technological advance that would enable our material needs to be met without sacrificing leisure. Universal leisure was likened to universal education and universal suffrage as one of the great experiments of the age.

There was, though, a warning, one that might well have been directed to such products of leisure as holiday camps. 'We have now a society with leisure but as yet without the tradition of leisure and without the education that is needed for the full intellectual and aesthetic enjoyment of leisure. If in such a society a man sets out to make a profit by providing mass pleasures, he will be apt to choose the pleasures that excite for the moment, rather than those that stimulate the intelligence or the imagination.'[27]

If the vision of a society of leisure receded in the 1940s (obscured by the war and by the subsequent period of austerity) it reappeared in bolder form in the 1950s as a cultural watershed between two worlds — the world of wartime Britain and its aftermath, and the world of 'affluence' with its 'growing prosperity, of a kind.'[28]

In the so-called affluent society of the late 1950s and, at least, the early 1960s the idea of leisure assumes a new and unprecedented importance. Partly, it is a

spin-off from economic and cultural developments in America in the post-war period. The conventional wisdom was that what was happening in America would spread naturally and logically to those societies that were pursuing comparable paths of capitalist development. And the image of America at the time was one where material standards were well in advance of those in Europe. Affluence was already entrenched and popular mythology had it that new technologies could be relied upon to increase productivity, reduce the need for labour, and thereby create an age of leisure where everyone enjoyed high living standards while the machines did all the work.

It was part of the vision that society would never be the same again. As the work ethic declined, so a new 'morality of happiness' would take its place.[29] Moreover, the benefits of technology, which would make all this possible, would extend no less to the non-work sector – seen as an 'advance into an era of breathtaking fun specialism – much of it based on sophisticated technology.'[30]

The image of affluent Britain was one where 'most of our people have never had it so good'.[31] It was an image of washing machines and television sets, of coffee bars and American-style juke boxes, of jeans and fashion boutiques, of mini cars and motorways, of cities ripped apart to implant new lifestyles. And, of course, in all this holiday camps flourished. There was money around and leisure was the thing of the future. Nearly a quarter of a century after Skegness, Butlin retained sufficient faith in the concept to open a new camp at Bognor.

Holiday camps in these boom years were not simply a market reaction to consumer demand. They were more than that, embodying within the camps the very essence of affluent society. Perhaps, though, the identification was too close, with holiday camps enclosing themselves within the bubble of affluence. For when the bubble burst (as inevitably it would) in the 1960s (a product of economic recession coupled with an underlying disaffection with undiluted material values), the original idea of the holiday camp was itself in danger of falling apart.

In fact, the changing social context from this period proved to be complex, with various cross-currents producing counter trends. On the one hand, the leisure idea did not disappear without trace. For certain sections of the population, leisure activities continued to prosper throughout the 1970s and 1980s. Within this, patterns of holidaymaking changed and holiday camps were forced to adapt. But at least a market remained (with the number of holidays taken in Britain not reaching a peak until 1974)[32] even if the camps could no longer claim to be the apotheosis of the whole holiday idea.

On the other hand, there was no longer serious talk of an impending age of leisure. Growing unemployment had given the very idea a new and unpalatable meaning. In any case, a whole anti-leisure critique had grown up. Kenneth Roberts points to a variety of observers who believe that work retains its traditional importance in modern society (in terms of hours worked and the way it is treated).[33] Moreover, time not spent at work is becoming less rather than more leisurely, with the work ethic spilling into spare time to reduce the enjoyment of what for centuries utopians believed would be the essence of the Golden Age.

We are left, in the second half of the 1980s, with a mixed picture. Holiday

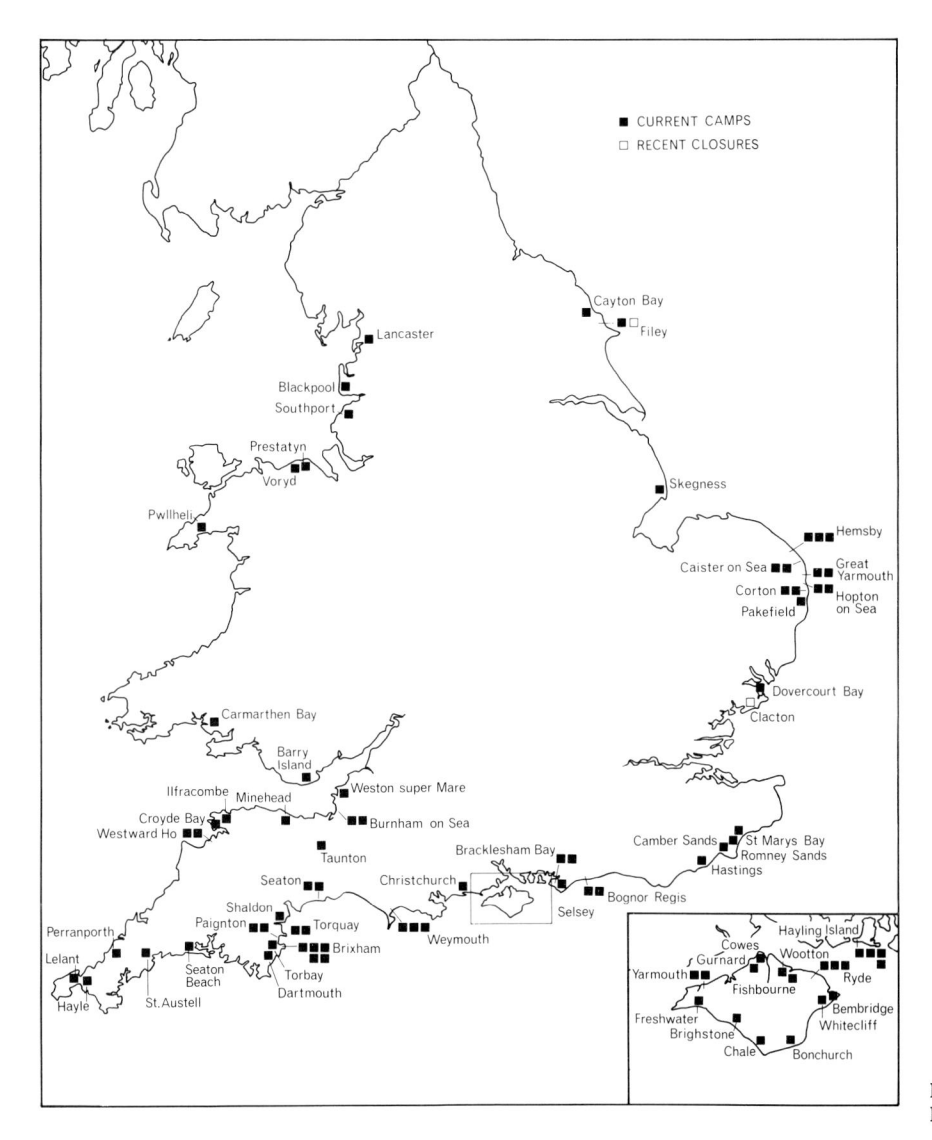

Holiday camp sites in England and Wales, 1986.

camps have certainly not been swept away by changing fashions and a social and economic context that is radically different from that of fifty years ago. Family holidays are still the mainstay of their trade (though now more often than not self-catering), with special interest weeks and arrangements with social service departments to extend the season. The map of holiday camps today would be recognizable to the camp entrepreneur of the 1930s.

And yet, at the same time, there is something anachronistic about those that remain. New coats of paint at the start of each season fail to conceal the fading messages beneath. At different times in the past holiday camps have accurately reflected and, in turn, exaggerated popular dreams. In the 1930s they offered

151

visitors from a grey industrial setting a glimpse of Hollywood, first-hand experience of the seductive glitter previously restricted to the view from a cinema seat. Then, in the 1940s, the camps were filled with holidaymakers, relieved that the war was over and attuned to the idea of doing things *en masse*. This period, in turn, was followed by the 1950s, when holiday camps could offer a package to meet the promise of an affluent age.

Since then, though, whether the camps can provide what society wants has become less clear. Some people still demand what they enjoyed a generation ago. But for others, holiday camps are something of a period piece, a source of nostalgia rather than the highlight of one's year. The quest for a world of make-believe is undiminished, but new concepts of holidaymaking have been developed to meet the needs of a new age. Package holidays to exotic places, coupled with more individualistic off-season breaks, increase the difficulties of the camps. Things which were once restricted to a holiday setting are now enjoyed all the year round. Much about the holiday camp is now commonplace. Perhaps they still offer good value for money and, on that basis, will continue as a feature of the holiday scene. It is doubtful, though, whether in broad social terms they are any longer 'such stuff as dreams are made on'.

The Culture of the Camps

> Every culture lives inside its own dream.
>
> (Quoted in Richard Hoggart, *Uses of Literacy*, Pelican, 1958).

It is one thing to explain the advent of holiday camps in terms of broader trends in leisure. But what does it all mean in terms of cultural development? Holiday camps have undoubtedly made their mark on the twentieth century and, in a sense, have become something of a symbol of their time. Yet is society any better or worse for their happening? What, if anything, have the camps contributed to the cultural well-being of the day?

One way of approaching these questions is to see holiday camps in the context of popular culture in the twentieth century. Holiday camps are very much a product of their age, and can be viewed in much the same way as other modern activities. Although it has not always been defined in such catholic terms, popular culture is now generally held to consist of 'the entire range of cultural activities that take place outside the celebration of religious, civic or artistic values enshrined in the official or dominant culture.'[34] It is, in effect, about everyday life.

With such a wide definition, research in this area has embraced activities as diverse as brass bands and women's magazines, television soap operas and sports clubs, newspapers and d.i.y. There is no difficulty in slotting holiday camps into one of the many popular culture pigeon-holes, but what is the point? What can this way of looking at the topic offer in terms of explanation?

Above all, an understanding of popular culture can help in attaching *meaning* to an event or activity. We are encouraged to look beyond a mere record of what happens, and to locate the object of study within a wider social canvas. Alternative viewing points, however, reveal contrasting impressions. A traditional perspective would locate holiday camps very much in terms of what was seen as a wider decline in standards. In contrast, a modern perspective might attempt to see holiday camps in their own terms, as a reflection of particular social circumstances and as evidence of a 'lived culture' in its own right. Each of these views can produce its own insights.[35]

Cultural Slumming

If we were to apply the traditional way of looking at popular culture to the example of holiday camps, the view would be clearcut. Holiday camps would be seen purely and simply, as further evidence of the moral and spiritual decline of established values and of society itself.

It is a pessimistic view which would find in the fun and gaiety of the campers only cause for further gloom. Although this is a view which has been challenged by more recent interpretations of popular culture, it is worth looking at more closely if only because it has been (and, to an extent, still is) applied to the modern holiday camp.

If one is to look for its origins, an important source of influence is Matthew Arnold's book published in 1869, *Culture and Anarchy*.[36] In this, Arnold interprets cultural developments in industrial society as a drift away from what was accepted as normal and proper. It is an elitist stance, where the yardstick of normality, against which everything else is measured, is defined and practiced by the dominant elements in society.

In effect, culture is equated with a classical notion of civilization, requiring a knowledge of philosophy and the arts and the development of qualities of physical fitness and fortitude that were associated with the lives of the elites in Ancient Greece or Rome. High culture in this sense is strictly for a minority. Inevitably, popular pursuits among the less privileged failed to measure up to the exacting standards of what is sometimes referred to as the 'culture and civilization' view. It was not just that such pursuits were different but rather that they represented a threat to high culture, if not to the stability of society itself. Undoubtedly they were regarded as inferior.

Although the culture and civilization view was articulated in the nineteenth century it provided a basis for refinement and application to changing circumstances until well into the present century. During the 1930s, in the face of a whole range of new activities (like the cinema, listening to the wireless, going on holiday, choosing furniture), custodians of the old values were spurred once again to defend the standards they believed were so essential to the integrity of the nation. T. S. Eliot, F. R. Leavis and others now carried the banner against what had become a formidable enemy, increasingly known as 'mass culture'.

Embracing, as it did, such a wide range of activities the culture and civilization lobby were themselves forced beyond a narrow, literary defence. Popular use of the environment, for instance, could be seen as an assault on our heritage, a symbol of the clash between old and new values. In one publication, *Culture and Environment*, school children were warned of the forces of standardization and levelling-down. As a fieldwork exercise to foster a consciousness of good taste they were asked to estimate the advantages and disadvantages of mass production as represented by the local branches of Woolworth's.[37]

It is entirely within this context, where culture and civilization set the standards by which all things could be judged, that a particular response to holiday camps can be understood. When the mass camps first made their mark in the mid-1930s they were so clearly standard-bearers of commercialism and the pervasive dilution of values that Arnold had detected as part and parcel of industrial society some seventy years previously.

Holiday camps (if viewed from that perspective) in their modern form exhibited all that was offensive in a changing world. Unlike the pioneer camps (simple places with familiar values) the new camps were brash, vulgar and generally in the poorest of taste. If the very concept of mass culture could be embodied in a single form it was here. Nostalgia and conservatism encouraged a backwards look to a model of folk culture that had been all but swept away by the tide of industrialization. The homespun leisure of agrarian labourers, reflecting the cycles of their work and the close-knit pattern of their lives, was now a thing of the past. Urbanization and a growth in leisure time in the nineteenth century led to new forms of activity, with commercial motives an important force. The recreation of the masses was seen less as indigenous, and more as an imposed culture with the word 'popular' meaning 'coarse' and 'inferior'.

Such trends were already well entrenched in the nineteenth century, although evidence of a traditional folk culture had by no means disappeared. Richard Hoggart argues that even through to the 1950s an urban working-class culture survived, resisting powerful forces of change and even adapting them to traditional ends.[38] To some extent the pioneer holiday camps were also consistent with this view of popular culture. Such camps were associated with healthy habits, they showed an appreciation for natural settings, there was even an element of 'improvement' in their programmes, and what was more their advocates were in the forefront of opposition to the new mass camps.

In contrast, Butlin's *et al.* were standard-bearers for culture with a difference. They were popular in more sense than one. People came to the camps in their thousands, not to be educated but to turn their backs on the world which dominated their lives for the rest of the year. They enjoyed the bright colours, the silly competitions, the make-believe backcloth of a Hollywood film set. Theirs was not to grieve over the loss of what others saw as heritage but to indulge in the sheer joy of 'sun, sea and sand' with the hungry appetites of people who had been denied for generations what others had assumed as their birthright.

The resultant clash of cultures was sharp and inevitable, and holiday camps were vilified for what they were and for what they symbolized. Although the culture and civilization view has declined in relative influence since the 1960s, it remains to this day a significant source of critique. From the 1930s onwards, holiday camps have attracted the kind of criticism that has its origins in the school of thought which can measure everything against a classical notion of heritage.

In a way, the scene had been set well before the 1930s. John Walton shows how in mid-Victorian times the arrival of thousands of working-class trippers to seaside resorts was enough to evoke a hostile response from those who feared that mass enjoyment posed a threat to the very fabric of society. Religious, moral and public order arguments were used to counter, in vain, the seasonal invasions. The religious voice was heard at its loudest in opposing fun and games on the Sabbath. In turn, moral concern was directed at the spectacle of drunkenness and sexual misdemeanours in the free-and-easy setting of the seaside resort. Public order was also an issue, with large crowds of working people seemingly unconstrained by some of the normal rules and codes of behaviour which dominated their everyday working lives.[39]

Although some of this outright fear and opposition mellowed in the post-Victorian period there was still a sense in which enjoying oneself in a popular resort was regarded as something of a fall from grace. For the moralists, if their arguments were to be accepted anywhere then holiday camps presented the obvious opportunity.

Sexual licence, intemperance and an absence of church-going were common sources of complaint. Sometimes the images of licentious living were based on tales of isolated incidents (like the Methodist minister who visited a camp in 1947 to see for himself whether stories of drunkenness were true, only to meet a man who proclaimed himself the week's Champion Beer Drinker).[40] More often than not they had no foundation at all. Life within the camps was not necessarily more or less libertarian than elsewhere.

An absence of evidence was not enough, however, to deter those who James Walvin refers to as 'those leisured critics whose holidays generally consisted of self-organised, self-improving visits to European cities, or invigorating walks over hills and mountains.'[41] Such critics despised holiday camps, if only for reputedly exploiting the indolence of people who want a holiday but are too lazy to organize it for themselves.

George Orwell was one who took a gloomy view of events of this kind in the 1940s. The main features of modern 'pleasure spots', he bemoaned, were that one is never alone, one never does anything for onself, one is never within sight of wild vegetation or natural objects of any kind, light and temperature are always artifically regulated, and one is never away from the sound of music.[42] Holiday campers could find little wrong in all that.

Reinforcing his view of cultural decline, Orwell cites the example of an entrepreneur's vision of a purpose-built paradise:

> His blue-prints pictured a space covering several acres, under a series of sliding roofs – for the British weather is unreliable – and with a central space spread over with an immense dance floor made of translucent plastic which can be illuminated from beneath. Around it are grouped other functional spaces, at different levels. Balcony bars and restaurants commanding high views of the city roofs, and ground-level replicas. A battery of skittle alleys. Two blue lagoons: one, periodically agitated by waves, for strong swimmers, and another, a smooth and summery pool, for playtime bathers. Sunlight lamps over the pools to simulate high summer on days when the roofs don't slide back to disclose a hot sun in a cloudless sky. Rows of bunks on which people wearing sun-glasses and slips can lie and start a tan or deepen an existing one under the sunray lamp. Music seeping through hundreds of grills connected with a central distributing stage, where dance or symphonic orchestras play or the radio programme can be caught, amplified, and disseminated.[43]

Also writing in the 1940s, when holiday camps were exposed to the full glare of social evaluation (what part would they play in post-war Britain?) J. A. R. Pimlott highlighted the questions that needed to be answered. 'Do holiday camps entail regimentation and standardisation to a degree which is unhealthy in a free society? Are there not dangers in the sacrifice of privacy and individual initiative? Is it not inevitable that as in the cinema the cultural level should fall to the lowest common denominator and be determined by purely commercial considerations?'[44]

These were questions which reflected the concerns of the 1940s, seeking to get the balance right between individual and collective interests, and putting high store in good taste and education as essential components of the Brave New World in the making. Culture and civilization might be redefined, but there was no question of lowering standards. Instead, what were prerogatives of the few would now be opened to the masses. If holiday camps could contribute to this, all to the good. But to be accepted they had first to meet the same exacting standards that were applied to other institutions in the new Britain.

Popular Pursuits

Evaluating popular culture from a traditional viewpoint has been likened to 'cultural slumming', in the sense that the likes of holiday camps would not be regarded as part of the normal territory of the observer. More than that, the inference is that one's own high standards are the measure against which the rest of the world can be judged. It is an approach which is nurtured by elitism (of the Left as well as the Right) in society generally, but which weakens in the face of more pluralist activity. It is in this context that the traditional approach is challenged at the end of the 1950s by a new way of looking at popular culture.

Drawing on historical evidence of the relationship between culture and society, both E. P. Thompson and Raymond Williams offer a new perspective. In a more idiosyncratic way, Richard Hoggart uses his own working-class childhood to illustrate that the 'lived cultures' of ordinary people are worthy of attention in their own right. Popular culture is not something to be viewed from the lofty peaks of elitism. Nor is it something which can be viewed (as conventional Marxists would do) in a deterministic way that explains culture as simply the outcome of a capitalist system. In this latter explanation, holiday camps would appear a logical outcome of capitalism, a cog in the apparatus designed to secure the reproduction of labour. What is denied in this explanation is a sense of personal involvement in the experience, and the part which ordinary people play in their own history.

Instead, what is referred to as 'culturalism' redefines culture as a semi-autonomous realm, where participants are able to influence as well as to receive in a passive sense. Popular culture as such can be defined as an area where ordinary folk can organize and express their own hopes and aspirations, feelings and preferences. Popular activities are not to be denied or scorned but understood as a part of modern society, linked to other structures, but also with a life of their own. A sensitive view (directed against critics of holiday camps in the 1940s) is that of H. D. Willcox, observing that 'no one is qualified to carp at spoon-fed leisure, bright lights and perpetual organisation, who has not spent years, like most of today's holiday-makers, on a routine job in a factory, and lived their lives in a factory town.'[45]

Popular culture becomes a product and a reflection of people with a shared experience and consciousness shaped by their place in society as a whole. Particular forms of popular culture, like holiday camps, can then be seen as a source of expression for a whole set of common experience. Holiday camps are popular precisely because they meet a common need to indulge in escapism, to break conventions and simply to relax in a setting which is sufficiently familiar to enable the participants to feel comfortable yet sufficiently different to induce a sense of excitement. If there is fantasy it has to be rooted in what is already known.

The class dimension of culture creates its own perspectives. Middle-class environmentalists have for long been suspicious, if not fearful, of a mass incursion of the countryside by working folk from the towns. At least, though, holiday camps held out some hope of containing the crowds. In the 1940s, Professor C. E. M. Joad wrote (somewhat indelicately) that the camps performed the same function as a drainage system. 'Just as a sewage farm accumulates and concentrates refuse and prevents it from spreading, so does the camp concentrate those very elements whose unchecked spread would overwhelm the countryside.' What is more, the camps might even be regarded in educational terms, as a kind of training ground where the 'untutored townsman' could learn how to behave. He explained that 'You cannot, after all, jump overnight from the Blackpool holiday in a mob to the mountain holiday with two or three. You must first be given the opportunity to see mountains and then perchance you may feel their spell and learn to love them,' and he thought that the camp at Pwllheli with its view of Snowdon would perform 'the office of a kindergarten for future mountaineers.'[46]

Joad's view may seem insensitive now, but Ray Gosling reminds us that 'We do forget that the fear the middle classes must have had for Butlin was real. They were — the ruling middle class — still treating the seaside rather like Charlotte Brontë — they came to breathe the air and gaze upon the waving waters: an act that always made Charlotte have a good cry. What else was there to do?' For Gosling, the 'regimentation' that the critics of holiday camps complained of was merely a way of helping people take the plunge. 'For we're all a little shy, aren't we, at first, of strange things and new places. That's why so many of us bank at the Trustee Savings bank, and why so many shop at the Co-op. After all, when the children of the English upper classes first made the Grand Tour of Europe, they were always accompanied by a tutor. When the Prince Regent first bathed at Brighton, he didn't just plunge himself into the sea; there was a class of maid called a dipper who did it to you.'[47]

The 1960s, which saw something of an explosion of popular cultural activity, provided an obvious spur to related changes in the way that culture itself was perceived. Ordinary people and ordinary places took on a new meaning. Coronation Street has been enjoying mass audiences since 1960. The Beatles were not simply a talented musical group but had the added attraction of being working-class lads from a working-class city. They symbolized in colourful terms the redefinition of culture at that time. Plays about working-class life, pop music and dance, boutique clothes in every High Street, and the impact of a mass market for consumer goods reflected and in turn forced a change in perspective.

Modern camps have been described as not an escape from the commercial world beyond the gates, but as an apotheosis of it.

In all this, holidays, now much more than a week in a boarding-house in Blackpool, inevitably opened new possibilities. Holiday camps thrived in the consumer boom before, in turn, being challenged by new competing package deals. But the camps, in spite of the challenge, remained a characteristic feature of this period, inextricably bound into the structure of a new consumer society.

Nicholas Mosley visited the Butlin's camp at Bognor when it opened in 1961 and found the whole concept 'not a change from the modern industrial world, but an apotheosis of it. You leave behind the worries of the factory, the responsibilities of the office, and go into the pipe-dream that lurks at the back of them anyway. It is like living *inside* commercial television...There are advertisements on the outside walls for every brand of cigarette; in the Camp Programme advertisements for most of the commodities used at Butlin's. Newspapers sponsor the innumerable competitions...There is half an hour a day of commercials over Radio Butlin's; many of the jokes in the shows are about commercials...If there is a criticism of Butlin's, it has to be criticism of a whole trend of western society.'[48]

It was this wider trend in society which Raymond Williams addressed in a book on Britain in the 1960s. Culture is examined in a context of social change, which in turn provides a helpful framework for locating the place of holiday camps. If people have turned away from more conventional notions of culture this has to be understood, in part at least, as a rejection of its class and privilege associations. In the same way, reflecting a divided society, much of popular culture is despised as the creation of an ignorant and disrespectful mass. The danger is that between the two extremes (high and popular culture) 'into the gap pour the speculators who know how to exploit disinheritance because they themselves are rooted in nothing.'[49]

This was seen as the cultural challenge of the 1960s. It was not that the idea of a genuinely popular culture based on modern communications was itself wrong, but rather that it might underestimate the intelligence, capacities, tastes and interests of ordinary people. If left entirely to commercial considerations the new process of mass communication would subvert rather than enhance the quality of life. So long as there is an emphasis on profit, the tendency would be to concentrate on things already known and safe, rather than attempting to offer new ideas and experience.

A debasement of culture, however, was by no means inevitable. Seen in the context of creating an educated and participatory democracy, the growth of large-scale organization and communications could be seen as a major human gain, far outweighing the real difficulties and confusion it had also brought. What needed to be done was to break out of the 'social situation in which it is taken for granted that the arts and learning are minority interests, and that the ordinary use of general communications is to get power and profit from the combination of people's needs and their inexperience.'[50]

If this wider debate is related to holiday camps it is conceivable that organizational and communication changes could have been used more imaginatively to enhance the quality and scope of the holiday experience. The idea of taking holidays together and of jointly pursuing fulfilling activities was widely appreciated in the pioneer camps of the 1930s. It is a paradox that when the means arrived to universalize this concept, the very process of applying modern communications served to subvert rather than to extend the promised opportunities. Holiday camps, in this sense, became a victim of the agents for their own potential.

Good Night, Campers

Good night, campers, I can see you yawning.
Good night, campers, see you in the morning.
You must cheer up, or you'll soon be dead –
I've heard it said that most folks die in bed
...Good night, campers, good night!

(Traditional campers' good night song, in *Holiday Camp Review*, June, 1938).

For all the changes in name and style of accommodation, and in spite of their continuing popularity, holiday camps have passed their peak. This is in no sense an obituary. But the 'togetherness' which characterized the heyday of the camps belongs to another era. They will never again attract the crowds who flowed to them with the ending of the Second World War, and who returned year after year in the 1950s. That particular pattern of collective fun has faded, along with the ubiquitous Odeon, the 'dogs' on a winter's evening and the provincial ballroom.

Nostalgia is now the vogue and yesterday's 'vulgarities' are today's collectors' items. People who would never have set foot in a holiday camp are free to revel in the antics of a modern television series set in 1959. Images are formed of a whole generation stepping through the gates wearing dowdy clothes and trusting expressions, exchanging routine lives for organized jollity. Inhibitions disappeared in dining rooms resounding with calls to the camp host, in the endless competitions, and on the side-by-side cycles that typify the camps. Such moments are treasured by a new generation which, strangely, sees a warmth and sense of real life in what were at the time reviled for their 'shiny barbarism', a mere 'candy floss world'.[51] A change in perception is not simply due to the passing of time. Certainly, the past invariably seems more alluring than the present. But, in addition to that, it is probably true that mass culture has, over the years, put more stress on 'mass' and less on 'culture'. What seemed brash and intrusive thirty years ago has now acquired a charm of its own.

Holiday camps have become something of a period piece, part of the popular folklore of the twentieth century. But this way of looking at them tells us more about our own times than about their original social setting. How should holiday camps really be remembered? They may be getting a good press now, but the weight of criticism in the past has to be acknowledged.

Some of the cultural aspects have been considered in the previous section. Such criticisms have focused around the transparency of this type of leisure provision, replicating and amplifying the worst aspects of modern commercialism. Related to this cultural critique is the no less fundamental issue of the place of the individual. Are holiday camps further evidence of what is seen as a persistent worsening of the role of the individual at the expense of mass trends in modern society?

Indicative of this view, Patrick Goldring has likened aspects of modern society to that of the broiler–house.[52] In the broiler–house, generations of chickens are bred under artificial conditions for the sole purpose of maximizing profits for their owners. He warns that a tendency similar to the factory farming process can be seen at work in our own society. While we are turning animals into factory products we are becoming broilerhouse inmates ourselves. In short, an increasing proportion of modern life is enacted in controlled environments where, it is argued, the role of the individual becomes ever more passive. Choice and spontaneity are in short currency.

It is tempting to extend the analogy to the controlled world of the holiday camp, where the very virtue of the camp is that everything is organized. Artificial environments were created to provide for every need of the holidaymaker, and from one camp to the next the mix was identical – the same pattern of entertainment, the same diet, the same type of accommodation, the same weekly routine. Whatever it was that attracted visitors to a holiday camp, choice of what to do (other than from a prescribed tariff) was not an obvious feature. 'Free-range' holidaymakers undoubtedly went elsewhere.

In the same vein, holiday camps exemplify the practice of packaging goods and services that has become a hallmark of life in the late twentieth century. Supermarket shoppers recall with mixed feelings childhood visits to the corner shop, where sugar was poured into separate bags, bacon was cut to order, and vinegar jars were refilled. Package holidays, modern estates, enclosed shopping precincts, chain store fashions and furniture warehouses are all witness to a way of life that is now firmly entrenched and widely accepted but which, when 'Butlinism' first made its mark, aroused widespread consternation.

To claim that holiday camps have contributed to the subjugation of the individual is a weighty indictment. But has it really been like that? Certainly, at the societal level, for those who wish to see more power and discretion resting with the individual this has hardly been a century to inspire optimism. Undoubtedly, control and centralization have been favoured by a whole variety of technical and political developments. The term 'mass society' is very much a product of our time. And yet, perhaps the critique is exaggerated.

For one thing, however much choice and individual freedom is limited, there is another sense in which these qualities are more finely developed than at any time previously. As he trudged round England in the 1930s, J. B. Priestley was perceptive enough to see that for all the monotony and standardization in the new social and cultural landscape, the fact was that it was opening new frontiers for a deprived majority.[53] Woolworth's was a frequent butt of scorn from elitists, but it had its own meaning for those who were tasting the first fruits of a consumer society. Materialism as an end in itself is an oppressive force, but (compared with the greyness of poverty) better material conditions were undoubtedly a force for good.

It is in this context, as a source of social opportunity that holiday camps earn their place in history. Although they have never been cheap they have been consistently recognized as 'good value for money'. As such they have lowered the social ceiling, enabling more people to enjoy a holiday with entertainment than was previously possible. 'A veritable Beveridge of Leisure' Ray Gosling has called them.[54] What they have done is to open the doors of the Grand Hotel or the luxury liner to millions rather than to a privileged few. This alone is no mean achievement.

There is another sense in which it is erroneous to tar as necessarily destructive everything that reflects a profile of 'mass society'. What such a critique implies is that there is somehow a causal relationship between the mass provision of goods and services and a progressive loss of individuality.

Certainly, the evidence of mass provision is all around us. But does this structure necessarily determine that individuality is lost? If anything, the evidence is to the contrary. The 1980s is alive with examples of individual and community initiative. 1984 has come and gone, and while there is plenty of which to despair there is also abundant evidence that the human spirit is alive and well.

The strength of this argument is not simply to rebut the inference that eating 'Mother's Pride' or wearing 'M and S' shirts is, in itself, a cause or effect of lost individuality. Rather, it is that the very process of confronting the daily evidence of mass trends may serve to evoke a commensurate response. The mass society takes its captives, but passive resistance is by no means universal and inevitable. It is entirely conceivable that a dialectic between individual and mass tendencies can produce its own creative impulses and its own changes. Society reflects a constant tension between opposing forces and it is to oversimplify the situation to suggest that one will automatically replace the other.

It was easy for critics to scorn holiday camps for their regimentation, and to dismiss them as yet another sign of society's fall from grace. But it is facile to claim that people, in choosing this form of holiday, necessarily abandon their individuality in the process. A week or two in a holiday camp is part of a complex tapestry of annual activities, in some of which a common theme might well be passivity. Equally, in many cases, the holiday camp experience will be part of a more varied mix, and staying in a camp will mean something very different in the lives of those who do it. Qualities of individuality are more subtle (and indeed more resilient) than to be determined solely by whether one lives in a tower block estate, works on a conveyor belt or stays in a holiday camp.

At the end of the day, then, we are left in something of a quandary. There are arguments both for and against holiday camps. Critics despise them for their assault on 'real culture' and for symbolizing the very worst of twentieth-century consumerism. Their advocates, on the other hand, point to the happy holidays that have been brought to millions. If numbers are to mean anything, the supporters of holiday camps retain a strong argument.

There is merit on both sides, and if a judgement is to be made one must perhaps step back to set the camps in a wider context. The merits or demerits of a particular institution can only really be judged in the context of the social setting in which it occurs. Holiday camps exemplify something of the best and worst of twentieth-century Britain. If they have not achieved their true potential (something of the promise shown in the pioneer camps), as places where individuality can flourish in a collective setting, then that is a failing that has occurred elsewhere in society too.

When J. L. Hammond, in the 1930s, linked leisure with education and universal suffrage as three great areas of twentieth-century change, he was looking in each case to their enormous social and political potential.[55] It would be hard to argue in any of these cases that this potential has been fully realized. Some progress has been made, but opportunities have been missed. And, looking back on the history of holiday camps as a small part of these wider transformations, that is perhaps how they too will be remembered.

NOTES

Chapter 1

1. Holding, T. H. (1897) *Cycle and Camp*. London: De Vere & Co.
2. Holding, T. H. (1908) 'A Camper's Story', in *The Campers Handbook*. London: Simkin Marshall.
3. Dutton, Ralph (1970) *Hampshire*. London: Batsford.
4. Dawes, Frank (1975) *A Cry from the Streets: The Boys' Club Movement in Britain from the 1850s to the Present Day*. Hove: Wayland Publishers.
5. Springhall, John (1977) *Youth Empire and Society: British Youth Movements 1883–1940*. London: Croom Helm.
6. *Ibid.*
7. Paul, Leslie (1950) *Angry Young Man*. London: Faber.
8. Paul, Leslie (1938) *The Republic of Children*. London: Allen and Unwin.
9. Schmitt, Peter (1969) *Back to Nature: The Arcadian Myth in Urban America*. New York: Oxford University Press.
10. Orwell, George 'Hop-picking', in *The Collected Essays, Journalism and Letters of George Orwell*, Vol. 1. London: Secker and Warburg, 1968.
11. Bignell, Alan (1977) *Hopping Down In Kent*. London: Robert Hale.
12. *Ibid.*
13. *Chamber's Book of Days*, 1869, quoted by Bignell *op. cit.*
14. Wood, Charles in *Argosy*, December 1883, quoted by Bignell *op. cit.*
15. Ray, Cyril (1960) *Merry England*, London: Vista Books.
16. Bignell *op. cit.*
17. Carpenter, Edward (1887) *England's Ideal*. London: Swan Sonneschein.
18. Lethaby, W. R. (1922) *Form in Civilisation*. Oxford: Oxford University Press.
19. 'Report of the Inter-departmental Committee on Physical Deterioration', quoted by Richard Titmuss in *Essays on The Welfare State*. London: Allen and Unwin 1958.
20. 'Nunquam' (Robert Blatchford) *Merrie England*. London: Clarion Office 1893, reprinted with a publisher's foreword, London: Journeyman Press 1976.
21. Bridgeman, Harriet and Drury, Elizabeth (1977) *Beside the Seaside*. London: Hamish Hamilton.
22. Southgate, Walter (1982) *That's the Way it Was: A Working Class Autobiography 1890–1950*. Oxted: New Clarion.
23. 'The history of Ladbrokes', in *Ladbrokes Life*, Journal of the Ladbroke Group, Vol. 2, No. 4, May/June 1973.
24. *Ibid.*
25. Stokes, George W., Letter in *The Sunday Telegraph* 30 October 1983.
26. *The Holiday Camp Book*, National Federation of Permanent Holiday Camps 1949.
27. Brunner, Elizabeth (1945) *Holiday Making and the Holiday Trades*. Oxford: Nuffield College.
28. *Geography*, September 1931.
29. MacKenzie, Norman and Jeanne (eds.) (1984): *The Diary of Beatrice Webb: Vol. Three, 1905–1924*. London: Virago.
30. *Ibid.*
31. Drower, Jill (1982) *Good Clean Fun: The Story of Britain's First Holiday Camp*. London: Arcadia Books.
32. *Ibid.*
33. *Ibid.*

Chapter 2

1. *Holiday Camp Review* was published monthly from April to September 1938, and from May to September 1939.
2. Editorial, *Holiday Camp Review*, Vol. 1, No. 1, April 1938.
3. Editorial, *Holiday Camp Review*, Vol. 1, No. 2, May 1938.
4. *Ibid.*
5. Letter from C. T. Norman, *Holiday Camp Review*, Vol. 2, No. 1, May 1939.

6. *Ibid.*

7. A note from the President to explain the Association was included in the *Holiday Camp Review*, Vol. 1, No. 2, May 1938.

8. See Chapter 1 for an account of the Cunningham Camp.

9. An article on camp history appeared in *Holiday Camp Review*, Vol. 1, No. 2, May 1938.

10. From an article, 'Looking Backwards: H. E. Potter of Hopton Beach tells you his story', in *Holiday Camp Review*, Vol. 2, No. 1, May 1939.

11. *Ibid.*

12. 'What we want from Campers', *Holiday Camp Review*, Vol. 1, No. 3, June 1938.

13. Information from Mr. Victor Dodd.

14. Hardy, Dennis and Ward, Colin (1984) *Arcadia for All: The Legacy of a Makeshift Landscape.* London: Mansell.

15. Wren, Philip (1981) Holiday Shanties in Britain, Unpublished dissertation, Hull School of Architecture.

16. From advertisements appearing regularly in *Holiday Camp Review*, 1938 and 1939.

17. The aims of the Holiday Fellowship and what it could offer were included in its annual brochures.

18. 'National Fitness Campaign Plans Holiday Camp', *Holiday Camp Review*, Vol. 1, No. 4, July 1938.

19. Information from Taylor Stoehr, comparing Wouk, Herman (1956) *The City Boy.* London: Jonathan Cape, with Goodman, Paul (1946) *The Break-Up of Our Camp.* Norfolk, Conn.: New Directions.

20. Sellers, Edith (1927) 'For England's Sake and their Children's', *Cornhill*, February.

21. *Parl. Debates (House of Commons) 1938–39.* Second Reading of Camps Bill, 29th March 1939 London: HMSO.

22. 'Holiday Camps: Some Notes on Recent Suggestions', *Industrial Welfare*, February 1939.

23. Dr Innes, Chief Education Officer for Birmingham, reported in *Holiday Camp Review*, Vol. 2, No. 2, June 1939.

24. *Parl. Debates, op. cit.*

25. *Parl. Debates, op. cit.*

26. Carrington, Noel (1939) 'Country Camps for School-Children', *Country Life*, 1 April.

27. Reid, William (1920) *History of the United Co-operative Baking Society Ltd: A Fifty-Years' Record 1869–1919*, Glasgow: UCBS.

28. 'Rothesay Camp to Close', *Co-operative News and Scottish Co-operator*, 20 September 1974.

29. Briscoe, Robert (1960) *Centenary History: A Hundred Years of Co-operation in Portsmouth.* Manchester: Co-operative Press Ltd.

30. 'Younger Generation Learns the Value of Communal Life', *Co-operative News*, 17 June 1938.

31. *Wheatsheaf*, Coventry Edition, July 1930.

32. 'Pioneer Holiday Camp on the North Wales Coast', *Co-operative News*, 15 July 1939. See also 'The Co-ops also have Camps', *Holiday Camp Review*, Vol. 2, No. 5, September 1939.

33. Harold Worthington, personal communication August 1985. See also Coventry and District Co-operative Society (1967): *A Century of Service.*

34. *Holiday Camp Review*, Vol. 1, No. 4, July 1938.

35. 'Leisure as an Architectural Problem', *The Architectural Review*, December 1938.

36. Survey of Ministry of Town and Country Planning, *Coastal Camps and Holiday Centres in England and Wales*, 1942 (PRO/HLG92/1).

37. Sources for the Derbyshire Miners Holiday Centre include Williams, J. E. (1962) *The Derbyshire Miners*. London: Allen and Unwin; and *Derbyshire Times*, 5 and 12 May 1939 and 3 June 1939.

38. 'Trade Unions will also have camps', *Holiday Camp Review*, Vol. 2, No. 4, August 1939.

39. 'Trade Union Camps: Hotel and Apartment Association Protest', *Holiday Camp Review*, Vol. 2, No. 5, September 1939.

40. Gilbert, E. W. (1939) 'The Growth of Inland and Seaside Health Resorts in England'. *Scottish Geographical Magazine*, January 1939. Quoted by Brunner, *op. cit.*

41. Brown, R. Douglas (1980) *East Anglia.* Lavenham: Terence Dalton.

42. 'Holiday Camps: Some notes on recent suggestions', *Industrial Welfare, February 1939.*

43. Brunner, Elizabeth (1945) *Holiday Making and the Holiday Trades.* Oxford: Nuffield College.

44. Brown, W. J. (1943) *So Far.* London: Allen and Unwin.

45. *Ibid.*

46. *Red Tape* (Journal of the CSCA) April and May 1924.

47. *Red Tape* August 1924.

48. *Red Tape* August 1925.

49. *Red Tape* December 1929.

50. *Red Tape* February 1930.

51. *Red Tape* June 1936.

52. *Red Tape* July 1936.

53. Brown, W. J. *op. cit.*

54. *White Collar Union: the history of NALGO 1965–1980.*

55. *Ibid.*

56. 'Holiday Facilities – Future planning policy'. NALGO Conference White Paper 1970.

57. *Path to Maturity: the history of NALGO 1965–1980.*

58. We are grateful for access to NALGO branch records (Middlesex Polytechnic) to see the various papers on this issue, circulated in 1976.

59. Personal Interview, July 1985.

60. 'Lambeth People to have their own Holiday Camp', *Holiday Camp Review*, Vol. 2, No. 1, May 1939. A full account of the sequence of events is to be found in the records of the Public Health Committee, Lambeth Borough Council, 1938 to 1939.

61. 'After the Lambeth Walk – The Lambeth Camp', *Holiday Camp Review*, Vol. 2, No. 2, June 1939.

62. Pimlott, J. A. R. (1947) *The Englishman's Holiday: A Social History.* London: Faber and Faber.

63. 'After the Lambeth Walk – The Lambeth Camp', *Holiday Camp Review*, Vol. 2, No. 2, June 1939.

64. 'Holiday Camps: Some Notes on Recent Suggestions', *Industrial Welfare*, February 1939.

65. *Parl. Debates, op. cit.*

66. 'Holiday Camps: Some Notes on Recent Suggestions', *Industrial Welfare*, February 1939.

67. 'Camps and A.R.P.', *Holiday Camp Review*, Vol. 2, No. 1, May 1939.

68. *Parl. Debates, op. cit.*

69. *Parl. Debates, op. cit.*

70. Lord Dawson of Penn, speaking on the Second Reading of the Camps Bill in the House of Lords, 1939.

71. George Lansbury, writing in *Holiday Camp Review*, Vol. 1, No. 1, April 1939.

72. Figure cited in 'Holiday Camps: Some Notes on Recent Suggestions', *Industrial Welfare*, February 1939.

73. Editorial, *Holiday Camp Review*, Vol. 1, No. 1, April 1938.

74. The cost for instance, of a week in 1938 at Atherfield Bay Camp on the Isle of Wight was from 45 shillings each; at Sussex Ideal Holiday Chalets at Bracklesham Bay between 47/6 and 55 shillings; and at the Constitutional Holiday Camp at Hopton-on-Sea charges were between 47/6 and 52/6 weekly.

75. Pimlott, J. A. R. (1947) *The Englishman's Holiday: A Social History.* London: Faber and Faber.

76. 'First Time at a Camp but Going Back for More', *Holiday Camp Review*, Vol. 1, No. 2, May 1938.

77. 'Holiday Camps and Why We Go There', *Holiday Camp Review*, Vol. 2, No. 3, July 1939.

78. *Ibid.*

79. *Ibid.*

Chapter 3

1. Sir James Carreras, interviewed in Butlin, Sir Billy with Dacre, Peter (1982) *The Billy Butlin Story.* London: Robson Books.

2. Bobby Butlin, interviewed in Butlin, *ibid.*

3. *Ibid.*

4. *Ibid.*

5. Butlin, *ibid.*

6. *Ibid.*

7. Cedric Belfrage, in the *Sunday Express* 15 January 1933, quoted in Butlin, *ibid.*

8. *Ibid.*
9. *Ibid.*
10. *Ibid.*
11. North, Rex (1962) *The Butlin Story*. London: Jarrolds.
12. Butlin, *op. cit.*
13. North, *op. cit.*
14. Phillips, Andrew (1985) *Ten Men and Colchester*. Chelmsford: Essex Record Office.
15. Hardy, Dennis and Ward, Colin (1984) *Arcadia for All: The Legacy of a Makeshift Landscape*. London: Mansell.
16. North, *op. cit.*
17. *Clacton Times and Gazette* 5 December 1936.
18. Butlin, *op. cit.*
19. North, *op. cit.*
20. Brown, J. H. (1983) 'Filey has coped with changing holiday habits'. *Scarborough Mercury*, 29 October.
21. Howes, David (1973) 'Filey – where nature is still king'. *Hull Daily Mail*, 17 August.
22. Brown, *op. cit.*
23. Butlin, *op. cit.*
24. *Ibid.*
25. Johnson, Derek E. (1985) *The Exodus of Children*. Clacton: Penny-farthing Publications.
26. *Ibid.* See also Tittmuss, Richard M. (1950) *Problems of Social Policy*. London: HMSO.
27. Butlin, *op. cit.*
28. Drower, Jill (1982) *Good Clean Fun: the Story of Britain's First Holiday Camp*. London: Arcadia Books.
29. North, *op. cit.*
30. Brown, R. Douglas (1980) *East Anglia 1939*. Lavenham: Terence Dalton.
31. Butlin, *op. cit.*
32. Lettercard in the John Tovey Collection.
33. Butlin, *op. cit.*
34. *Ibid.*
35. *Ibid.*
36. *Ibid.*
37. North, *op. cit.*
38. *Ibid.*
39. For the shifts in official perception of the wartime 'Home Front' see Mack, Joanna and Humphries, Steve (1985) *London at War*. London: Sidgwick and Jackson.
40. Westall, Robert (1985) *Children of the Blitz*. London: Viking.
41. Butlin, *op. cit.*
42. Godfrey Winn: Unpublished account cited in Butlin, *op. cit.*
43. Butler, R. H. (1943) *Hansard* (House of Commons) 3 June.
44. Lloyd, John (1983) 'The Scottish Camp Schools, 1940–1945: An experimental expedient'. *Scottish Educational Review*, **15** (2), November.
45. *Ibid.*
46. *Ibid.*
47. British Tourist and Holidays Board (1949) *Survey of Holiday Accommodation in Britain*.
48. Rolph, C. H. (1951) 'Southend's Little Sister'. *New Statesman*, 4 August.

Chapter 4

1. Ward, Colin (1963) 'Direct action for houses: the story of the squatters'. *Anarchy* 23, **3** (1), January.
2. Sir Fred Pontin, interview 14 May 1985.
3. The history of Ladbrokes, in *Ladbrokes Life*, Journal of the Ladbroke Group Vol. 2 No. 4, May/June 1973.
4. Recollection from Ron Griffiths, 5 August 1985.
5. North, Rex (1962), *The Butlin Story*. London: Jarrolds.

6. *Ibid.*
7. *Investors Chronicle* 9 December 1960.
8. *The Times*, 28 July 1980.
9. Clark, Eric (1984) 'Camps wake up to the 80s'. *Marketing*, 30 August.
10. *East Anglian Daily Times*, 23 October 1985.
11. Goffman, Erving (1961) *Asylums: Essays on the Social Situation of Mental Patients and Other Inmates*. New York: Anchor Books.
12. Pradeep Bandyopadhyay, 'The Holiday Camp' in Smith, Michael, Parker, Stanley and Smith, Cyril (1973) *Leisure and Society in Britain*. London: Allen Lane.
13. Recollection from Harold Worthington, 6 September 1985.
14. *Management Today*, November 1974.
15. Jones, David (1985) 'Maplin's was never like this.' *News of the World*, reproduced in *Butlin's Holidays, Students Guide*, Spring.
16. *Ibid.*
17. Bandyopadhyay, *op. cit.*
18. Mars, Gerald and Nicod, Michael (1981) 'Hidden rewards at work: the implications from a study of British hotels' in Henry, Stuart (ed.) *Can I Have it in Cash?* London: Astragal Books.
19. Mars, Gerald (1982) *Cheats at Work: An Anthropology of Workplace Crime*. London: George Allen and Unwin.
20. Bandyopadhyay, *op. cit.*
21. Kerridge, Roy (1985) *Bizarre Britain: A Calendar of Eccentricity*. Oxford: Basil Blackwell.
22. Roberts, Yvonne (1977) 'Is Everybody Happy?' *New Statesman*, 26 August.
23. Pithers, Malcolm (1974) 'Pontin's staff accused of 'get out or else' threat', *The Guardian*, 10 August.
24. *Ibid.*
25. Roberts, *op. cit.*
26. Silverton, Pete (1985) 'Going red in Skegness', *Radio Times*, 6–12 July.
27. Sue Ann Scott, interviewed in *Just 17*, 20 September 1985.
28. Kavanagh, P. J. (1966) *The Perfect Stranger*. London: Chatto and Windus.
29. We are grateful to many people for their recollections of working in camp, and especially to Jim Dumsday, Shirley Stuart, Della Chapman, Lynn and Brian Edwards, Sylvia Sutcliffe and Roger Milne.
30. Myerscough, John (1977) Introduction to new edition of Pimlott, J. A. R. *The Englishman's Holiday*. Brighton: Harvester Press.
31. Arthur Foster, interview November 1984.
32. Richard Page, interview July 1985.
33. '400 ill with suspected food poisoning at Norfolk holiday camp' *Daily Telegraph* 6 Sept 1979. 'Affected camp to close' *ibid* 7 Sept 1979.
34. Bandyopadhyay, Pradeep (1973) 'The Holiday Camp' in Smith, Michael, Parker, Stanley and Smith, Cyril *Leisure and Society in Britain*. London: Allen Lane.
35. Myerscough, *op. cit.*
36. Margaret Jones, interview November 1985.
37. 'Holiday Camp Champ' *Sunday People* 14 March 1982.
38. Creasey, John (1954) *The Toff at Butlin's*. London: Hodder and Stoughton.
39. Deal, Paula (1961) *Nurse at Butlins*. London: Arthur Barker.
40. Richards, Frank (1961) *Billy Bunter at Butlin's*. London: Cassell.
41. Butlin, Sir Billy with Dacre, Peter (1982) *The Billy Butlin Story*. London: Robson Books.
42. Lea, Timothy (1972) *Confessions from a Holiday Camp*. London: Sphere Books.
43. *Ibid.*
44. Taylor, Laurie (1984) 'The Costa del Hanky-Panky', *The Observer*, 9 December 1984.
45. Jones, David (1985) 'Maplin's was never like this.' *News of the World*, reproduced in *Butlin's Holidays, Students Guide*, Spring.
46. Information kindly provided by Mr F. F. Marshall, 14 Marine Drive, Barry, Glamorgan CF6 8QN.
47. Wollaston, Nicholas (1965) *Winter in England: A Traveller in His Own Country*. London: Hodder and Stoughton.
48. *Ibid.*
49. Theroux, Paul (1983) *The Kingdom by the Sea*. London: Hamish Hamilton.
50. The Rev. Wilf Curtis, interviewed in 'Goodnight Campers.' BBC1 31 January 1984. Produced by Mark Rowland.

51. Lindley, Kenneth (1973) *Seaside Architecture*. London: Hugh Evelyn.

52. Solzhenitsyn, Alexander (1973) *The Love Girl and the Innocent*, Act 1, Sc. iii., trans by N. Bethell and D. Burg. Harmondsworth: Penguin Books.

53. North, *op. cit.*

54. Healy, William and Alper, Benedict (1941) *Criminal Youth and the Borstal System*. New York: The Commonwealth Fund.

55. Llewellin, W. W. (1936) 'The North Sea Camp – A Fresh Borstal Experiment', *The Howard Journal*, Vol. IV, No. 3.

56. Behan, Brendan (1958): *Borstal Boy*. London: Hutchinson.

57. Clark, Eric (1984) 'Camps wake up to the 80s', *Marketing*, 30 August.

58. Kerridge, Roy (1985) *Bizarre Britain: A Calendar of Eccentricity*. Oxford: Basil Blackwell.

59. Hughes, Jacqui and Pitharas, Lysandros (1985) 'Welcome to the Pleasure Dome', *City Limits*, 21 December – 3 January.

60. Walker, Ian (1983) 'Welcome to the House of Fun', *Observer Magazine*, 12 June.

61. Fred Gray kindly drew our attention to this letter in the collection of holiday material in the Mass Observation Archive in the library of the University of Sussex.

62. Butlin, Sir Billy with Dacre, Peter (1982) *The Billy Butlin Story*. London: Robson Books.

63. Pimlott, J. A. R. (1947) *The Englishman's Holiday: A Social History*. London: Faber and Faber.

64. *The Times* 12 June 1959.

65. 'Butlin's early call is put to rest', *The Guardian*, 4 August 1979.

66. Interview with Tony Wright, marketing director of Butlin's in *Management Today* November 1981.

67. 'Butlin's adjust their image for 1961', *The Observer*, 28 May 1961.

68. 'Butlin's: same formula, new image', *The Times*, 1 September 1981.

69. *Sunday Mirror*, 4 January 1981.

70. Walvin, James (1978) *Beside the Seaside*. London: Allen Lane.

71. 'Camp Followed', *New Society*, 12 January 1978.

72. 'Butlin's adjust their image for 1961', *The Observer*, 28 May 1961.

73. Theroux, Paul (1983) *The Kingdom by the Sea*. London: Hamish Hamilton.

74. Martyn Harris, 'Costa del Butlins', *New Society* 9 August 1985.

75. 'Butlin's to spend £15m to change its image', *Financial Times*, 29 October 1985.

76. Bob Webb, managing director of Butlin's Holiday Centres, addressing the annual convention of the Association of British Travel Agents, Sorrento 28 October 1985.

Chapter 5

1. 'Holidays with pay', *Journal of the Town Planning Institute*, January 1939.

2. Town and Country Planning Act 1932: Circular 1750, 'Control of Premature or Unsightly Development in the Country and on the Sea Coast'.

3. Reported in 'Holiday Camps', *Journal of the Town Planning Institute*, October 1939.

4. 'Holiday Camps', *Journal of the Town Planning Institute*, October 1939.

5. Stephenson, Gordon (1939) 'Making the Best of Camp Sites', *Holiday Camp Review*, June.

6. Thomas Adams, letter to *The Times*, 28 December 1939.

7. Mr. Elliot, Minister of Health, in *Parl. Debates (House of Commons) 1938–39* Second Reading of Camps Bill, 29 March 1939, London: HMSO.

8. *Ibid* (Mr. Noel-Baker).

9. Lock, Max and Ledeboer, Judith (1939) 'Architects' ideas on how camps should be planned', *Holiday Camp Review*, August.

10. Bennett, Frank (1939) 'Holiday Camps: their design and planning', *The Builder*, 3 March, 17 March, and 7 April.

11. Bennett, Frank (1939) 'Holiday Camps: their design and planning', *The Builder*, 3 March.

12. *Ibid.*

13. The two aspects were considered by Hamlyn, William H. (the designer of Prestatyn Holiday Camp) in a paper, 'Camps: Design, Construction and Hygiene', *The Builder*, 12 April 1940. Fuller consideration of the public health aspects is provided in an article by Brant, Herbert (1938) 'Holiday Camps', *Journal of the Royal Sanitary Institute*, January.

14. 'Current Notes on Planning; Holiday Camps', series of articles by 'E and O.E.' in *The Architect and Building News*, 10 February, 17 February, 24 February, 3 March, 17 March, 24 March, 31 March, 7 April 1939.

15. Pilcher, Donald (1938) 'Leisure as an Architectural Problem', *Architectural Review*, December.

16. Helpful reports of Prestatyn Holiday Camp were published in *The Builder*, 30 June 1939, *The Architect and Building News*, 7 July 1939 and *The Journal of the Royal Institute of British Architects* 17 July 1939.

17. *The Builder*, 30 June 1939.

18. In 1942 Regional offices of the Ministry of Town and Country Planning conducted a survey, *Coastal Camps and Holiday Centres in England and Wales* (PRO/HLG/92/1). Results of the survey are presented in terms of Civil Defence Regions. The Lincolnshire Coastline is included in Civil Defence Region 3.

19. *Ibid.*

20. In his report on Coastal Preservation and Planning (PRO/HLG/92/80) J. A. Steers included a section, *Shacks, Huts and Camps*, in which he made various observations on holiday camps.

21. *Ibid.*

22. *Ibid.*

23. Internal correspondence (June 1942), Ministry of Works and Planning, relating to Coastal Surveys (PRO/HLG/92/1).

24. Council for the Preservation of Rural England (1942) *Second Report of the Coastal Preservation Committee*, October (PRO/HLG/92/1).

25. Internal correspondence (June 1944), Ministry of Town and Country Planning, relating to Coastal Planning (PRO/HLG/92/1).

26. *Parl. Debates (House of Commons) 1938–39*, Second Reading of Camps Bill, 29 March 1939. London: HMSO.

27. *Ibid* (Mr. Noel-Baker).

28. *Ibid* (Mr. Creech Jones).

29. *Ibid* (Major Sir Ralph Glyn).

30. Internal correspondence (July 1942), Ministry of Works and Planning, *op. cit.*

31. Steers, *op. cit.*

32. Report from Regional Planning Officer (South East Region), Ministry of Town and Country Planning, 6 October 1944 (PRO/HLG/92/1).

33. 'Holiday Centres: W.T.A. Competition Award', *The Builder* 14 June 1946.

34. *Ibid.*

35. Post-War Holidays Group (1946) *Report to the Catering Wages Commission on the subject of Post-War Holidays*. London: National Council for Social Service.

36. It was commonly predicted in the 1940s that the demand for holiday camps would continue to exceed supply, unless there was a considerable increase in provision. In 1949, for instance, the Home Holidays Division of the British Tourist and Holidays Board arrived at a similar conclusion to that of the Post-War Holidays Group. In a publication, *Survey of Holiday Accommodation in Great Britain*, it was estimated that the demand at that time for accommodation in seaside holiday camps amounted to 1,216,000 places annually. This figure compared with an existing supply of 874,000 places. Interestingly, in relative terms, the shortfall for countryside places was even greater – a demand of 454,000 but only 30,000 places.

37. *Ibid.*

38. *The Bognor Regis Post*, 28 September 1957.

39. Estimates of the camp's impact are cited in a series of local newspaper reports between 1957 and 1960, as contained in the Gerard Young Collection.

40. *Bognor Regis Observer*, 12 February 1960.

41. *The Bognor Regis Post*, 28 September 1980.

42. *Ibid.*

43. *Bognor Regis Observer*, 4 October 1959.

44. Cited in Young, Gerard (1983) *A History of Bognor Regis*. Chichester: Phillimore, p. 252.

45. *Ibid.*, p. 252.

46. *Bognor Regis Observer*, 4 October 1959.

47. View expressed by a local hotelier, in *Portsmouth Evening News*, 26 September 1957.

48. Report of Public Inquiry (Application No. BR/142/57), Ministry of Housing and Local Government, 10 March 1958.

49. View expressed in *Portsmouth Evening News*, 26 September 1957.

50. *The Bognor Regis Post*, 26 September 1959.

51. *The Bognor Regis Post*, 31 October 1959.

52. *Bognor Regis Observer*, 12 February 1960.

53. Norton, Rex (1962) *The Butlin Story*. London: Jarrolds, p. 140.

54. Cited in Young *op. cit.*, p. 252.

55. Mosley, Nicholas (1961) 'Butlins.', *Time and Tide*, 15 June.

56. A letter was sent by the authors in September 1984 to all County Planning Departments and to selected District Planning Departments in England and Wales to gain information on current policies for holiday camps. The authorities were asked whether there are currently specific policies for holiday camps, whether there have been any special reports and whether case histories are available. References to individual authorities in the rest of this section are extracted from the response received.

57. Information supplied by Dr. Fred Gray, including a report on the opening of the baths (Municipal Review, July 1933) and current publicity literature for the Hastings Holiday Centre.

58. 'Welcome to The Fitties...A Holiday Camp to be proud of', *Evening Telegraph*, 30 July 1984.

59. English Tourist Board (1982) *Raising the Standard: Improving Holiday Caravan and Chalet Sites*. London: English Tourist Board.

60. *Ibid* (Mr. Wilson).

61. 'Butlin's closes Filey camp', *Scarborough Evening News*, 18 October 1983.

62. Woodcock, Roy (1983) 'Filey update too little, too late', *Hull Daily Mail*, 19 October.

63. 'Butlin's at Filey sold in big deal', *Hull Daily Mail*, 17 January 1985.

64. 'Butlin's closure shock', *East Essex Gazette*, 21 October 1983.

65. 'Butlin's site in poor state says tourist board', *East Essex Gazette*, 11 November 1983.

66. 'Spectacular Essex theme park plan', *East Anglian Daily Times*, 25 February 1984.

67. 'Leisure park sale imminent', *East Essex Gazette*, 29 November 1985.

68. Clark, Eric (1984) 'Camps wake up to the 80s', *Marketing*, 30 August 1984.

69. Hoggart, Richard (1958) *The Uses of Literacy*. Harmondsworth: Pelican.

70. Hebidge, Dick (1982) 'Towards a Cartography of Taste, 1935–62', in Waites, B., Bennett, T., and Martin, G. (eds.) *Popular Culture: Past and Present*. London: Croom Helm.

71. Hoggart, *op. cit.*

72. Orwell, George (1939) *Coming up for Air*. London: Gollancz.

73. Unattributed article, 'Do you want neon lights and chromium at your camp?', *Holiday Camp Review*, August 1939.

74. Lindley, Kenneth (1967) *Coastline*. London: Hutchinson.

Chapter 6

1. These are various versions of the peasants' dream, *The Land of Cokaygne*. This extract is included in the version in Morton, A. L. (1978) *The English Utopia*. London: Lawrence and Wishart.

2. Sir Walter Citrine, giving evidence on behalf of the T.U.C. before the Holidays with Pay Committee in 1937, spoke of the growing holiday habit since 1918, but also of the scope for the further development of this habit if paid holidays were to be fully enjoyed.

3. Helpful general sources on the social history of holidaymaking are Pimlott, J. A. R. (1947) *The Englishman's Holiday: A Social History*. London: Faber and Faber; Walvin, James (1978) *Beside the Seaside*. London: Allen Lane; Walton, John K. (1983) *The English Seaside Resort: A Social History 1750–1914*. Leicester: Leicester University Press; and Walton, John K. (1983) *Leisure in Britain 1780–1939*. Manchester University Press.

4. This popular day for outings was granted as part of the 1871 Bank Holidays Act.

5. Citrine, *op. cit.*

6. This was the estimate of Political and Economic Planning (Planning, No. 194), cited in Brunner, Elizabeth (1945) *Holiday Making and the Holiday Trades*. Oxford: Nuffield College.

7. London Cooperative Society spokesman, quoted in Brunner, *op. cit.*

8. This was the view of Pimlott, *op. cit.*, writing at that time.

9. Ernest Bevin's views were reported in *The Times*, 23 July 1946, and those of Sir Stafford Cripps in *The Times*, 26 February 1947.

10. Figures cited in Walvin, *op. cit.*

11. Central Statistical Office (1985) *Social Trends*. London: HMSO.

12. Walvin, *op. cit.*
13. Hoggart, Richard (1958) *The Uses of Literacy.* Harmondsworth: Pelican.
14. *Ibid.*
15. Walvin, *op. cit.*
16. Gilbert, E. W. (1939) 'The Growth of Inland and Seaside Health Resorts in England', *Scottish Geographical Magazine*, January.
17. Brunner, *op. cit.*
18. Pimlott, *op. cit.*
19. *Ibid.*
20. Brunner, *op. cit.*
21. Glasser, Ralph (1970) *Leisure: Penalty or Prize?* London: Macmillan.
22. 'Holiday Camps' Popularity', *The Times*, 10 January 1949.
23. The sociology of leisure and the implications of current trends are clearly discussed in two books by Roberts, Kenneth: *Contemporary Society and the Growth of Leisure*, (1978) London: Longman, and *Leisure* (2nd edition, 1981), London: Longman. Another valuable source is Smith, Michael, Parker, Stanley and Smith, Cyril (1973) *Leisure and Society in Britain*. London: Allen Lane.
24. Dumazedier, Joffre (1967) *Toward a Society of Leisure.* New York: The Free Press.
25. *The New Survey of London Life and Labour*, Vol. IX. 1935, London: P. S. King.
26. Hammond, J. L. (1933) *The Growth of Common Enjoyment.* London: Oxford University Press.
27. *Ibid.*
28. Hall, Stuart (1974) 'Between Two Worlds', one of a BBC Radio 4 series, and published in Barker, Theo (ed.) (1978) *The Long March of Everyman.* Harmondsworth: Penguin.
29. Dumazedier, *op. cit.*
30. Toffler, Alvin (1971) *Future Shock.* London: Pan Books.
31. From a speech by Harold Macmillan at Bedford in July 1957, quoted in Hall, *op. cit.*
32. Holiday trends between 1951 and 1980, produced from the British Tourist Authority's British National Travel Surveys, in Grahame Thompson (1981), *Holidays*, Unit 11, Course U203, Milton Keynes: The Open University.
33. Roberts (1978), *op. cit.*
34. Bennett, Tony (1981) *Popular Culture: History and Theory*, Unit 3, Course U203. Milton Keynes: The Open University.
35. A helpful overview and introduction to the study of popular culture is provided by the course material, *Popular Culture* (U203), first produced by the Open University in 1981.
36. Arnold, Matthew (1869) *Culture and Anarchy.* London: Smith, Elder and Co.
37. Leavis, F. R. and Thompson, Denys (1933) *Culture and Environment.* London: Chatto and Windus.
38. Hoggart, *op. cit.*
39. Walton, J. K. (1983) *The English Seaside Resort: A Social History 1750–1914.* Leicester: Leicester University Press.
40. Walvin, *op. cit.*
41. *Ibid.*
42. Orwell, George (1946) 'Pleasure Spots', in *Collected Essays*, Vol. 4. Harmondsworth: Penguin, (reprinted 1970).
43. *Ibid.*
44. Pimlott, *op. cit.*
45. Willcock, H. D. (1946) 'Boarding House or Butlin's', *Geographical Magazine*, July.
46. Joad, C. E. M. (1946) *The Untutored Townsman's Invasion of the Country.* London: Faber and Faber.
47. Gosling, Ray (1978) 'Workers' Playtime', BBC Radio 4, 31 July.
48. Mosley, Nicholas (1961) 'Butlins!', *Time and Tide*, 15 June.
49. Williams, Raymond (1962) *Britain in the Sixties: Communications.* Harmondsworth: Penguin.
50. *Ibid.*
51. Terms used in Hoggart, *op. cit.*
52. Goldring, Patrick (1969) *The Broilerhouse Society.* London: Leslie Frewin.
53. Priestley, J. B. (1934) *English Journey*, London: Heinemann (reprint).
54. Gosling, *op. cit.*
55. Hammond, *op. cit.*

INDEX

176